Diagnosis and Remediation
of
Reading Disability

Diagnosis and Remediation
of
Reading Disability

EMERALD DECHANT

PARKER PUBLISHING COMPANY, INC., *West Nyack, N.Y.*

PRINTED IN THE UNITED STATES OF AMERICA

B&P

To my wife, Deloris,
and our children,
Randy
Lori
Pami

Why This Book Was Written

The reasons for writing this book are many. One of the more obvious is the fact that today, with expanded federal programs, we are able to offer reading programs, especially corrective and remedial programs, that a few years ago many local school districts could not even consider. We have opportunities for greater quantity but also greater quality. In our consultive work across the country, we have been asked many questions concerning the nature of such programs and the roles of the various teachers that staff or will staff these programs. In some states, state-wide meetings have been held to help educators to answer some of the questions that are being asked.

Teachers of reading are becoming vitally concerned with the respective roles of the classroom reading teacher, the reading specialist, and the reading consultant. They are asking:

1. What training should each of these have?
2. With whom should each work?
3. What is the role of the specialist and the generalist?
4. What happens when we take the best teacher out of the classroom and make him the specialist? Is the replace-

ment going to create more problems than the special teacher can remediate?

5. What is the importance of getting the pupils back into the classroom?

6. What knowledge about the reading process, about the nature of the child, and the nature of the learning process is essential to the reading teacher?

7. How can we shift the emphasis from correction and remediation to prevention?

8. What are the basic ingredients of good diagnostic procedure? How do we identify the pupil's potential and his actual achievement?

9. How can the teacher of reading become a better observer of the symptoms of reading disability?

10. How can the teacher of reading become more expert in hooking symptoms to their proper cause?

11. What special tests are available to aid in the diagnostic process?

12. Do children have a preferred mode of learning?

13. What are the advantages and disadvantages of various methods of teaching reading both in developmental and remedial settings?

14. Who is the retarded reader, the slow learner, the reluctant reader, and the disadvantaged reader and how should each of these children be taught?

15. How does the remedial program differ from the corrective and the developmental program?

16. What materials are available to the classroom and the remedial teacher? How can money be used wisely in the selection of materials?

In this book, we have set out to answer these and similar questions. Our first concern has been the presentation of guidelines, procedures, and techniques for preventing, diagnosing, and remediating reading problems. The book thus is directed primarily at the *classroom teacher* who is after all the key person in reading. The best prevention of reading disability is still early identification and remediation in the regular classroom.

The book nevertheless should have equal value for the teacher who will be working in a corrective or remedial setting. It provides the *remedial teacher* with a ready source of principles, reading tests, materials, and diagnostic and remedial procedures useful in arriving at and carrying out educational decisions that will lead to correction of reading disabilities. It attempts to be as practical as possible in suggesting methods of diagnosis and treatment. It seeks to develop the concept of classroom teacher and remedial teacher working together to remove the pupil's reading deficiency.

We would hope that the book also would be most helpful to the *reading consultant,* that person whose major task is to work with other teachers toward the solution of the reading problem; to *administrators* who have a need to understand the roles of the teachers and special teachers in the areas of diagnosis and remediation; and to personnel in *State Departments of Public Instruction* as they plan and help plan with local school personnel programs in remediation.

In attempting to answer the questions suggested above and to meet the needs of the classroom teacher and the above-listed professionals, we have divided the book into the following chapters: *Identifying the Difficulty; The Diagnostic Process—Diagnostic Testing; Fully Investigating the Causes of Reading Disability; How to Organize and Implement Remediation; A Survey of Reading Methods; Meeting Individual Needs; Materials for Teaching Reading.*

This book is a sequel to *Psychology in Teaching Reading* [1] and *Improving the Teaching of Reading.* [2] The first of these was primarily concerned with the identification of the basic psychological principles upon which reading method is founded. The second was concerned more with reading method and the actual teaching of reading. Here we are concerned with what needs to be done for the pupil who has already drifted into trouble, for

---

[1] Smith, Henry P. and Dechant, Emerald. *Psychology in Teaching Reading.* Prentice-Hall, Inc., Englewood Cliffs, 1961.

[2] Dechant, Emerald. *Improving the Teaching of Reading.* Prentice-Hall, Inc., Englewood Cliffs, 1964.

the pupil who is not advancing in reading achievement the way he should.

We believe that the book has the following strengths:

1. It puts special emphasis on prevention.
2. It leads the reader step by step through diagnostic procedure, showing him how to determine whether a pupil is a retarded reader or not, how to identify reading potential and actual achievement, what tests to use, how to evaluate test results, how to administer a reading inventory, both informal and formal, how to use oral reading tests in diagnosis, how to use diagnostic tests, and how to identify the causes of reading disability.
3. It lists and discusses causes of reading disability, but in addition seeks to develop in the reading teacher a *modus operandi*, a *savoir-faire*, in testing out the specific cause in a given reading disability case. It thus shows the teacher how to tie together symptom and cause.
4. It shows how the teacher can identify the pupil's preferred mode of learning, so that he can use correctly either a configuration, phonic, kinesthetic, or combination method in remediation.
5. It provides the teacher with a philosophy of test interpretation, a look at the deficiencies of reading tests, and techniques for interpreting reading test profiles.
6. It provides a survey of reading methods and offers suggestions as to when each might be used.
8. It offers a compilation of proven remedial and psychotherapeutic principles and techniques and suggests applications.
9. It offers differential remedial programs for the retarded reader, the slow learner, the reluctant reader, the disadvantaged reader, the severely emotionally-disturbed retarded reader, and the dyslexiac.
10. It supplies the teacher with an up-to-date list of reading materials, including basal readers, materials designed to develop comprehension and word-recognition skills, audio-visual materials, mechanical devices, programmed materials, professional books, and lists of publishers.

11. The appendices provide the teacher with lists and descriptions of intelligence tests, readiness tests, reading survey and diagnostic tests, and oral reading tests.

We owe special thanks to the many people who have permitted us to quote from their materials; to the students in my reading classes; to President M. C. Cunningham and Fort Hays Kansas State College without whose support a project of this type would not be possible; to Allen McCune, Specialist in Education, whose suggestions greatly improved the manuscript; and to my wife, Deloris, who spent many hours typing and checking the manuscript.

Contents

Basic objective

The basic objective of this book is to present guidelines, procedures, and techniques for preventing, diagnosing, and remediating reading problems. The book thus is directed primarily at the classroom teacher.

Chapter 1   Identifying the Difficulty • 1

This chapter begins with a discussion of the prevention of reading disability and ends with a detailed procedure for carrying out the first diagnostic process. It describes the screening process and shows how to identify those pupils in a classroom of 30 who are actually retarded and who need remedial teaching. It draws a clear distinction between the slow learner, reluctant reader, disadvantaged reader, and retarded reader. It shows how to identify reading potential and reading achievement. Step I of the diagnostic process is primarily concerned with the identification of the difficulty. It helps to differentiate those pupils who are genuinely retarded and who need corrective and remedial instruction from those who simply need adapted instruction.

Chapter 2 Diagnostic Testing • 26

This chapter describes the beginning of detailed analysis of the reading problems of pupils identified in Step I as retarded readers through the use of the *Personal Data Sheet,* the *Learning and Behavior Checklist,* the formal and informal inventory, the oral reading test, and the diagnostic reading test. The significance of Step II is that it is an intensive study of the symptoms of reading disability. It is an important step because many reading disabilities become disabilities because someone either ignored or misinterpreted the symptoms of reading disability. The result is that some reading needs are not met, and it is these unmet reading needs that lead to disability cases. The chapter concludes with a discussion of developmental, corrective, and remedial instruction and with a case study illustrating the use of the above diagnostic techniques.

Chapter 3 Fully Investigating the Causes of Reading Disability • 54

Chapter 3 describes Step III of diagnostic procedure which is a thorough analysis of the reading disability leading to an identification of the causal factors involved. The chapter looks at inadequate language background, inadequate maturation, inadequate intellectual development, inadequate social-emotional development, lack of motivation, instructional inadequacies, and inadequacies in physical development as factors that interfere with learning to read.

The most important section of this chapter is the one that shows the teacher how to hook symptoms to their proper cause. The special or remedial teacher is by definition an expert in tying together symptom and cause. Chapter 3 concludes by hooking symptom to cause, using the case study begun in Chapter 2 to illustrate the procedure.

Chapter 4 How to Organize and Implement Remediation • 109

Diagnosis is not complete without remediation. Chapter 4 discusses Step IV of the diagnostic process which is remediation. It helps the teacher to formulate a plan for remediation, outlines principles of remediation, and offers suggestions on how to organize for corrective and remedial reading. The chapter closes with a look at the case study begun earlier, outlining remedial procedure.

Chapter 5   A Survey of Reading Methods • 140

Since the book takes the position that corrective or remedial methods are in reality developmental and that remedial reading is not a hocus-pocus of special methods, but a more intense and personal application of those methods that are effective in the regular class-room, Chapter 5 looks at various methods of teaching reading. It surveys, in addition to the more common methods, ITA, the Diacritical Marking System, the Unifon System, the Ten-Vowel Modification Model, Words in Color, Linguistic Systems, Programmed Learning, Language-Experience Approach, and such mediational approaches as that of Delacato. The chapter makes an evaluation of reading methods and encourages the teacher to select from the great variety of approaches that one or combination of approaches which best meets the needs of the pupil. It concludes with the following statement:

In evaluating the trend in reading method, we should like to quote from our book, *Improving the Teaching of Reading*, p. 195:

> In reading, good teaching seems to mean that the teacher must devise techniques of instruction which help the pupil to construct a generic code or a coding system that has wider applicability in reading than would the rote identification of individual words. The code has wider application than in the situation in which it was learned. The child learns to "read off" from this generic code information that permits him to attack other words. . . . The child, in a sense, must be taught to be a better guesser by knowing the language system and the phonogram-phoneme interrelationships.

The newer approaches in reading, in one way or another, seem to be carrying out the implications of the above statement.

Chapter 6   Meeting Individual Needs • 162

The first portion of Chapter 6 deals with those pupils who need even more individualized attention than the average retarded reader. The slow learner, the disadvantaged reader, the reluctant learner, the severely emotionally-disturbed retarded reader, and the dyslexiac reader each needs a slightly different program of remediation. The chapter shows how to differentiate instruction for these pupils.

Chapter 6   Meeting Individual Needs (*cont.*)

The second part of the chapter, proceeding on the assumption that there is no one best remedial or corrective method, introduces the reader to the following remedial methods: the visual method (Gates); the Monroe Method; the Fernald Method; the Unified Phonics Method; the Color Phonics System; the Progressive Choice Reading Method; and the Gillingham Method.

The chapter concludes with a discussion of ways to determine the effectiveness of various remedial procedures in terms of the gains in reading achievement. It shows how to evaluate improvement from remedial teaching.

Chapter 7   Materials for Teaching Reading • 194

The materials surveyed in this chapter include materials for both developmental and remedial instruction. To provide for the specific needs of slow learners, disadvantaged children, the reluctant readers, and the retarded readers a great variety of remedial and special help programs are needed. There is no panacea for reading problems, but the newer media can help. The chapter thus suggests guidelines in choosing materials and lists materials in each of these areas:

1. Skill-Improvement Materials
   a. The Basal Reading Series
   b. Reading Laboratories
   c. Comprehension Development Materials
   d. Word Attack Materials

2. Audio-Visual Materials

3. Mechanical Devices
   a. Tachistoscopes
   b. Accelerating Devices
   c. Reading-Related Machines

4. Professional Books

Epilogue

Not all children progress at the same rate. Even among pupils of adequate ability, some meet problems that delay or block learning. The effective developmental reading program is thus built on a foundation of early diagnosis of inadequacies, careful evaluation of needs and

Epilogue (*cont.*)

abilities, and the utilization of professionally designed methods and materials.

A basic thesis in the book has been that diagnostic procedure ought to be aimed at prevention as well as remediation; that prevention is best accomplished by an early identification of the symptoms of incipient reading disability; and that when it is not possible to prevent, when in fact the pupil has already become a reading disability case, that every effort be made to identify the causes and to provide the proper remediation.

Remedial reading instruction is not going to remove all reading disabilities from the educational scene. This would be expecting too much, but remedial instruction has amply proved its effectiveness. Its greatest benefit may be that it focuses the teacher's attention on the pupil's difficulties. Remedial instruction is not magic. Often it is simply a matter of teaching the skills that the pupil does not have.

In summary, diagnosis and remediation are essential elements of a sound developmental program. They are no longer the special privileges of the slow or retarded learner. They must be extended to every child in the classroom.

Appendices

Diagnosis and Remediation
of
Reading Disability

1

Identifying the
Difficulty

While this book is focused on diagnosis and specific remedies for reading difficulties, it should be pointed out that many educators today are concerned about the overemphasis on remediation and the frequent ignoring of prevention. Their fears are not entirely groundless. In too many instances the best teachers are removed from regular classroom teaching and put into the role of special or remedial reading teacher. This can only lead to poorer instruction in the classroom and increased numbers of children with reading problems. It may well be that we are thus producing retarded readers at a rate much faster than we will ever be able to remediate.

Although we have done a better job of remediation than of prevention, it is naturally better to prevent than to remediate; it is far better that we deal with the problem in the classroom than wait until the pupil becomes a reading disability. And because of the important relationship between diagnosis and prevention, this book will offer tested guidelines that will help the reader anticipate a potential reading problem.

Prevention is not an easy task. No one has found the appropriate solutions or we would not have the number of reading disabilities that we do have. Perhaps we have not looked for ways of preventing reading disability. We may well have been satisfied with cures.

Reading failures can be prevented only if every lesson is a diagnostic, and in a sense, a remedial lesson. Perhaps even then many failures could not be prevented, but the teacher must operate on the assumption that failures can be prevented, and it is only through accurate and continuous diagnosis of the child's needs and difficulties, of his assets and strengths, that the teacher can modify instruction to meet these needs. Diagnosis is a blueprint for instruction. Continuous diagnosis is a "must" in the reading classroom. Prevention is an end-product of diagnosis. Diagnosis identifies minor difficulties before they become disabilities and thus occasions adjustments in instruction that might remove these difficulties.

One of the lessons we have learned the hard way in combating cancer is that many people die from cancer because someone either ignored the symptoms or did not read them correctly. Children likewise become reading disability cases because someone ignored or did not read the symptoms of reading disability correctly.

It is not uncommon for the teacher to observe within the classroom children who fit the following descriptions. Jane has completed the readiness program, but still cannot identify rhyming words. Dick has missed a significant amount of reading instruction because he was ill. June has an abnormal amount of difficulty with similar-appearing words such as *them* and *then*. Pat, in reading orally, gets the meaning but cannot say some of the words. Jim has difficulty remembering such high frequency words as *in* or *the*.

Others are developing habits of word-by-word reading, of vocalizing, of back tracking, of daydreaming while reading, of rereading, of plodding along at a snail's pace, of word blocking, of following words with their finger, or of moving the head from side to side rather than moving their eyes across the page.

Serious problems? No, but these innocuous difficulties tend to snowball. Most remedial cases are probably instances of "an accumulation of unmet reading needs." Reading deficiency begins with simple inadequacies. Despite the good work of the classroom teacher, some pupils lose increasingly more ground with each year of school attendance. Retardation is cumulative.

To detect and diagnose the incipient reading problems, then, is a prime responsibility of the teacher and it is at this point that prevention of reading disability begins. Prevention of reading difficulties thus begins before the child begins formal reading instruction and continues throughout his entire school year. It begins in the readiness program and is best brought about by diagnosis of and constant alertness to any incipient or existing difficulty.

It doesn't make sense to delay remedial instruction until the third grade. We cannot permit children to become imprisoned in faulty learning habits. At any time the teacher notices that the child is not progressing satisfactorily, diagnostic study and appropriate remedial education seem indicated. As Eisenberg [1] notes:

> We would not hear of delaying therapy for rheumatic fever because not every patient incurs a valvulitis; we would not consider deferring laparotomy for a suspected appendicitis because diagnosis is imprecise and not every appendix perforates.

From what we have said thus far one point stands out. The teacher, if he is to prevent reading disabilities, needs to become somewhat of an expert diagnostician. He needs to be "on top of the situation," as it were. Furthermore, he needs to become a diagnostic teacher who has command of various instructional techniques and methods.

Let us begin then by making some generic observations about diagnosis.

Definition of diagnosis

Diagnosis is defined in *Webster's New Collegiate Dictionary* as the art or act of recognizing disease from its signs and symptoms. Bruecker [2] notes that educational diagnosis refers to the techniques by which one discovers and evaluates the strengths and weaknesses of an individual. The diagnostician gathers data and then on the basis of the analysis and interpretation of these data suggests developmental or remedial measures.

Tiegs [3] adds that educational diagnosis

> . . . is the basis of intelligent teaching. Its function is to facilitate the optimum development of every pupil. The following activities should become routine: determining for each pupil (1) which of his factors of intelligence are strong and which are weak, (2) whether he learns better through language or non-language materials and situations, (3) what his unattained objectives are, and (4) the nature of his desires, his fears, and his frustrations.

Diagnosis is an identification of weakness or strength from an observation of symptoms. It is an inference from performance. It must include assessment of both level of performance (reading retardation) and manner of performance (inability to integrate visual stimuli). It is concerned with determining the nature of the problem, identifying the constellation of factors that produced it, and finding a point of attack.

The heart of diagnosis is an intelligent interpretation of the facts. It is not simply testing. The diagnostician must possess both theoretical knowledge and practical experience, know what questions to ask, what tests and procedures to use to get the needed facts, and how to interpret the findings. He needs to be able to draw up a plan for correction and remediation.

Principles of diagnosis

As one scans the literature on diagnosis, a few general principles emerge:

1. Diagnosis begins with each pupil's unique instructional needs—
   a. What can he do?
   b. What are his difficulties?
   c. What are the causes for his difficulties?
   d. What can be done to remedy his difficulties?
2. Diagnosis is a continuous process.
3. Diagnosis should be directed toward formulating methods of remediation.
4. Diagnosis and remediation are no longer the special privi-

leges of the slow or retarded learner—they are extended to the gifted and the average as well.

5. Diagnosis may be concerned merely with the symptomatology, but genuine diagnosis looks toward the causes of the symptoms. The diagnostic viewpoint is that behavior is caused. The teacher thus needs to understand the causes of inadequate performance rather than to blame the pupil for it. The child should not be labeled dumb or lazy, even though each characteristic may be a cause once in a while.

6. The causes of pupil inadequacy are usually multiple rather than single or unitary.

7. The teacher needs more than simply skill in diagnosing the causes of the child's difficulty. He needs ability to modify instruction to meet the need identified by diagnosis.

8. Decisions based on diagnosis should flow from a pattern of test scores and a variety of other data.

9. The analysis of reading difficulties is primarily an *educational-analysis* task; it is best done by an experienced teacher who knows the essential elements in reading instruction.[4]

Steps in diagnosis

Diagnosis leads to an ever more detailed study of the problem. It begins in reading with simple observation and possibly a survey test and ends up with a hypothesis for remediation. It involves the identification and description of the problem, the discovery of the causes, and projection of remediation required. More specifically, the steps of the diagnostic procedure may be the following:

I. The Overall Screening Process—Compare expected functioning level as determined by IQ and other test and personal data with actual functioning level as determined by the reading survey test or by other less formal procedures. This is the level of *survey diagnosis* and consists chiefly of classroom screening.

II. Diagnostic Testing—Describe the condition more specifically, checking on such specifics as knowledge of vocabulary, inability to associate sound with the beginning consonant, inability to phrase correctly, or reversal problems. Informal observations of the pupil's reading and diagnostic testing will help to identify the difficulties. This is the level of *specific diagnosis* and is identified with individual diagnosis.

III. Detailed Investigation of Causality—Make an analysis of the disability, looking for the correlates of disability. If the test results in Step II show a weakness in phonic skills, the pupil's auditory discrimination might be checked. This is the level of *intensive diagnosis* and is associated with identifying the underlying causes of the reading disability.

IV. Remediation—Finally, draw up a program of remediation. Diagnosis is complete only when remediation occurs.

We have devoted four chapters to the diagnostic process. This first chapter will deal with the initial step in diagnosis. Chapters 2, 3 and 4 will take up the remaining steps in the diagnostic process.

Step I: The screening process

Let us assume that we have a typical elementary school that has about 500 children and in which the administration and staff want to begin a special reading program for those children who are more or less retarded in reading. The immediate aim will be to reduce the number of pupils for this special education to somewhere below 500.

Screening separates those persons who are most likely to need special attention from those who are not likely to need it. It is commonly applied to large groups of pupils by classroom teachers. This first step tends to be comprehensive in *breadth;* the later steps in diagnosis are more comprehensive in *depth.* Screening procedures should be simple, fairly quick, inexpensive, valid, reliable, and productive.

For many children we do not need a detailed diagnosis. A more general diagnosis is sufficient. It is enough in most instances that we acquire sufficient knowledge about the 500 children or the 30 children in a given classroom so that instruction might be adjusted to the group. This overall screening process should identify the overall reading proficiency of the group or class, help to adjust instruction to individual differences within the group, and locate those pupils who are in need of further analysis of their disability.

There needs to be adequate provision for remediation of most reading disability cases in the regular classroom. We simply cannot refer everybody to the remedial teacher. If the remedial teacher is to accomplish his task, he needs to be able to work with fewer pupils than the regular teacher. It doesn't make sense to overload the remedial teacher to the point where he cannot provide for the special needs of those pupils who are referred.

One factor that operates against remediation in the regular classroom is the high pupil-teacher ratio. It is difficult to provide individual remediation when there are 30 children all clamoring for the teacher's time and attention. There thus needs to be a reduction in this ratio in the remedial setting. Other reasons for reducing the ratio might be cited. For one, the pupils needing special attention exhibit a wider range of individual differences, have more frequent and greater psychological and physical limitations, and show a greater variation of reading difficulties. Secondly, the remedial teacher needs more time for individual diagnosis and remediation, for record-keeping, and for consultation with parents and classroom teachers. Probably no more than eight youngsters with special reading problems should be assigned to the special teacher at any given time. The smaller the group, the greater the returns for each child tend to be.

Furthermore, the reading specialist cannot become the dumping ground for all children who are a problem in school. The special reading class cannot become a place where teachers, administrators, and parents dump the child who is a problem to them. If this should happen, the teacher soon becomes overburdened and frustrated.

THE NATURE OF RETARDATION

Perhaps the first prerequisite for anyone associated with the reading program, and indeed the educational program, is to have a clear conception of the meaning of retardation. There is a difference between slow learners, reluctant readers, experientially deprived readers, and retarded readers. *See Figure 1-1,* which delineates some of these differences.

Retardation generally is defined in relation to level of general development, with perhaps the greater emphasis being on mental development. Retardation is associated with slower progress than is expected. A retarded reader is one whose reading capacity is considerably greater than his reading achievement.

A retarded reader has been described as one with normal intelligence who has had ample opportunity, has tried, but is unable to learn. Bryant notes that disability is always dependent upon the material and methods used in instruction. A child may not be able to learn by one method; but he may not be "disabled" if a different method is used.[5] Bryant adds that disability is the result of a complex interaction of multiple factors.

A reader is also more or less retarded. The retarded reader of fifty years ago was more likely to be a pupil who could not read. Today, he often is a pupil who is not reading as well as he might. Durrell[6] notes that a retardation of six months at the first-grade level is more serious than is a retardation of six months at the sixth-grade level. Harris[7] does not consider a first-grade child retarded unless his reading age is at least six months below his mental age. The difference between performance and potential might be at least nine months for children in grades four and five and about a year in grades six and above.

Certainly, retardation is a matter of degree. There are general levels of retardation and each level tends to be characterized by its own symptoms and requires its own remedial techniques.[8] Retardation may be general or specific. General retardation refers to a generally low level of reading ability as compared with mental age. The child lacks overall maturity in reading. Specific retardation is the term used to designate weaknesses in a specific area or areas of reading. Retardation also can be in the nature of a limiting disability or a complex disability. The child with limiting disability is one who has serious deficiencies in basic reading skills which impede his entire reading growth. In the case of a child with a complex disability there is severe reading retardation as shown by a marked discrepancy between his achievement and his ability and in addition he shows symptoms of personal problems, tension, and antipathy to reading.

Characteristics of Various Poor Readers

A	B	C	D
Slow Learner	Reluctant Reader	Disadvantaged Reader	Retarded Reader
↓	↓	↓	↓
ability level below 90 IQ	can read but will not	potential often far exceeds performance	is usually of average or above average intelligence, although a retarded reader could also be a slow learner
↓	↓	↓	↓
generally reads on ability level	the root of the reading difficulties is the mental attitude of the pupil	generally can learn and wants to learn	does not read on ability level
↓	↓	↓	↓
generally reads below grade level	solution to the reading problem begins with a change of attitude	lacks adequate oral language because of inadequate experience	may or may not be reading below grade level
↓		↓	↓
instruction needs to be adapted to his limited ability— the pace of instruction and teacher expectations must be realistic		does not look upon reading as life-related	may show blocks to learning, especially emotional or neurological, which keep him from learning to read
		↓	
		often feels alienated from the larger social structure	
		↓	
		often is deficient in auditory attention	
		↓	
		needs to learn how to learn	

Figure 1–1

READING POTENTIAL

The first diagnostic step involves an analysis of (1) reading potential or reading expectancy level and (2) reading achievement. It presents the teacher with a knowledge of what the child's present level of achievement is and to what level he might progress.

Various ways of assessing reading potential have been tried. The tests most frequently used to assess reading potential are intelligence or scholastic aptitude tests. The purposes of these tests and guidelines for their use are outlined in *Figure 1–2*. These

Values and Limitations

of

SCHOLASTIC APTITUDE OR
INTELLIGENCE TESTS

1. The tests sample learnings that almost everybody has had an opportunity to learn.
2. Their primary purpose is to gear the instructional program to the ability level of the pupil.
3. Effective use of intellectual ability depends on drive, interest, opportunity, and one's self-concept.
4. Intelligence is measured through a small sample of a pupil's behavior—the sample therefore needs to be fair.
5. The child's performance needs to be interpreted in terms of the curriculum to which he has been exposed.
6. Preschool experience differentiates intelligence scores more highly at grade 5 than at grade 1. Deprivational influences have a greater effect at later developmental stages than at earlier times.
7. The tests do not discriminate between ignorance and stupidity.
8. The child with language and reading difficulties will not be able to show his true intellectual level on a verbal intelligence test.
9. The child who does not have adequate sensory mechanisms to acquire experience or to acquire it adequately tends to show up poorly on intelligence tests.

Figure 1–2

tests often provide IQ or mental age scores. The mental age is a fairly good indicator of the level at which the child should be reading and IQ is a pretty good indicator of the level that the child will ultimately attain.[9]

Since the idea is to obtain intelligence or scholastic aptitude test scores on all 500 children, or perhaps on a class of 30, it is recommended that the first test be a group paper-and-pencil test. Tests useful for this purpose are:

- California Test of Mental Maturity
- Kuhlmann-Anderson IQ Test
- Kuhlmann-Finch IQ Test
- Otis-Lennon Mental Ability Test
- SRA Primary Mental Abilities Test

Each of these tests is described in Appendix I. Most primary tests use pictures and thus can generally be used with retarded readers. Tests for fourth grade and higher usually require reading. Some of these, however, provide nonverbal scores and these scores can give clues for diagnosis. When the verbal score is substantially lower than the nonverbal score, the teacher might suspect that the pupil's performance on the verbal sections is limited by the lack of reading ability. The test is thus an unfair test for him. It often places the poor reader in the dull-normal category, thus underestimating his real ability.

Probably, every child whose IQ score falls below 90 or below the 25 percentile on a test requiring reading should be given another intelligence or scholastic aptitude test. Another IQ test should also be given when the pupil's reading level score as determined by a reading achievement test is significantly below his grade level. This means that perhaps 25 per cent or 125 pupils of the original group of 500 need retesting. It may mean that from six to eight pupils in a given classroom need to be retested. Their abilities need to be measured by a test that does not require reading to get the correct answer. Here is a list of tests that are specifically designed to deal with this problem. Some of them may be administered to a group of children and others must be given individually. Some of the latter require special training for their administration.

Group

- Chicago Nonverbal Examination
- IPAT Culture Fair Intelligence Tests

Individual

- Columbia Mental Maturity Scale
- Full-Range Picture Vocabulary Test
- Peabody Picture Vocabulary Test
- Quick Test
- Slosson Intelligence Test for Children and Adults
- Stanford-Binet Intelligence Scales
- Wechsler Intelligence Scale for Children

Each of these tests is described in Appendix I.

Let us look at three of the tests listed. The *IPAT Culture Fair Intelligence Test*,[10] in that it is a group nonverbal test, is very useful to the reading teacher. It attempts to measure intelligence apart from educational and experiential influences. It seeks to single out basic mental capacity apart from the accidental circumstances of better or poorer schooling, social class, or experience. Scale 1 is for children four to eight years of age; Scale 2 is for pupils of age eight to fourteen; and Scale 3 is used with bright high school youngsters or adults. The test may be administered either singly or in groups. The test has two parts, each made up of four subtests.

Test 1 (*Series*) from Scale 2 requires the student to answer the question: "Which one would come next in the series?"

Part I: Sample 1:

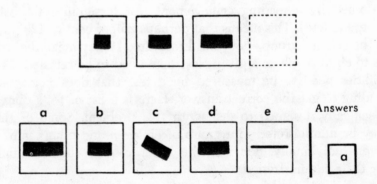

Test 2 (*Classification*) requires the examinee to answer the question: "Four are the same, one is different. Which one is different?"

Part I: Sample 1:

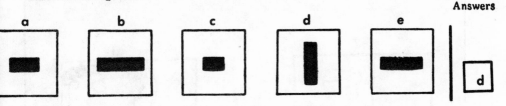

Test 3 (*Matrices*) requires the examinee to answer the question: "Which one shall we put in the box to make it look right?"

Part I: Sample 1:

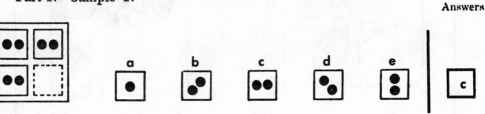

Test 4 (*Conditions*) tells the examinee to look at the dot or dots in a sample configuration and then select a configuration in which dots can be placed in an analogous way.

Part I: Sample 1:

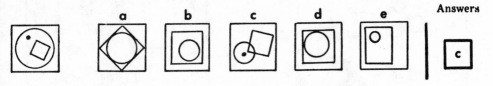

The *Quick Test* [11] consists of three plates, each with four drawings. The pupil is shown the plate and then fifty words of increasing difficulty are read to him. He must associate the word with one of the four pictures (*see Figure 1–3*).

The administrator starts out by saying something like: "I'm going to show you some pictures, and say some words. When I

Figure 1–3
Quick Test

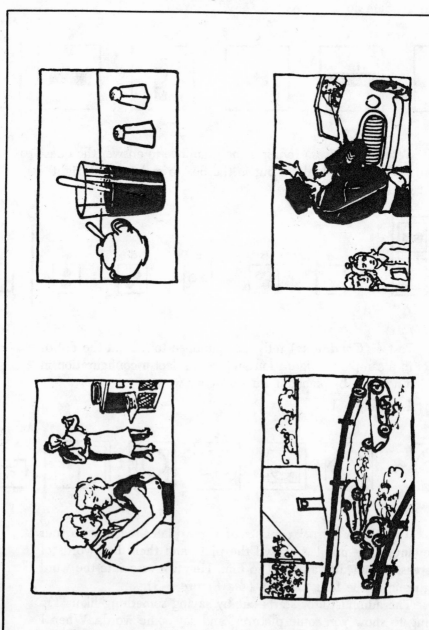

say a word, show me which of the pictures best fits it. Show me _____."

The following instructions might also be used: "This is a kind of picture game. I am going to show you some pictures and read some words. You point to the best pictures for the words. Some of the words will be very easy and some of the words will be hard. You won't know all the words. If I read a word that you don't know, just tell me that you don't know, and I will go on to another word."

The following words are used with Form 1:

belt	drink	pepper	track	respectful
dancing	wreck	racing	school	betting
traffic	music	salt	partner	daring
whistle	medicine	woman	couples	stadium
fence	gun	sugar	rail	pedestrian
graceful	crystallized	velocity	intimacy	cacophony
fluid	turntable	decisive	concoction	miscible
solution	saccharin	laceration	conviviality	amicable
discipline	immature	foliage	chevrons	pungent
bleachers	cordiality	imperative	condiment	imbibe

The test, even when all three forms are administered, takes only ten to fifteen minutes. The test allows for testing for IQ from the ability level of one-and-a-half-year-old children to superior adults. It is especially designed for small children, the severely physically handicapped, and children who have reading or other communication difficulties. Testing continues until the pupil has failed six consecutive words.

The WISC (Wechsler Intelligence Scale for Children) is an individual test and requires special training on the part of the administrator. It consists of eleven subtests. It has proved very useful in diagnosis. The research [12] shows that on this test poor readers score low on the Arithmetic, Coding, and Information subtests, and score relatively higher on the Picture Arrangement and Picture Completion. On the Illinois Test of Psycholinguistic Abilities (ITPA) poor readers were found to score lower on Auditory-Vocal Automatic (a verbal grammar test) and Visual-Motor Sequential (visual sequential memory). On the Stanford-

Binet poor readers tend to perform poorly on defining words, auditory memory of non-meaningful material, and on the completion of sentences read to or by the examinee. These studies indicate that poor readers:

1. Do poorly on tests which measure school learning as indicated by the low information score on the *WISC* and poor reading scores on the Binet.
2. Do poorly on auditory and visual memory tasks which contain non-meaningful material as is indicated in the Coding test on the *WISC* and on the Visual Motor Sequential subtest of the *ITPA*.
3. Are not able to organize separate auditory and visual stimuli into meaningful wholes and are thus unable to blend sounds.

Reading potential or readiness for reading instruction on the kindergarten–first grade level also may be assessed through readiness tests. Readiness tests are closely related to scholastic aptitude tests, and in general, measure much the same area of development. They appraise various types of mental functioning that are related to success in reading, such as ability to perceive likenesses and differences in letter and word forms, ability to follow directions, and auditory memory and discrimination. In addition, they measure other skills more indicative of other types of readiness.

Some reading readiness tests that we can recommend are the following:

- Diagnostic Reading Tests
- Reading Readiness Booklet
- Gates Reading Readiness Test
- Harrison-Stroud Readiness Tests
- Lee-Clark Reading Readiness Test
- Metropolitan Readiness Test
- Murphy-Durrell Diagnostic Reading Readiness Test

Each of these and other tests commonly used to assess the child's readiness for reading are discussed in Appendix II.

A program called KELP (Kindergarten Evaluation of Learning Potential), available from McGraw-Hill Book Company, offers another way of evaluating learning potential. It includes measures of auditory perception, visual discrimination, language skills, number concepts, physical adeptness, and social interaction.

There is a third way of estimating the pupil's potential. The pupil's listening ability is a good indicator of the level on which the pupil could be reading. Reading might be defined as listening through print. The following tests provide a measure of the pupil's listening comprehension:

- *Stroud-Hieronymus Primary Reading Profiles,* Houghton Mifflin Company.

  This test is designed for first-second grade level and measures aptitude for reading, auditory association, word recognition, word attack, and interpretation and comprehension. Test 1, *Aptitude for Reading,* is a listening test, requiring no reading of any kind. Its purpose is to indicate the pupil's aptitude to understand spoken language, informative language, and directions, as well as his ability to associate the meaning of the pictures with what he hears.

- *Botel Reading Inventory,* Follett Publishing Company.

  This inventory for grades 1-12 has a section entitled "Word Opposites Listening Test." There are ten multiple-choice items at each level. Each item consists of four or five words and the pupil must find a word in each line that is opposite of the first word.

- *Sequential Tests of Educational Progress,* Listening, Cooperative Test Division, Educational Testing Services.

  This listening test is part of a larger battery of tests usable on grade levels four to fourteen.

- *Brown-Carlsen Listening Comprehension Test,* Harcourt, Brace, and World.

  This test for grade nine and above measures five important listening skills—immediate recall, following directions, recognizing transitions, recognizing word meanings, and lecture comprehension.

- *Durrell-Sullivan Reading Capacity Test,* Harcourt, Brace, and World.

  This test for grades two-and-a-half to six requires from

thirty to forty-five minutes. It measures word and paragraph meaning, spelling, and written recall. It requires no reading and is basically a listening comprehension test.

Studies indicate that up to fifth grade, students tend to be better listeners than readers. We need to capitalize on this ability of the student. We also need to use the pupil's listening ability as a gauge of the level on which he might be reading.

READING ACHIEVEMENT

Having discovered the potential of the 500 youngsters, or the 30 in the individual classroom, it is next necessary to get an estimate of their reading achievement. A reading survey test should be administered to each of the pupils.

The survey test is concerned with general achievement and typically is the first reading achievement test that the teacher will use. Usually it emphasizes vocabulary knowledge, comprehension of sentences or paragraphs, and perhaps speed of comprehension. It gives a general picture by identifying broad areas in which the pupil excels or is weak. It may tell, for example, that a certain child is reading at a level typical of children one or more grades above or below his present grade level. It indicates the general level of pupil progress and provides data for determining a pupil's proper grade placement and the reading materials that he should be expected to use with understanding.

Some survey tests that we can recommend are the following:

- California Reading Test
- Durrell-Sullivan Reading Capacity and Achievement Test
- Gates-MacGinitie Reading Tests
- Iowa Silent Reading Test
- Metropolitan Reading Test

Each of these and numerous other survey tests are described in Appendix III.

After having obtained the intelligence test score and the survey reading test scores, it is possible to identify the number of students whose reading scores are significantly below their intelligence or scholastic aptitude test score.

The following data are from an elementary class in a western state, data which can surely be duplicated in many other schools. This was a class of twenty-eight eighth graders, fifteen boys and thirteen girls. The IQ data were obtained through testing with the *Kuhlmann-Finch IQ Test*. The reading scores were obtained by administering the *Gates Reading Survey Test*. The tests were given one day apart, February 28 and March 1, 1967, and thus the class was on about 8.6 grade level. The chronological ages of the pupils ranged from thirteen years and two months to fourteen years and four months.

The teacher's question is generally this: "I have the data, but what do I now do with them?" In the next few pages we have tried to outline the steps in using the information.

Begin treatment of the data by grouping the reading and intelligence scores into two columns. The reading scores of the twenty-eight pupils ranked from high to low are given in column I. Each pupil's corresponding IQ score is given in column II. The reading scores should be reported as age or grade scores. Here they are reported as grade scores.

Pupil	Reading Score at Grade Level	IQ Score	Pupil	Reading Score at Grade Level	IQ Score
1	11.6	122	15	8.0	114
2	11.5	120	16	8.0	105
3	11.5	124	17	7.9	98
4	11.3	116	18	7.9	117
5	11.3	125	19	7.8	101
6	10.7	96	20	7.7	100
7	10.4	107	21	7.5	117
8	10.2	114	22	7.5	97
9	9.8	107	23	7.0	102
10	9.4	111	24	7.0	103
11	8.8	102	25	6.5	101
12	8.7	115	26	6.1	113
13	8.3	107	27	6.0	101
14	8.3	122	28	4.9	83

The range in reading performance in this group was from 4.9 grade level to 11.6 grade level, suggesting that about six-and-a-half grade levels differentiated the best from the poorest reader.

The IQ range was from 83 to 125. The median reading score was 8.15; the median IQ was 107. The scores plotted on a scattergram, *Figure 1–4*, look as follows:

The scattergram is divided into four quadrants. Each quadrant tells us something:

Quadrant A.   The IQ score is in the upper half of the class, but the reading score is in the lower half.

Quadrant B.   The IQ score is in the upper half of the class, and the reading score is in the upper half.

Quadrant C.   The IQ score is in the lower half of the class and so is the reading score.

Quadrant D.   The IQ score is in the lower half, but the reading score is in the upper half.

It is our feeling that pupil No. 28 should be retested with another IQ test, preferably one of the individual tests we suggested previously, because his IQ was identified as below 90; we recommend, in addition, that pupils 25, 26, and 27 (and 28 of course) be similarly retested because their reading score is significantly below grade level, thus indicating a reading problem. This reading problem unquestionably prohibited them from revealing their real potential on a group, paper-pencil test of intelligence.

An analysis of the scattergram reveals:

1. That pupils 15, 18, 21, and 26 are probably genuinely retarded in reading.

2. Since the reading performance of pupils 6 and 11 is in the upper half of the class, but their IQ scores are in the lower half, one might be suspect of the IQ score. Students who score thusly often are called over-achievers. Remember, however, that pupil 11 has an above average IQ (102—the average is 100) and his reading performance is 8.8, just slightly above his grade level which is 8.6. His scores probably are correct. Pupil 6 presents a different picture. He should be retested. His IQ score is just slightly below average, but his reading performance is significantly above grade level.

3. Pupils 14, 16, 19, 20, 23, 24, 25, and 27 all have average

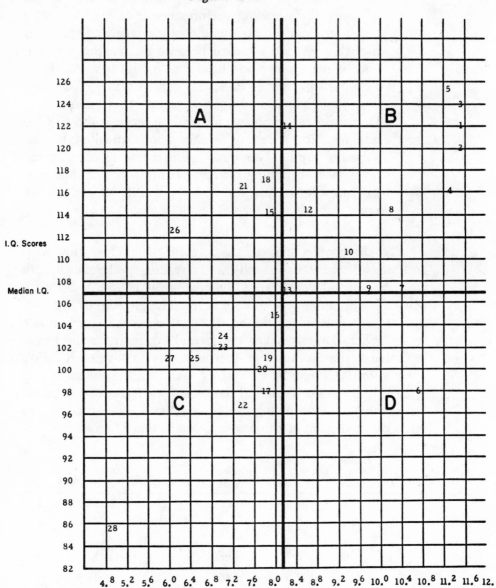

Figure 1–4

(100) or above average IQs, but each is performing below grade level. It is probable that pupils 16, 23, 24, 25, and 27, since their reading performance is at least one year below grade level, are significantly retarded. Pupil 14 is probably severely retarded because his reading performance is not up to grade level, but his IQ is substantially better than average. The same can be said for pupil 12, even though he is reading at or slightly above grade level. One of the real problems for reading teachers today is the administrator, parent or teacher who is unwilling to consider the pupil to be retarded if he is reading above grade level, even though his reading performance might be considerably below his ability level. Pupils 19 and 20 are more difficult to interpret.

To check upon some of the foregoing hypotheses and suggestions, let us compare each pupil's reading performance with his or her mental age. It would be possible, of course, to compare it with his listening performance score. The purpose of this procedure is to determine whether the reading score (reading age score) is substantially below the mental age score, or the listening score as the case may be. It is necessary to have each child's age and his IQ. Begin by converting the reading grade score into a reading age score. Then find the mental age. This may be done (as shown) by multiplying the age by the IQ, being careful to put a decimal point at the proper place in the IQ score.

Pupil	Reading Grade Score	Reading Age (RA) Score	Chronological Age	IQ Score	Mental Age	Difference between MA & RA
1	11.6	16.9	14.0	122 (14 x 1.22)	17.0	— .1
2	11.5	16.9	14.0	120 (14 x 1.20)	16.8	+ .1
3	11.5	16.8	14.0	124 (14 x 1.24)	17.4	— .6
4	11.3	16.6	13.6	116 (13.6 x 1.16)	15.8	+ .8
5	11.3	16.5	13.3	125 (13.3 x 1.25)	16.6	— .1
6	10.7	16.0	13.3	96 (13.3 x .96)	12.7	+3.3
7	10.4	15.9	13.8	107 (13.8 x 1.07)	14.7	+1.2

8	10.2	15.5	13.2	114 (13.2 x 1.14)	15.0	+ .5
9	9.8	15.0	14.4	107 (14.4 x 1.07)	15.3	— .3
10	9.4	14.6	13.8	111 (13.8 x 1.11)	15.3	— .7
11	8.8	14.0	13.8	102 (13.8 x 1.02)	14.0	—
12	8.7	13.9	13.4	115 (13.4 x 1.15)	15.4	—1.5
13	8.3	14.8	13.6	107 (13.6 x 1.07)	14.5	+ .3
14	8.3	13.5	13.9	122 (13.9 x 1.22)	16.9	—3.5
15	8.0	13.2	13.2	114 (13.2 x 1.14)	15.0	—1.8
16	8.0	13.2	13.9	105 (13.9 x 1.05)	14.5	—1.3
17	7.9	13.3	13.5	98 (13.5 x .98)	13.2	+ .1
18	7.9	13.1	14.1	117 (14.1 x 1.17)	16.4	—3.3
19	7.8	13.0	13.4	101 (13.4 x 1.01)	13.5	— .5
20	7.7	13.0	13.5	100 (13.5 x 1.00)	13.5	— .5
21	7.5	12.8	13.5	117 (13.5 x 1.17)	15.8	—3.0
22	7.5	12.6	13.5	97 (13.5 x .97)	13.0	— .4
23	7.0	12.3	13.1	102 (13.1 x 1.02)	13.3	—1.0
24	7.0	12.2	13.4	103 (13.4 x 1.03)	13.8	—1.6
25	6.5	11.5	13.2	101 (13.2 x 1.01)	13.3	—1.8
26	6.1	11.3	14.2	113 (14.2 x 1.13)	16.0	—4.7
27	6.0	11.1	13.3	101 (13.3 x 1.01)	13.4	—2.3
28	4.9	10.0	14.0	83 (14.0 x .83)	11.6	—1.6

An analysis of the foregoing data indicates:

1. That pupils 12, 14, 15, 16, 18, 21, 23, 24, 25, 26, 27, and 28 are reading significantly below their mental age level. The discrepancy between their mental ages and reading ages is more than a year and so it is assumed that genuine retardation exists.

2. Of these, the scattergram had clearly identified only 15, 18, 21, and 26.

3. Our projection that pupils 12, 14, 16, 23, 24, 25, and 27 were probably retarded was correct. Pupil 28, although a slow learner, is nevertheless retarded.

4. Pupil 6 is identified as reading supposedly 3.3 years above his ability level. This needs to be further investigated.

5. Pupil 7, since he is supposedly reading 1.2 years above ability, should be given another intelligence test.

6. Pupils 14, 18, 21, and 26, each retarded more than three years, were boys.

Summary

Step I is primarily concerned with the identification of the reading difficulty. It is a process of screening and selecting. If reading retardation is to be prevented, the identification of reading difficulties must come soon after they arise. Remediation can then be initiated before the problem mushrooms into a severe disability. By completing Step I, we should have greatly reduced the number of pupils who need special attention. We should have differentiated pupils who are genuinely retarded and who need corrective and remedial instruction from those who simply need adapted instruction.

----

[1] Eisenberg, Leon. "Epidemiology of Reading Retardation," in *The Disabled Reader*, ed. by John Money, Johns Hopkins Press, Baltimore, 1966.

[2] Bruecker, Leo J. "Introduction," *Educational Diagnosis*. Thirty-fourth Yearbook of the National Society for the Study of Education, Public School Publishing Company, Bloomington, 1935, pp. 1-14.

[3] From *Educational Bulletin No. 18*, "Educational Diagnosis," 1959 Revision, by Ernest W. Tiegs by permission of California Test Bureau, a Division of McGraw-Hill Book Company, Del Monte Research Park, Monterey, California, p. 5.

[4] Durrell, Donald D. *Improving Reading Instruction*. World Book Company, New York, 1956, pp. 354-355.

[5] Bryant, N. Dale. "Learning Disabilities in Reading," *Reading as an Intellectual Activity*. International Reading Association Conference Proceedings, Scholastic Magazines, New York, 1963, pp. 142-146.

[6] Durrell, Donald D. *The Improvement of Basic Reading Abilities*. World Book Company, Yonkers, New York, 1940, p. 270.

[7] Harris, Albert J. *How to Increase Reading Ability*, 3rd edition, David McKay Company, Inc., New York, 1961, p. 299.

[8] Bond, Guy L. and Tinker, Miles A. *Reading Difficulties: Their Diagnosis and Correction*. Appleton-Century-Crofts, New York, 1967, pp. 95-99.

[9] These concepts are explained more fully in Chapter 3 under the heading, "Inadequate Intellectual Development."

[10] Reproduced by permission of the Institute for Personality and Ability Testing, 16024 Coronado Drive, Champaign, Illinois.

[11] Reproduced by special permission of Psychological Test Specialists, Missoula, Mont. Copyright 1962.

[12] Neville, Donald. "Learning Characteristcis of Poor Readers as Revealed by Results of Individually Administered Intelligence Tests." *Vistas in Reading*, Proceedings of the Eleventh Annual Convention, International Reading Association, Newark, 1967, pp. 554-559.

2

The Diagnostic Process–
Diagnostic Testing

Chapter 2 continues the diagnostic process begun in Step I. Step II, diagnostic testing, is the beginning of detailed diagnosis. It is directed toward defining the actual nature of the individual's reading difficulties and with identifying the conditions causing them. It is a detailed investigation of the symptoms of reading disability, leading to a clinical diagnosis. On this level the teacher is not satisfied to know that the pupil is reading on a second-grade level when in fact he might be able to read on a fourth-grade level. The teacher wants to know the specific reasons for the overall low performance: Is it the inability to attack words? Is it the limited vocabulary? Is it the failure to use context? Is it the lack of ability in auditory blending? Is it an orientational difficulty? Or, is it a combination of factors?

Smith and Carrigan [1] note that diagnosis must be based on a careful investigation of the symptoms, on psychological test behavior, and often on intensive clinical case studies. "Such dead-end diagnosis as 'he isn't trying'; 'he needs more discipline'; 'he's neurotic'; 'too much pressure from his parents'; 'the trouble is, the schools don't teach phonics any more'—such conscience balms must be replaced with a clinical diagnosis."

Step II thus is a specific, an individual, and a clinical diagnosis. It is a detailed analysis of the reading problems of the pupils identified in Step I as retarded readers. Let's assume that about 20 per cent of the pupils studied in Step I are actually retarded in reading. It is now necessary to determine what their specific difficulties are and where, whether in the regular classroom or in the remedial room, their difficulties might best be taken care of.

In many schools, the classroom teacher is still the person primarily responsible for the diagnosis and remediation of reading problems. In others, the teacher is assisted by a remedial teacher or a reading specialist. The special reading teacher might then direct the diagnostic process or actually do the diagnosing himself.

Step II should include, if possible, the personal data sheet, a learning and behavior checklist, and a formal or informal inventory, an oral reading test, or a diagnostic test. Let us begin with the personal data sheet.

Personal data sheet

The first report on each pupil who was revealed in Step I to be reading significantly below his ability should summarize personal data on the pupil. *This report might be used as the referral form from the classroom teacher to the special teacher if this becomes necessary. It might also be sent to the pupil's new teacher when the pupil moves from one grade to another.* In this way, the new teacher would have some knowledge of the pupil's needs and could then adjust his instruction to the pupil.

The personal data sheet includes such data as: pupil's name, age, grade level, address, previous grades, attendance record, statements about his health, standardized test results, a compilation of the anecdotal reports by other teachers, and, most of all, the reason for the referral. The reason may be that the pupil is not reading up to ability level. The statement might simply read: "The test results indicate that he is reading about one grade level below his ability"; "He has a mental age of ten, but is reading like the average eight year old"; or, "His reading level is substantially below his listening comprehension level."

Whether the pupil is referred or kept in the regular classroom, it is imperative that the teacher know at least in a general

PERSONAL DATA SHEET

Pupil's Name_____ Birth date_____

                                    Mo. Day Year

Parents' Name_____ Age_____ Grade_____
Address_____ Phone_____

Academic Progress

   Report last year's grade (s)

Attendance Record

   Number of days absent for each grade: K__1__2__3__4__
                                           5__6__7__8__

Health

   (List physical infirmities, accidents, and severe illnesses as listed
   in school record.)

Standardized Tests

   Include all test results available—intelligence tests, achievement
   tests, etc.

| *Date Given* | *Name of Test* | *Score by* | |
| | | *Grade Level* | *Percentile* |

Reason for Referral

Anecdotal Reports or Comments of Former Teachers (Report on
back of this page)

                              Signed _____
                              Position _____

Date of report_____ 19__

Figure 2–1

sense what the problem is. The remaining instruments discussed
in this chapter delve more deeply into the pupil's more specific
problems and symptoms.

   A form similar to Figure 2–1 might be used to compile the
basic information on a pupil.

LEARNING AND BEHAVIOR CHECKLIST

There is also a need for another report, detailing the pupil's behavior and learning problems in the classroom. It is designed to summarize information about the child's usual scholastic performance and interaction in classroom affairs. A checklist, such as the following might be completed by the teacher on each pupil who is significantly retarded in reading. Each of the items should be answered as *Yes* or *No*.

Learning and Behavior Checklist

Name .... Sex..................

Age in years..................... and months................

IQ............................ MA............................

	YES	NO
1. Background of Previous Experience		
a. Has attended kindergarten		
b. Has a foreign language background		
c. Is from a low-level socioeconomic home ...		
d. Is intellectually dull-normal		
2. General Mental Development		
a. Perceives likenesses and differences		
b. Remembers word forms		
c. Has appropriate memory and attention span ..		
d. Thinks clearly and in sequence		
e. Can express his thoughts in his own words ...		
f. Associates symbols with pictures, objects, or facts		
g. Sees the relationship of the part to the whole		
h. Can think on an abstract level		
3. General Language Development		
a. Has appropriate vocabulary for his age		
b. Enunciates clearly		
c. Articulates clearly		
d. Pronounces words accurately		
e. Expresses himself clearly to others		
f. Is sensitive to sentence structure		

YES | NO

g. Talks in simple sentences .... ———|———
h. Understands that what can be said also can be
   written .... ———|———

4. General Physical and Physiological Development
   a. Has sufficient visual acuity .... ———|———
   b. Manifests refractive errors: myopia, hyperopia,
      astigmatism .... ———|———
   c. Eyes aim in different directions .... ———|———
   d. Eyes are in focus .... ———|———
   e. The visual images are different in shape and
      size .... ———|———
   f. Has a conductive hearing loss .... ———|———
   g. Has a high tone hearing loss .... ———|———
   h. Has good health .... ———|———
   i. Has suffered a neurological injury .... ———|———
   j. Has clearly developed eye-preference .... ———|———
   k. Has clearly developed dominance .... ———|———
   l. Makes reversals in speech, reading, and/or
      writing .... ———|———
   m. Has been converted from left to right-handed-
      ness .... ———|———

5. Motivational, Emotional and Social Development
   a. Is interested in learning to read .... ———|———
   b. Is interested in books .... ———|———
   c. Is interested in interpreting pictures and printed
      symbols .... ———|———
   d. Is curious about the shapes of words .... ———|———
   e. Works well with a group .... ———|———
   f. Is responsive to instruction .... ———|———
   g. Has a feeling of adequacy and belonging .... ———|———
   h. Has learned to help himself .... ———|———
   i. Has developed some tolerance for failure .... ———|———
   j. Exhibits a normal amount of self-confidence .. ———|———
   k. Tends to withdraw from the situation .... ———|———
   l. Is acceptant of authority .... ———|———
   m. Is normally communicative in the classroom .. ———|———
   n. Is usually attentive .... ———|———

6. Educational Development
   a. Can concentrate on or attend to learning ac-

	YES	NO

     tivities ....

  b. Can follow directions ....

  c. Instructional materials are adequate ....

  d. Has had training in efficient work habits ....

  e. Has attended regularly ....

  f. Has changed schools ....

7. Deficiencies in Comprehension
  a. Lacks vocabulary ....
  b. Uses context effectively ....
  c. Understands organization ....
  d. Uses structural clues to meaning ....
  e. Reads for main ideas ....
  f. Reads for details ....
  g. Reads to learn ....
  h. Reads critically ....
  i. Knows technical vocabulary ....

8. Deficiencies in Word Attack
  a. Associates sound with total word ....
  b. Knows the names of the letters ....
  c. Associates sound with beginning consonant ..
  d. Associates sound with medial vowel ....
  e. Uses configuration clues ....
    1. Inflectional endings ....
    2. Compounds ....
    3. Roots, prefixes, suffixes ....
    4. Contractions ....
  f. Handles consonant blends or digraphs (speech consonants) ....
  g. Has difficulties with long vowels ....
    1. a e i o u ....
    2. long vowels plus silent e ....
    3. vowel digraphs ....
    4. diphthongs ....
  h. Has difficulties with er, or, ir, ur ....
  i. Has difficulties with silent consonants ....
  j. Has difficulties with syllabication ....

9. Deficiencies in Oral Reading
  a. Has an inappropriate eye-voice span ....
  b. Phrases correctly ....

	YES	NO
c. Makes constant repetitions	____	____
d. Enunciates poorly	____	____
e. Pronounces poorly	____	____
f. Has inadequacies in pitch and volume	____	____
10. Deficiencies in Study Skills		
a. Has adequate dictionary skills	____	____
b. Has adequate reference or locating skills	____	____
c. Can use indexes, glossaries, maps, etc. effectively	____	____
d. Uses library resources effectively	____	____
e. Organizes data	____	____
11. Deficiencies in Rate of Comprehension		
a. Makes right-to-left movements	____	____
b. Regresses frequently	____	____
c. Vocalizes	____	____
d. Can skim and scan	____	____
e. Adjusts rate to materials	____	____

Formal or informal inventory

A teacher's prime task (or the special teacher's as the case might be) with the retarded may be to identify the pupil's frustration, instructional, and independent reading level. To do this, he may administer additional individual intelligence tests such as the *Wechsler Intelligence Scale for Children* or the *Revised Standford-Binet Scale* and additional achievement tests, but he certainly makes use of informal and formal reading inventories.

Betts [2] considers a child to be reading on a frustration level if he reads with less than 75 per cent comprehension and less than 90 per cent of accuracy. He reads on an instructional level if he reads with 75 per cent comprehension and 95 per cent accuracy in word recognition. And, he reads on an independent level if he reads with 90 per cent comprehension and with 99 per cent accuracy in word recognition.

INFORMAL INVENTORIES

The classroom teacher has probably already used informal procedures in gauging the reader's achievement as well as his frustration, instructional, or independent level. The classroom

teacher frequently determines the level of the child's performance through an informal analysis of the pupil's oral reading.

Generally, the teacher will select a passage for the pupil to
read orally. The teacher ought to have picked out the passages,
made a readability [3] check on each, and have some questions
prepared to measure pupil competency before he uses a given
book to make an informal check on a pupil's reading. The reading
by the pupil tells something of the pupil's background of experience, of his vocabulary knowledge, of his reading habits (slowness in reading, lip movements, or finger pointing), of his comprehension, and of his specific difficulties.

As the child reads, the teacher looks for pupil interest in materials, pupil concentration or apathy, the speed with which he
completes his work, the willingness to read orally, and the ability
to follow directions. The first sign indicative of poor reading is
often the pupil's attitude toward reading. A pupil who does not
read well generally is not willing to read aloud. He would rather
hear others. The teacher notes whether the child's oral reading
indicates deficiencies in sight-reading, in vocabulary, in structural
or phonetic analysis, in comprehension, in eye-voice span, in
phrasing, or in inflection. The teacher notes whether in his silent
reading the pupil follows instructions, reads for meaning, and
uses the context to determine the meaning of the story. He is interested in whether the learner hears and sees likenesses and differences in letters and words. He evaluates the pupil's expressive
and receptive abilities in the oral language area.

Smith in *Graded Selections for Informal Reading Diagnosis:
Grades One Through Three*, 1959, and in *Graded Selections for
Informal Reading Diagnosis: Grades Four Through Six*, 1963,
both published by New York University Press, lists passages for
use in informal diagnosis. The reading passages are presented with
questions and answers and with vocabulary checks useful in detecting word recognition difficulties.

Inventories are especially helpful in making continuous evaluations of the pupil's progress during the major transitional
changes in reading development.[4] Stage I occurs in the latter
half of grade 1 and during grade 2 and is identified with the
development of independence in reading through the addition
of phonic and structural clues to the earlier-used configuration,
context, and picture clues.

The second stage occurs when the child learns to recognize quickly larger word elements such as syllables and common word endings. It is a transition from phonic clues to the use of visual structural clues. He now sees the word *walk* not as *w-a-l-k*, but perhaps as *w-alk*.

The third stage occurs when the pupil learns to use reading for the acquisition of a knowledge of the content areas. It is in the fourth, fifth, and sixth grades that this occurs.

Inventories administered at each of the previously mentioned critical stages help the teacher to determine changes in instructional, frustration, and independent reading level and to detect improvements or continuing inadequacies in dealing with individual reading skills. They provide a good measure of the child's true growth. Other devices such as the following may be used to aid informal diagnosis.

1. Keep samples of classroom work.
2. Make an anecdotal record of the child's reading behavior.
3. Have the pupil write a reading autobiography.
4. Place a transparency over the book from which the child reads to check errors that can be analyzed later.
5. Make a tape recording of the pupil's reading.

FORMAL INVENTORIES

Many classroom teachers use formal or standardized inventories to gauge a child's reading level. These are usually compilations of graded reading selections, with questions prepared in advance to test the reader's comprehension.

Frequently the formal inventory is administered by the special or remedial reading teacher to pupils identified as retarded readers. He is especially interested in a more detailed diagnosis of the pupil's reading deficiencies. He is not satisfied with an overall estimate of the pupil's reading ability. He wants to know specific strengths and weaknesses.

Two good standardized inventories are the *Botel Reading Inventory* and the *Classroom Reading Inventory*.[5] The *Botel Reading Inventory*, designed for grades 1-12 and published by Follett Publishing Company, obtains an estimate of the pupil's instructional, independent, and frustration reading level. It is useful only when the reading level is below fourth grade. The inventory consists of two tests: *Phonics Mastery Test* and the *Reading Placement Test.*

The *Phonics Mastery Test* is a group test. Level A measures single consonant sounds, blending consonants, consonant digraphs and rhyming elements. Level B tests vowel sounds; level C measures syllabication; and level D, nonsense words, measures recognition of phonetic elements.

The *Reading Placement Test* consists of a Word Recognition Test and the Word Opposites Test. The Word Recognition Test is an individual test and is a measure of oral reading. It consists of twenty word samples at each reading level, from preprimer through fourth grade. The Word Opposites Test evaluates pupil comprehension. There are Word Opposites Reading Tests and Word Opposites Listening Tests. The Word Opposites Test is a group test. As a listening test, it indicates the discrepancy between reading performance and reading potential. The pupil listens for the word that is opposite of the first word read (strengthen: strong—weaken—support—luncheon).

The test's basic purpose is to determine how difficult a book the pupil can read. It is based on the assumption that about ten to fifteen million children in regular classrooms attempt to read books that are too difficult for them and that this interferes with reading progress. It is based on the assumption that informal tests, which are based upon reading materials used in the classroom, rather than standardized testing methods, are the best basis for planning classroom instruction.

The Botel inventory suggests that a pupil is reading on an instructional level when the pupil can recognize and pronounce 70-90 per cent of the words in the Word Recognition Test and when he can comprehend 70-80 per cent of the words in the Word Opposites Test. The pupil is reading on a frustration level when he fails to recognize more than 5 per cent of the running words in the Botel inventory (this is equivalent to 70 per cent on other lists) and shows less than 70 per cent comprehension. Pupils reading on this level tend to dislike reading, are anxious, read orally with poor rhythm and timing, and point to words.

Another inventory, the *Classroom Reading Inventory*, has recently been developed by Nicholas Silvaroli and is published by Wm. C. Brown Company, 135 South Locust Street, Dubuque, Iowa. It is designed specifically for teachers who have not had prior experience with individual diagnostic reading measures. The chief purpose of the inventory is to identify the frustration, instructional and independent reading level of the pupil. It is useful in grades 2 through 8.

The *Classroom Reading Inventory* is composed of two main parts: Part I, Graded Word Lists, and Part II, Graded Oral Paragraphs. Part III, A Graded Spelling Survey, may also be administered. Parts I and II must be administered individually; Part III may be administered to groups. The inventory may be administered quite easily in about 15 minutes.

DOLCH BASIC SIGHT WORD LIST

Other inventories or checks that isolate specific areas might be constructed. For example, the classroom or special teacher will learn much about a child's reading by having him respond to a test over the Dolch Basic Sight Word List.

If the pupil knows up to 75 of these words, he may be reading on a preprimer level; up to 120, on the primer level; up to 170, on the first reader level; up to 210, on the second reader level; up to 220, on the third reader level. A child is given credit for knowing the word if he can pronounce it or if he corrects the word immediately after mispronouncing it.

Inventories have an advantage in that they provide some clues as to why a pupil pronounced the word in a peculiar way, why he reversed letters, or why he skipped a word. In diagnosing, we are especially interested in the causes of errors. Our interest does not cease with a yes-no answer. We want to know why and how the child got his answer. It is, for example, quite common at the first-grade level for a child to recognize a word by means of irrelevant clues (e.g., identification of words with an erasure mark or a torn edge in the book or on the word card).

In using inventories we generally are trying to determine what books a child can read for enjoyment and how difficult an assigned reading can be and still be used as instructional material. Although, unfortunately, grade-level designations furnished by the publishers of many books are far from accurate, the experienced teacher can select a suitable set of books and other materials for use in informal determinations of children's reading abilities.

The classroom teacher should forward to the remedial

teacher or to the reading clinic the results of any informal or formal inventories that he administered to the retarded reader while he was in the regular classroom.

Oral reading tests

Oral Reading Tests are helpful both in measuring pupil reading achievement (especially in oral reading) and in making diagnostic evaluations. They possess many of the same advantages as the reading inventories, in that they permit the teacher to detect the errors made by the pupil and to identify the reasons why the error was made.

Here is a list of some common oral reading tests:

- Gilmore Oral Reading Test
- Leavell Analytical Oral Reading Test
- Slosson Oral Reading Test
- New Gray Oral Reading Test

Each of these tests is described in Appendix VI. Let us look more closely at the *Gilmore Oral Reading Test.*

The *Gilmore Oral Reading Test* provides teachers with a means of analyzing the oral reading performance of pupils in grades 1-8. It measures accuracy of oral reading, comprehension of material read, and rate of reading. There are ten oral reading paragraphs with five comprehension questions for each paragraph. The test takes from 15 to 20 minutes for administration. As the pupil reads, errors, time required for reading, and responses to comprehension questions are recorded. The test manual describes how errors are recorded. Here are these directions.[6]

TYPE OF ERROR	RULE FOR MARKING	EXAMPLES
Substitutions		
A sensible or real word substituted for the word in the paragraph.	Write in substituted word.	*black* The boy is back of the girl.
		girl See the girls.
		most He is almost ready to go.

Type of Error	Rule for Marking	Examples
Mispronunciations A nonsense word which may be produced by (1) false accentuation; (2) wrong pronunciation of vowels or consonants; or (3) omission, addition, or insertion of one or more letters.	Write in word phonetically (if time permits) or draw line through word.	*sim-bol-ik* (1) symbolic (or) ~~symbolic~~ *bles-fool* (2) blissful (or) ~~blissful~~ *blent* (3) bent (or) ~~bent~~
Words Pronounced by Examiner A word on which subject hesitates for five seconds.[7] (The word is then pronounced by the examiner.)	Make two checks above word pronounced.	✓ ✓ It is a fascinating story.
Disregard of Punctuation Failure to observe punctuation.	Mark punctuation disregarded with an "x."	Jack, my brother,[x] is in the navy.
Insertions (including additions) A word (or words) inserted at the beginning, in the middle, or at the end of a sentence or line of text.	Write in inserted word (or words).	*the* The dog and cat are fighting. *I* [8] See the girl.
Hesitations A pause of at least two seconds before pronouncing a word.[8]	Make a check above the word on which hesitation occurs.	✓ It is a fascinating story.
Repetitions A word, part of a word, or group of words repeated.[9]	Draw wavy line beneath word (or words) repeated.	<u>He thought</u> he saw a whale.
Omissions One or more words omitted. (If a complete line is omitted, this is counted as one omission error.)	Encircle the word (or words) omitted.	Mother does all (of) her work with great care.

Sample

Mother waves goodby to Father each morning. She begins
the housework(soon)after he leaves. Bob and Jane help her before
      start   *Then*   *wun*
they go to school.   ∧   They dry the dishes and clean their own
rooms.

We have reproduced in the following section paragraphs 1
and 5 from the comprehension section of the test. Included also
are the comprehension questions over these paragraphs and the
list of errors to be checked.

    1. I see two boys.
       Here is a man.
       I can see Mother.
       She looks at the boys.
       They look at the toys.
       I see a flower.

Time_____Seconds

_____1. How many boys are there?
_____2. What is Mother doing?
_____3. What are the boys doing?
_____4. What other person do you see?
_____5. What do you see that grows?

    Number right_____

ERROR RECORD	NUMBER
Substitutions	
Mispronunciations	
Words pronounced by examiner	
Disregard of punctuation	
Insertions	
Hesitations	
Repetitions	
Omissions	
Total Errors	

5. On Saturday the two boys do things they enjoy. For them this is the nicest day of the week. Sometimes they help with different household duties. In warm weather Tom and Father mow the lawn. If Mother is especially busy cooking for Sunday, Ned is glad to run errands for her before lunch. The family does not always spend the day working. In summer they often visit a lake near the city, where they spend happy hours swimming and boating. In winter the boys sometimes attend a movie; or, in freezing weather, they skate with their parents. The family takes real pleasure in Saturday activities.

Time_____Seconds

_____1. What is the most pleasant day of the week for the boys?
_____2. What do Tom and Father do on Saturdays in warm weather?
_____3. What does Ned do for Mother?
_____4. Where does the family go in summer?
_____5. What do the boys do with their parents in the winter?

Number right_____

ERROR RECORD	NUMBER
Substitutions	
Mispronunciations	
Words pronounced by examiner	
Disregard of punctuation	
Insertions	
Hesitations	
Repetitions	
Omissions	
Total Errors	

This test, like the other oral reading tests, is most useful in the diagnosis of reading difficulties. There is strong evidence to suggest that the oral reading errors of a pupil tend to be carried over to silent reading. *The oral reading test thus reveals pupil strengths and weaknesses and suggests the kinds and types of reading experiences which should be provided. Analysis of pupil errors should help to identify areas where most of the mistakes occur and toward which remedial teaching ought to be directed.*

Diagnostic reading tests

Up to this point, we have described the following instruments that might be used in diagnosis: The Personal Data Sheet, the Learning and Behavior Checklist, the informal and formal reading inventory, and the oral reading test. Let us now look at the diagnostic reading test.

The diagnostic reading test, like some of the instruments already described, seeks to discover specific strengths and weaknesses. It is especially useful in planning remedial procedures. It is no doubt possible to make a successful diagnosis without using any objective test measures, just as it is possible for a physician to diagnose a disease correctly without X-ray. However, for the most part diagnostic tests prove useful.

The survey test, the type given in Step I, tells us that a boy or girl who is in fifth grade is reading at a level typical for third graders. The diagnostic test, on the other hand, identifies the pupil's specific deficiencies, his inability to work out unfamiliar words, his inability to blend sounds, or his tendency to reverse. It helps to locate those areas of deficiencies that need to be investigated further. It also may indicate which instructional adjustments are needed. It provides the basis for planning remedial teaching of such specifics as word analysis or phonic skills.

The following diagnostic tests have demonstrated their usefulness in diagnosis:

- Bond-Clymer-Hoyt Silent Reading Diagnostic Test
- Doren Diagnostic Reading Test
- Durrell Analysis of Reading Difficulty
- Gates-McKillop Reading Diagnostic Test
- Roswell-Chall Diagnostic Reading Test
- Spache Diagnostic Reading Scales

Each of these diagnostic tests, along with others, is described in Appendix V.

The *Durrell Analysis of Reading Difficulty,* as an example, is designed for grades 1-6. Testing time is usually from thirty to forty-five minutes. It consists of the following subtests:

1. Oral Reading Test

2. Silent Reading Test
3. Listening Comprehension Test
4. Word Recognition and Word Analysis Test
5. Naming Letters
6. Identifying Letters Named
7. Matching Letters
8. Writing Letters
9. Visual Memory for Words
10. Hearing Sounds in Words
11. Learning to Hear Sounds in Words
12. Learning Rate
13. Phonic Spelling of Words
14. Spelling Test
15. Handwriting Test

The teacher may want to give tests such as the following to evaluate even more closely a pupil's problem:

- Roswell-Chall Auditory Blending Test
- Mills Learning Methods Test
- Screening Test for Identifying Children with Specific Language Disability
- California Phonics Survey Test
- Auditory Discrimination Test
- Leavell Hand-Eye Coordination Test
- Perceptual Forms Test
- Phonics Knowledge Survey
- Phonics Mastery Test
- Robbins Speech Sound Discrimination and Verbal Imagery Type Tests
- McKee Inventory of Phonetic Skills
- Marianne Frostig Developmental Test of Visual Perception

Each of these tests is discussed at length in Chapter 3.

A case study

As illustrative of how the data gathered about a pupil might be used, we selected pupil 26 from the group of boys and girls whose reading and IQ scores were given in Chapter 1, page 19, to report in more detail. This pupil was found to have a reading level of 6.1 grade level or a reading age of 11.3. He had an IQ score of 113 on the *Kuhlmann-Finch IQ Test.* On the basis of these data, it seemed that he was reading about 4.7 years below what was expected of him.

The regular classroom teacher completed the *Personal Data Form* on this pupil and it revealed that as of September 20, 1966, he had the following grade placements on the *Stanford Achievement Test.*

Paragraph Meaning	5.0
Spelling	5.4
Language	5.2
Arithmetic Computation	4.4
Arithmetic Applications	4.4
Social Studies	8.3
Science	8.3
Total	5.3

It is important to note that these test scores are comparable for the most part to the reading score which was based on the *Gates Reading Survey* given on February 28, 1967. The pupil showed the following progressions and variations in grade-level reading performance from grade four through eight:

	Sept.	*May*
4th grade	3.7	3.1
5th grade	3.9	5.3
6th grade	5.7	6.2
7th grade	5.8	7.1
8th grade	6.1	

On the eighth grade test, his speed grade-level score was 5.8; his vocabulary score was 5.6; and his comprehension score was 6.9.

Important data appeared on the cumulative record. The pupil took the *Otis IQ Test* in 1966 and the IQ score obtained was 91. Contrast this score with the one on the *Kuhlmann-Finch:*

Reading Grade Score	Reading Age Score	Chronological Age	IQ	MA	No. of Years Retarded
6.1	11.3	14.2	113	16.0	4.7
6.1	11.3	14.2	91	12.9	1.6

These variant IQ data mean that if the Otis IQ score is used, the pupil is only 1.6 years retarded rather than 4.7 years, as indicated by more recent test data. Which IQ score is the correct one? On which score should the teacher rely to make an evaluation of the pupil's degree of retardation? Since the Otis test is an all-verbal test, it probably underestimated the pupil's actual ability. At any rate, the IQ scores are different enough that additional testing should be done. The pupil probably should be given the *Wechsler Intelligence Scale* or at least the *Culture Fair Intelligence Test*. In any case, the pupil is retarded and should be able to improve in reading.

We asked pupil 26's regular teacher to complete the *Learning and Behavior Checklist*. The teacher felt that the pupil was deficient in the following areas:

Mental and Language Development

1. Is deficient in memory and attention span.
2. Cannot think clearly and in sequence.
3. Cannot express himself in his own words.
4. Cannot see relationships of parts to whole.
5. Cannot think on abstract level.
6. Does not enunciate, articulate, or pronounce clearly.

Motivation Development

1. Is not interested in reading or in books.
2. Is not responsive to instruction.
3. Does not have a feeling of adequacy and belonging.
4. Has not learned to help himself.
5. Does not exhibit a normal amount of self-confidence.
6. Is not communicative in the classroom.
7. Is not usually attentive.
8. Cannot concentrate on learning activities.

Deficiencies in Comprehension

1. Cannot read for details.

2. Cannot read to learn.
3. Cannot read critically.

Deficiencies in Study Skills

1. Does not have adequate dictionary, reference, or locating skills.
2. Cannot organize data.

Deficiencies in Oral Reading

1. Has an inappropriate eye-voice span.
2. Does not phrase correctly.

Deficiencies in Rate of Comprehension

1. Regresses frequently.
2. Vocalizes.
3. Cannot skim or scan.
4. Does not adjust rate to materials.

Even though the foregoing factors may explain some of the pupil's reading deficiencies, the teacher needs to look to the positive elements, to those elements on which he can build. The checklist revealed that the pupil:

1. Perceives likenesses and differences.
2. Remembers word forms.
3. Associates symbols with pictures, objects, or facts.
4. Understands that what can be said also can be written.
5. Has adequate vision, hearing, and clearly developed dominance.
6. Does not reverse.
7. Can follow directions and has good work habits.
8. Can use structural clues to meaning.
9. Associates sound with the total word.
10. Knows names of letters.
11. Can handle beginning consonants, consonant blends, speech consonants and vowels.

It would appear from an analysis of these factors that the pupil's prognosis is good. His major difficulties are not in the word-attack, identification-recognition area, but rather in the motivational-self-concept area. He has difficulty with speed reading, with oral reading, and with abstraction. He has not learned to read intensively or for study purposes. The lack of motivation and the inadequacy of his self-concept seem very significant.

An interview with the stepmother gave the following information which substantially confirmed the teacher's view that the pupil did not like school and felt insecure in the school setting. The stepmother pointed out that the boy had been deserted by his real mother when he was two years old.

The boy's father remarried when the boy was four years old. After the marriage, the stepmother and father found it impossible to leave the boy anywhere, even for short intervals, since he seemed to have an extreme feeling of insecurity. He seemed to be in constant fear of being deserted again.

The boy had to be forced to go to kindergarten. The stepmother now thinks that the child would have gained confidence and a feeling of security if he had been allowed to skip kindergarten and stay home with her. She stated that the boy has never liked school. Both the father and stepmother want the boy to go to college, but they are beginning to wonder if he will master enough of the basic fundamentals to succeed in high school, much less college.

This is as far as the teacher went with the boy in testing. The administration of an inventory, an oral reading test, or a diagnostic test might be the next logical step to take.

The symptomatology of reading disability

What is the significance of Step II? It is an intensive study of the symptoms of reading disability. At this level we are still concerned primarily with identifying the areas of difficulty. We are dealing with symptomatology.

Many reading disabilities develop because teachers are not familiar with some of the symptoms of disability. The result is that some reading needs are not met, and it is these unmet reading needs that lead to disability cases. It is obvious that a clear identification of the symptoms of reading disability is needed.

Symptoms are observable characteristics which help the teacher to make some educated guesses about the pupil's reading problems. Symptoms rarely appear singly. There usually is a pattern of symptoms, a syndrome that characterizes the individual reading disability case. The teacher needs to know the pattern, must attempt to understand it, and must have the educational know-how to deal with the syndrome. The diagnostic responsibility of the teacher is to identify the pattern of symptoms, relate it to the appropriate skill area or areas, and plan a program to correct the deficiency. The interpretation of the syndrome pattern is much more significant than the data themselves.

As the teacher works with the symptomatology in a given case, he should ask himself four questions: [10]

1. Did the pupil make the same error on both easy and difficult material or were his errors chiefly the result of having to read material which for him was on a frustration level? Diagnostic conclusions and remediation should not be based on errors made on material that is clearly too difficult for the pupil.

2. Were his slowness in reading and his constant need to regress while reading the result of poor reading skill or simply of his desire to read carefully? Diagnostic conclusions should not be based on comprehension errors made over material the pupil did not have time to read. Sometimes the pupil's reading grade-level is inaccurate because he answered questions incorrectly on a test that he did not have time to finish.

3. Was the pupil's performance reliable or was it poorer than usual because he was nervous, upset, or distracted during the testing situations?

4. Was the pupil's poor reading performance basically in the area of comprehension skills, word-identification skills, rate skills, oral reading, or a combination of these?

The developmental reading program

Let us again look at pupils found to be retarded. Our concern is to decide the type of help the pupil needs and where he can best receive help. Perhaps at this time we should take a look at various phases of the total reading program. Authorities in the field speak of the developmental reading program, the corrective reading program, and the remedial reading program.

The developmental program emphasizes reading instruction that is designed to develop systematically the skills and abilities considered essential at each level of reading advancement. It thus encompasses also the corrective and remedial program. Perhaps we should then speak of developmental, corrective, and remedial instruction. Developmental instruction is the type of instruction that is given to the majority of children in the regular classroom.

Corrective instruction consists of remedial activities usually carried on by the regular classroom teacher within the framework of regular classroom instruction. Corrective instruction is provided when the entire class or a small group of pupils is deficient in a particular skill. Corrective reading deals with the problems of that type of pupil who can identify words and comprehend what he reads, but only with great difficulty. This pupil is a partial disability case. The pupil may not have been ready for initial reading experiences, instruction may have consistently been above or below his level of ability, or classroom stimulation may have been inadequate.

Remedial instruction consists of remedial activities taking place outside of the framework of regular class instruction and is usually conducted by a special teacher of reading. Remedial instruction should thus be restricted to a small clinical group with severe symptoms of reading retardation. It is the group that has difficulty mastering even the simplest mechanics of reading. The learner is identified as the word-blind or dylexiac learner. He has difficulty in remembering whole word patterns, does not learn easily by the sight method, and shows orientational difficulties.

The total reading program might schematically be portrayed as follows:

DEVELOPMENTAL READING PROGRAM

Developmental Reading Instruction	Corrective Reading Instruction	Remedial Reading Instruction

DEVELOPMENTAL
READING
INSTRUCTION

↓

Systematic and
continuous
instruction
in all skills
on all levels by
all teachers
↓
Regular
Classroom

If the pupil has a reading problem and if he is not a slow learner, a reluctant reader, or a disadvantaged reader, he needs corrective or remedial instruction and should be able to be classified as either a case with general retardation, specific retardation, limiting disability, or complex disability.

CORRECTIVE
READING
INSTRUCTION

*General
Retardation*
↓

The reading level is substantially lower than the mental age, but no other specific problem exists.
↓

He is a pupil who learns only after undue and laborious effort; he is like the underweight child whose eating habits are not conducive to gaining weight but who, if he follows the proper diet, will gain.
↓

The pupil may not have been ready for initial reading experiences, and thus fell farther and farther behind as his schooling continued.
↓

Instruction may have been above

*Specific
Retardation*
↓

There is a definite weakness in a given area. This is usually a skill weakness.
↓

This is a case of reading retardation not complicated by neurological difficulties.
↓

Learning capacity is adequate, but deficiencies in regard to certain specifics in word analysis or comprehension indicate that he has not profited from regular class work as well as he might. He has missed or has not profited from basic instruction in a given area.
↓

Although each pupil presents a

the pupil's level of ability.

↓

He perhaps was not stimulated to learn because instruction was below his ability level.

↓

He perhaps was absent from school at critical periods.

↓

The reading profile of the generally retarded pupil is relatively uniform.

↓

He needs more experience in reading, including systematic instruction at his level of ability. There is a need for major adjustment in materials and instruction and for a reading program that motivates the pupil to learn.

↓

On the secondary level, the pupil may be referred to the remedial teacher.

↓

The pupil should be kept in the regular classroom.

distinct pattern of acquisition and remediation, there will usually be others in the class with similar problems.

↓

His overall reading performance may be adequate, but deficiency in a given area may impede appropriate growth.

↓

The reading profile may show him to be high overall in relation to his ability, but diagnostic testing will reveal a low subscore on a test.

↓

There is usually a need for training in the area of weakness rather than a need for total remediation in the basis skills.

↓

The pupil should be kept in the regular classroom in which reading is taught to groups of three to five.

REMEDIAL READING INSTRUCTION

↓

Remedial instruction is designed for the pupil who is not benefitting from the corrective program because the classroom teacher either is not able or does not have the time to deal with the problem. The disability is either total or at least of an extreme nature.

Limiting Disability	Complex Disability
The pupil is deficient in even the most fundamental basic reading skills. It is almost as though the pupil had never been in school.	Instructional techniques alone do not come directly to grips with the pupil's reading problem.
There may be associative learning disability, making it impossible for him to associate experiences with symbols or to associate symbol with symbol. There are inadequacies in memory span and deficiencies in concept formation.	This learner has need for individual attention, often of a psychotherapeutic nature.
The pupil cannot deal with letters and words as symbols and thus cannot integrate the meaningfulness of written material.	Emotional and/or neurological difficulties are major factors in the prevention of learning. The pupil is not emotionally ready to face his problem or may be neurologically unable to do so.
He may be totally deficient in word attack or in comprehension. The reading profile will show this weakness.	He is actually prevented from becoming a reader by factors outside of his control. He may hate school and may be afraid of learning.
He needs total re-education.	
The pupil should be put in a remedial class in which reading is taught to groups of three to five.	The pupil should be put in a remedial class or in a reading clinic where he may have the benefits of one-to-one instruction and where he may be evaluated by a team—teacher, optometrist, nurse, neurologist, psychiatrist, etc.

Experience tends to indicate that most retarded readers fall in the general or specific retardation groups and should be helped in the regular classroom. Thus only a small percentage of pupils should be taken out of the regular classroom.

Pupil 26 seems to be in need of corrective instruction. He seems to be a case of general retardation. His reading level score is substantially lower than his mental age score; he learns only after real effort; he probably was emotionally and motivationally not ready for early reading experiences; his reading profile is relatively uniform; and he needs more experience in reading, a major adjustment in materials and instruction, and a reading program that is motivating. He should definitely be kept in the regular classroom.

Summary

Chapter 2 outlines the procedures for identifying and analyzing the symptoms of reading disability. The initial analysis through the use of the *Personal Data Sheet* and the *Learning and Behavior Checklist* is quite general, but the formal and informal inventories, the oral reading tests, and the diagnostic reading tests become increasingly more detailed until the pupil's specific difficulties in reading are isolated.

---

[1] Smith, D. E. P., and Carrigan, Patricia M. *The Nature of Reading Disability,* Harcourt, Brace and Company, Inc., 1959, p. 91. Reprinted by permission.

[2] Betts, Emmett A. *Foundations of Reading Instruction.* American Book Company, New York, 1957, pp. 538 ff.

[3] The Flesch, Dale-Chall, and the Spache readability formulas may be used to estimate the reading levels of materials.

[4] Unpublished paper of Dr. Hulda Groesbeck, Fort Hays Kansas State College, Hays, Kansas.

[5] *The Standard Reading Inventory,* by Robert A. McCracken, is available through Pioneer Printing Company, Bellingham, Washington. It is usable on pre-primer through seventh-grade level.

[6] Reproduced from the Gilmore Oral Reading Test, Manual of Directions. Copyright, 1952, by Harcourt, Brace and World, Inc. Reproduced by special permission of the publisher.

[7] If the subject hesitates on a word for two seconds, a check mark is placed above the word to indicate a hesitation (see Hesitations). If the word is pronounced by the examiner, a second check mark is made above the word. This counts as *one error*—a "words pronounced by examiner" error.

[8] If a pupil hesitates and then makes a mispronunciation or substitution error, this is counted *only* as a mispronunciation (or substitution) error.

[9] Even if a pupil repeats a word, part of a word, or group of words several times, this is considered as *only one error*. If a pupil makes a mispronunciation or substitution error and then corrects himself immediately, do not count as a repitition error, but only as a mispronunciation (or substitution) error.

[10] Wilson, Robert M. *Diagnostic and Remedial Reading*. Charles E. Merrill Books, Inc. Columbus, 1967.

3

Fully Investigating
the Causes of Reading
Disability

Step III of diagnostic procedure is a thorough analysis of the reading disability leading to an identification of the causal factors involved. It is the level of intensive diagnosis. It is a detailed study of the correlates of disability.

In Chapter 1 we noted that many specialists seem unwilling to investigate the real causes of reading disability. Often the few who do, get mired in the marshes of correlation.[1] Sometimes they get mired in their pet theory. The theory causes them to look for and to find a single cause in *all* disability cases. It is far too easy to assume that some factor is a cause when it may not be so. The teacher must identify the symptoms, study them, and seek the cause for these symptoms. The breakdown in remediation of reading disability cases often occurs because no one connects the symptoms with the *proper cause*.

The meaning of correlation

There are many factors, as we shall see later, that are related to reading disability. This is another way of saying that there is a fairly high correlation between the presence of certain conditions and reading disability, but a correlation does not necessarily imply a causal relationship. The term, "correlation," means simply relationship. The correlation coefficient (r) is an expression of the degree of relationship between two variables.

Correlation coefficients range from a − 1.00 to a + 1.00. The highest possible relationship is 1.00: a coefficient of − 1.00 indicating a perfect negative correlation and a coefficient of + 1.00 indicating a perfect positive relationship. We know that the relationship between the circumference of a circle and its diameter is perfect. The circumference is always 3.1416 times the diameter. This relationship would be expressed as 1.00. When the correlation coefficient is ± .00, the relationship is nil.

We already have noted that a correlation coefficient implies a relationship between two factors. When the two factors vary in the same direction (as, for example, when *high* test scores tend to be associated with *high* grades) we have a positive relationship. When the factors vary in an inverse direction, we speak of a negative relationship. In the latter instance, high test scores would be associated with low grades.

In each instance when there is a relationship between two factors, the reading teacher must decide when the factor in question is:

a. A basic cause of the reading disability.
b. A secondary effect (feeling of inadequacy that accompanies reading failure).
c. A contributing difficulty (frequent absences from school do affect reading).
d. A correlating resultant (usually when there is a reading disability, there is a lack of motor coordination, even though the two may not be causes of each other but the result of a common third factor).
e. An incidental factor (reading failures frequently come from homes where there are many arguments).

It is simple fact that too often we look for the reason for the disability in the wrong place. It is so easy to overplay the role of some of the correlates of reading disability that sometimes we may overlook the significant. The measurable and the observable simply are not identical at times with the significant. A cause may well be shared in common by reading disability and by its correlates.

The factors related to reading disability are so varied that the poor reader becomes the object of inquiry of many people, not always to his own advantage. The optometrist may discover an instance of exophoria and immediately conclude that this is the chief cause. The psychiatrist notices the pupil's anxiety and may conclude that this is the chief problem. Daddy and Mama simply notice the boy's laziness. And yet, proceeding as though correlation meant causation is not entirely without its heuristic values. Perhaps this is why it is so easy to equate the two. Correction of the visual problem, removal of the anxiety, or motivating the pupil may be the best that we can do and it is often better than nothing.

As we examine possible causal factors in reading disability, it is necessary to remember that sometimes the same behavioral characteristic may be both symptom and cause. A poor reader generally develops anxiety and perhaps even a dislike for reading. In this instance, anxiety and dislike for reading are symptoms. In another case, or even in the same case, anxiety may initiate the reading disability by prohibiting the use of the pupil's intellectual energies. In the latter instance, anxiety may be the cause.

The premises of this chapter are simply the following:

1. Reading is *a response* made by a learner and must *be learned* by a learner.
2. Reading achievement is thus interrelated with the learner's total growth and development.
3. Growth and development of the learner are variable and so is achievement in reading. Each child's growth is unique.
4. It becomes imperative that the teacher understand the *causes* for this variability in achievement.
5. Those factors (adequate experience, etc.) that are associated with good achievement in reading, if absent (lack of experience), may become causes of reading deficiency.
6. There is for each child a *teachable moment* for learning each of the reading skills. This teachable moment depends on those factors with which this chapter deals.

The teacher needs to ask himself: "When is the pupil ready to read?" When is the pupil ready to advance to the next stage of instruction? The learner must have an adequate experiential background, he must be intellectually ready, have adequate physical development, adequate visual and auditory readiness, and adequate neural development. He must have had an adequate language background and must be able to enunciate, articulate, and pronounce accurately, to express himself clearly to others, and to speak in simple sentences. He must have adequate social-emotional development and must be interested in becoming a reader. He needs to be able to detect perceptual differences, to perceive likeness and differences, to remember word forms, and to associate symbols with pictures and objects.

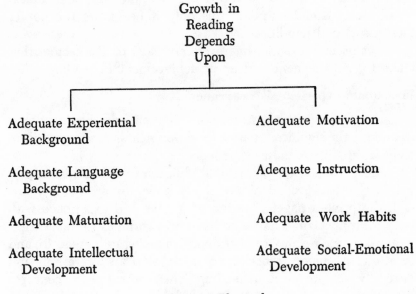

Growth in
Reading
Depends
Upon

Adequate Experiential
Background

Adequate Motivation

Adequate Language
Background

Adequate Instruction

Adequate Maturation

Adequate Work Habits

Adequate Intellectual
Development

Adequate Social-Emotional
Development

Adequate Physical
Development

Figure 3–1

Figure 3–1 identifies the basic correlates of reading achievement and deficiency. Perhaps of even greater significance is the fact that the child must be ready in each of the areas identified. The teacher must examine the composite of factors and on the basis of them must identify each pupil's specific readiness for reading. If there is one factor that interferes with learning to read, it needs to be identified. The effect of inhibitory factors is multiplicative rather than additive. Thus a pupil may be ready for reading in all areas except motivation. This factor alone may keep the pupil from learning. We all realize that if the pupil does not want to read, no reading will occur.

It is illogical to expect to produce a successful reader by promoting growth and development in only certain specifics. The teacher of reading must give consideration to all aspects of development. There commonly is a group of interacting factors, each in its own way contributing to the reading disability or preventing future growth. The teacher must make sure that the child is ready on all crucial levels. He must provide for readiness in all areas. And he can do this only if he knows the pupil's total assets and liabilities.

Let us now examine more closely each of the factors that make for achievement or lack of achievement in reading.

Inadequate experiential background

Experience is the basis for all educational development, and frequently the significant reason for differences in reading achievement is the differential in experience.

Most studies have shown that children from homes that provide a rich background of experience generally are ready to attack the printed page. Children who have had experience with books and magazines and who have opportunities to make trips, to go to summer camp, to hear good language, to be read to, and to attend a nursery school tend to develop an interest in and generally are proficient in reading. Their potential for concepts and meaning is greater than that of children who lack this background. They are ready to bring meaning to the printed page. The symbols on the page are empty unless the reader endows them with meaning. For this the pupil needs the appropriate experience.

The duty of the school and of teachers seems clear. If the child comes from an environment that does not stimulate experiential and perceptual growth, the school must provide the preparatory experiences. There is a special need to supply children from experientially deprived groups with stimulating nursery school and kindergarten experiences, with neighborhood reading centers, and with summer reading programs.

Of even greater significance in teaching these children is the realization that their reading achievement scores frequently are low because the reading materials in school present experiences alien to their own. As one teacher put it, these children read stories about "Saturday Night on Madison Street," but either can't or won't read "Dick and Jane." They find little material in the "Dick and Jane" stories that is familiar to them. When they work with stories and other materials, prepared by themselves or by the teacher, which use words familiar to their own experiences, their interest is stimulated and they begin to make progress. The value of teacher-prepared or pupil-prepared materials is readily apparent.

The teacher cannot overlook the wide diversity in experience between the country child and the city child; between the youngster whose family lives in a slum and the child who comes from a wealthy home. And he must remember that each child's reactions to the printed page are limited by his environment.

In summary:

1. Experience is one factor that accounts for differences among children and lack of experience may be a cause of reading disability.
2. Experience and maturation are the basis of all educational development. Behavior and development depend upon the state of the person and the environmental conditions. To predict behavior both the person and the environment must be considered as a constellation of interdependent factors.
3. Differences in learning ability of children are related to their biological potentials, but also to the environmental opportunities. Some children become reading disability cases because the environment does not call forth their potential.
4. It is impossible to predict the learning of the pupil without knowing the structure of his social environment, without knowing the types of behavior that are rewarded, and the types of rewards that are provided.
5. The child from the middle class home has an advantage because his home contains "a hidden curriculum" [2] which

permits him to deal appropriately with first school experiences.

Inadequate language background

One of the more obvious experiential deficiencies of some children is inadequate language development. Reading is a language experience and progress in reading occurs most readily when it is taught as one phase of the total communicative process. The pupil's proficiency in the communication and language skills, both speaking and listening, is the best indicator of the child's readiness for beginning reading and for subsequent reading instruction. A common cause of poor reading is poor language ability.

LISTENING ABILITY

Let us look first at listening. The ability to listen has an important effect on the development of competency in reading.

It is common knowledge that the capacity for mastering new sound discriminations diminishes with age.[3] A child learns to speak the language that he hears; an adult, with fixed habits of listening, does not hear the subtle sound distinctions and will learn to speak with an "accent." He hears the phonetic elements of the language that he is learning as though they were identical to those of his native tongue.

There are many children with different subcultural backgrounds that experience the same difficulty. The implications for the learning of phonics is obvious. Many reading disability cases may find their start right here. But even apart from that, here are other considerations:

1. Listening provides the vocabulary and the sentence structure that serve as a foundation for reading. Reading success depends upon the child's aural-oral experience with words. In a very real sense the child reads with his ears, mentally pronouncing the words to himself.
2. Ability to listen to and provide an ending for a story is a good indicator of potential progress in reading.
3. Words easily read are those that have been heard and spoken.

4. Listening ability (if scores on a listening comprehension
   test are higher than the scores on a reading comprehension test) is an indicator of the pupil's potential ceiling
   in reading ability.

The child learns language by ear. The vocabulary and skills
in language structure that he brings to school were learned first
through listening. In fact, if it were not for these learnings the
child would not, or at least only rarely, learn to read. The teacher
of reading must take advantage of these previous learnings. He
should help the child to associate the visual symbols with the
sounds previously learned.

PROFICIENCY IN SPEECH

Experience has shown that the pupil also must have reached
a certain level of oral language maturity before beginning reading. The reading teacher is interested in the "speech age" of the
learner. He must know how many phonemes the pupil uses consistently and how frequently the pupil substitutes because of an
inability to use a certain sound. A major concern is that pupils
learn to articulate all the vowels and the consonants without dis-
tortion, omission, substitution, addition, or transposition. Children must be taught to enunciate all syllables clearly. They must
be taught to pronounce accurately. They must give the total visual
form its proper sound and must accent the appropriate syllable
or syllables. Children generally must learn the alphabet of sound
before they can be taught the alphabet of letters.

Van Riper and Butler [4] point out that most articulatory
errors made by children involve *r, s, k, l, sh, th, ch,* and *f,* and that
elementary school children have most difficulty with *l, r, s, th.*
Many children show even more serious deficiencies in language
structure. They cannot formulate sentences or turn ideas into
words.

Artley [5] has outlined the language areas in which the child
needs special preparation before beginning to read. He suggests
that the readiness teaching should include the following:

1. Developing awareness of oral words as language units.
   For example, "Gimmethe" is three separate words.
2. Enriching oral vocabulary.

3. Strengthening meaning associations.
4. Formulating sentences.
5. Organizing ideas into language units.
6. Using narrative expressions.
7. Improving articulation.
8. Developing a sensitivity to inflectional variants.
9. Developing awareness of sentence structure.

Not all children, even in the upper grades, have equal proficiency in these areas or have mastered them all. The slow learner generally has a difficult time interpreting speech and expressing himself. Children from lower socioeconomic levels and from home environments in which English is perhaps secondary to another language do not develop the vocabulary and the accuracy in pronunciation and sentence construction that is found among children with more favorable surroundings. Above everything else, in learning to read, the child must perceive the relationships between the spoken and the written language. He must learn that what can be said also can be written.

In summary:

1. Reading success depends upon the child's aural-oral experience with words. Development in reading closely parallels development in listening and speech. Tyack [6] noted that reading involves the same language, the same message, and the same code as hearing of spoken words. The only difference is that in reading the contact is made on the central nervous system by light vibrations through the eyes; in hearing, it is by sound vibrations through the ears. The teacher will always experience difficulty teaching a child to read if the child cannot use sentence language in conversation. If the child cannot do this, it may well be a cause of reading disability.

2. To prevent reading disability, language training should accompany reading instruction every step of the way.

3. Training in listening develops auditory discrimination which in turn serves as a basis for phonetic analysis in reading.

4. Listening and speaking provide the vocabulary and the sentence patterns for reading.

5. If the pupil cannot sound the individual phoneme, he probably will not be a good oral reader. He will have difficulty with phonics. He also may have more difficulty in transmitting meaning.

    The child's proficiency in reading, and certainly his word identification and recognition skill, is dependent upon his ability to articulate, enunciate, and pronounce the sounds met in his language.

6. Genuine reading proficiency may mean the ability to read language structure. The best reader may be one mentally aware of the stresses, elongations of words, changes of pitch and intonation, and rhythms of the sentences that he reads. If he reads the way the writer would like it to have been said, true communication of meaning may be possible. Buswell [7] noted that the first goal and obligation in teaching reading is to help the child to derive meaning from the printed symbols with the same degree of functional efficiency that he has attained in deriving meaning from spoken words.

    The following words of Lefevre cannot be stressed too much: "While aware of complex causations of reading disability, I believe misapprehending the relationships between spoken and printed language patterns . . . to be the most decisive element in reading failures." [8]

    Another writer [9] says that the ultimate purpose of reading is comprehension through a process of converting printed symbols to their sound equivalents.

7. As noted in Chapter 1, reading is language: language involves thought; and reading is a thinking process.

8. Pupils who are retarded in reading and slow learners generally perhaps should be given frequent training in oral language and listening. Instruction should begin with familiar materials, materials that represent the child's speech. Experience charts are especially helpful.

Inadequate maturation

Even though we began this chapter by emphasizing experience, maturation cannot be ignored. The pupil's achievement depends as much on maturation as on experience. Baller and Charles [10] note that maturation is an unfolding or "ripening" of potentials that an individual possesses by virtue of his being a member of a given species or, more specifically, by virtue of his biological inheritance from a particular heritage.

We generally assume that the child receives his biological inheritance through maturation, while he acquires his social inheritance through learning. Maturation, however, is a prerequisite to much learning, and environment and experience are prerequisite to maturation.

Harris [11] aptly notes, "Without maturation the child cannot learn; without experiences he has nothing to learn."

Maturational changes usually are orderly and sequential. Wide variations of environmental conditions have little effect on maturation. The nervous system develops regularly according to its own intrinsic pattern. There thus seems to be very little benefit in rushing the maturation process. For example, we don't teach the child to swing a bat before he is capable of lifting a bat. The child learns to talk only after he is old enough. Practice needs to wait for maturation.

Teaching and other environmental stimulations are not useless. Children need appropriate environmental stimulation if maturational development is to progress at an appropriate rate. In many instances the child has inadequacies in his experiential background. The teacher should not overemphasize either maturation or experience-learning. Too much emphasis on maturation may lead to useless postponing of what could be learned; too much emphasis on learning or experience may lead to futile attempts at teaching that for which the child is not ready.

If teachers of reading are expert in evaluating children, they will not push children beyond their maturational level. The timing of instruction is especially important in preventing reading disability.

Instruction must march slightly ahead of development. "It must be aimed not so much at the ripe as at the ripening function." [12] However, it might be better to be wrong by going too slowly than by going too fast.

Rousseau [13] put it aptly when he wrote:

> I would much rather he (Emile) would never know how to read than to buy this knowledge at the price of all that can make it useful. Of what use would reading be to him after he had been disgusted with it forever.

Reading disability too often is caused by starting the child in a reading program before he is ready for it. Such a child cannot handle the day-by-day learning tasks and finds himself farther and farther behind as the time goes by. He becomes frustrated and develops antipathy towards reading. He actually learns *not to read*. This is quite different and far more serious than not learning to read. Bond and Tinker [14] note:

> Reading disability is frequently caused by starting a child in a standard reading program before he has acquired the readiness which will assure success in classroom reading activities. Due to his lack of experience, verbal facility, intellectual or emotional maturity, or a combination of these, he is unable to achieve enough of the learnings day by day to handle satisfactorily what is coming next. He gets farther and farther behind as time goes on. Inability to cope with the assignments produces frustration which leads to feelings of inadequacy, inferiority, insecurity, and perhaps even rebellion. Such a child is likely to develop an attitude of indifference to reading. He may even come to hate reading and all persons and activities connected with reading activities.

Another caution seems indicated. It may be dangerous to emphasize one phase of education at the expense of another. Although we can teach very young children to read and to type, we agree with Bugelski [15] that "typing is not a substitute for geography, nor is reading a substitute for tying one's shoes."

It may be good to introduce formal reading instruction to *some* three-, four-, or five-year-old children, but *en masse* introduction to such children can only cripple the spirits of these children. "Tomorrow's problems can wait. Indeed, for the best development of the child, they must wait."

It would be a serious indictment of us as teachers if children became reading disability cases because we did not know the child's ability—because we introduced him to reading too early or because we pushed him beyond his level of endurance. As Bond and Tinker [16] so aptly note:

> In general, the writers believe that most disability cases are made rather than born that way. Reading disabilities are sometimes the result of predisposing conditions within the child that are unrecognized, but for the most part they are brought about by factors in the child's environment at home, at play, and in school.

In summary:

1. The pupil develops reading skills most readily if they are built upon the natural foundation of maturational development.
2. Children should not be forced into readiness for either beginning reading or for any subsequent reading skill before maturational development is adequate. Such premature training may lead either to no improvement, to only temporary improvement, or to actual harm and to reading disability. The pupil may learn to fear, dislike, or avoid the task. Premature training may destroy the natural enthusiasm for a given activity, and it is doubtful that drill and exercises will ever be a substitute for maturation.
3. Generally the more mature that the learner is, the less training is needed to develop a given proficiency.
4. Thoreau, in *Walden* noted: "If a man does not keep pace with his companions, perhaps it is because he hears a different drummer. Let him step to the music which he hears, however measured or far away."

Inadequate intellectual development

Success in reading is built upon certain intellectual skills. The pupil must perceive likenesses and differences, must be able to remember word forms, and must possess certain thinking skills. He must have developed an appropriate memory and attention span. He must be able to tell stories in proper sequence, to interpret pictures, to associate symbols or language with pictures, objects and facts, to anticipate what may happen in a story or poem, to express his thoughts in his own words, and to think on an abstract level. He must be able to give identity and meaning to objects, events, and symbols. He must be able to categorize or to associate the particular object or experience with the appropriate class or category.

MENTAL AGE

The pupil's intelligence or his scholastic aptitude is usually measured by intelligence tests and is expressed as a mental age or an intelligence quotient score. Mental age (MA) refers to the *level* of development that the person has attained. It is the pupil's score on an intelligence test expressed in age units. Thus the average five-year-old child has a mental age of five; the average child of ten, a mental age of ten; and the average youth of fifteen, a mental age of fifteen.

THE INTELLIGENCE QUOTIENT

The intelligence quotient (IQ) refers to the *rate* of mental development. We all remember the simple formula: Distance equals Rate multiplied by Time ($D = R \times T$).

We may use an analogous formula in thinking about mental age and IQ: thus, $MA = IQ \times CA$. In the formula, MA refers to the distance that the pupil has traveled mentally; the IQ refers to the rate at which he has been going; and the CA refers to the length of time that he has been at it.

If we think of an IQ of 120 as meaning that the person has advanced at the rate of 1.2 years mentally for each year of chronological life (up to the age of fifteen or sixteen), and of an IQ of 80 as meaning that he has advanced 0.8 of a year mentally for each year of chronological life, the formula ($MA = IQ \times CA$) is easy to understand and to use. A ten-year-old boy with an IQ of 120 has a mental age of twelve ($MA = IQ \times CA$ . . . 1.2×10). Another ten-year-old with an IQ of 80 has a mental age of eight ($MA = IQ \times CA$ . . . 0.8×10). The first boy has attained the mental level of the average twelve-year-old; the second, the mental level of the average eight-year-old.

The IQ certainly is not an adequate criterion for reading achievement. However, it is significant in that it puts a ceiling upon individual achievement. Individuals with an IQ below 25 have little chance of learning to read; those with an IQ below 50 will experience difficulty with abstract materials; and those with IQs between 50 and 70 rarely will be able to read above a fourth-grade level.

The IQ also is an important long-range predictor of the child's performance. The child with a 150 IQ who is only six years old may not be as efficient a reader as the child with a 100 IQ who is ten years old. With time, however, the chances are that he will reach a higher level of reading proficiency.

Mental age, generally, is a much better indicator of reading readiness and achievement than is IQ, especially at the early levels. To be able to read, many skills are necessary that come only with age.

Even though the relationship between intelligence and reading achievement is high, it is not perfect. Intelligence is not the sole, nor necessarily the best, indicator of reading readiness or achievement. High intelligence does not guarantee success in reading. Research indicates that the great majority of poor readers have IQs between 80 and 110 and that frequently the most severely retarded readers in relation to their mental age have IQs of 130 or more.

In summary:

1. Intelligence or intelligence tests scores account for differences among children and low intelligence test scores are associated with reading achievement scores that are often below grade level.
2. Intelligence may well be a product of inherited structure developed by environmental stimulation and opportunity —it is an alloy of endowment and experience. Intelligence is subject to environmental variation. Intelligence tests do not discriminate between ignorance and stupidity.
3. The teacher thus needs to stimulate children; they do not develop best on their own. The child needs challenging

encounters with his environment. The teacher must be essentially an environmentalist.

4. The measured IQ of some children, especially the experientially deprived, diminishes with increasing age, apparently as a cumulative result of environmental deprivation.

5. Intelligence test scores serve their primary purpose by helping the teacher to gear the instructional program to the ability level of the pupil.

6. The teacher needs to be very careful when he interprets low intelligence test scores as a cause of reading disability because:

   a. A child who does not have adequate sensory mechanisms to acquire experience or to acquire it adequately tends to do poorly on intelligence tests. The cause of reading disability thus may be the inadequate sensory development.

   b. Intelligence test performance depends on drive, interest, and opportunity.

   c. The concept of reading disability is meaningful only in terms of one's potential. The slow learner often is not a retarded reader.

7. We may need to expand the intelligence level of some children in much the same way that we have extended the life expectancy of all Americans. Long life spans typify some families, but the life spans of all can be improved.

Inadequate social-emotional development

To help children both to develop adequate personalities and to become successful readers, the teacher of reading needs to understand the facts, principles, and symptoms of social and emotional development of the child. He must know how a child's social and emotional reactions influence his reading and how reading failure or success influences his emotional and social development.

The self-image of the learner is so obviously a significant determinant of learning that sometimes it does not receive the attention that it deserves.

Emotions are an important aspect of human development. Without emotional behavior, life would be dull and personalities would be flat and uninteresting. Few individuals would achieve, for none could feel the joy of success or long for the esteem of others.

However, sometimes emotional development is maladjustive. Thus, studies show that the incidence of maladjustment among poor readers is greater than among good readers. It is not always easy to establish whether personality maladjustment is the cause, the effect, or a concomitant circumstance. Frequently it is impossible to tell whether emotional and/or social maladjustment causes reading failure, or whether reading failure causes maladjustment. Some studies have failed to find a positive correlation between reading failure and personality maladjustment. Not all emotionally disturbed pupils are poor readers, nor are all poor readers emotionally disturbed.

Research tends to indicate that most children come to school with rather well-adjusted personalities. Personal maladjustment seems more frequently to be an effect of rather than a cause of reading failure. However, in some cases, personal maladjustment seems to precipitate problems with reading. Educational malfunctions, most commonly those of reading, frequently signify emotional problems.

Reading is a developmental task. It is a task that the pupil must perform in order to satisfy his own needs and so that he may satisfy the demands made upon him by society. There is no adequate compensation for success in reading. Failure in reading prohibits the actualization of the pupil's potentialities. It threatens self-esteem and the pupil's esteem in the eyes of others. It is a continuing block to normal development. Without success in reading, success in almost any other area becomes an improbability, if not an impossibility.

However, painful emotional events during early efforts at reading may turn the young learner against reading. The young reader may also at times transfer feelings of resistance from his mother to the teacher, or from his eating to his reading. A pupil may seek gang approval by not learning to read. Finally, he may exert so much energy in repressing hostile impulses that he has little left for intellectual effort.

There are numerous other factors of an emotional nature

that may hinder success in learning generally. Difficulties in adjusting to a new environment make it impossible for the child to expend the energies needed for learning. Poor parent-child relationships, sibling rivalry, unfair comparisons with a neighborhood prodigy, lack of encouragement from the home, and negative attitude of parents to learning in general may lead to failure.

The child may be afraid that he is "no good" and thus is sure that he cannot learn to read. Reading makes such a child feel "bad inside." Another child may be afraid of making mistakes. He doesn't want to be wrong because at home he has learned that it is "bad" to be wrong. A third child may literally punish himself by not learning to read. He feels a deep sense of guilt and atones for it by receiving the reprimands that accompany failure. A fourth may use failure as a way of punishing the adult. He demonstrates his independence by refusing to read. His attitude is: "I'll show you."

The teacher must be slow in attributing the reading difficulties of even *one* child to emotional and/or social problems. Poor readers do not have an identifiable personality. Poor readers may be adjusted or maladjusted; they may run the gamut of personal deviation.

The relationship between reading disability and emotional and social maladjustment frequently is circular in nature. Early reading failure leads to maladjustment and personal maladjustment in turn prevents further growth in reading. It is quite conceivable that in certain cases reading failure and personal maladjustment have their own distinct causes. Generally, if the reading failure is emotional in nature, the child will have difficulties in other academic areas also. If the emotional problem was caused by failure in reading, the emotional difficulty is reduced when the child learns to read.

In summary:

1. Emotions are reactions to environmental stimuli that also motivate behavior.
2. Some types of emotion facilitate learning and some hinder or prevent learning.
3. The relationship between maladjustment and learning to read might be any of the following:
   a. Maladjustment causes reading failure.

   b. Reading failure causes maladjustment.

   c. Maladjustment and reading failure have a common cause.

   d. Maladjustment and reading failure each have their own distinct cause.

   e. The relationship often is circular: maladjustment causes reading failure and the reading failure in turn increases the maladjustment, or reading failure causes the maladjustment which in turn increases reading failure.

Lack of motivation

Readiness for and achievement in reading are dependent also on the pupil's motivational readiness, and poor reading or reading failure may be caused by lack of interest. To achieve in reading the child must want to learn.

Interests arise through the interaction of our basic needs and the means we use to satisfy them. The child who is interested in reading is usually the child for whom reading satisfies the basic needs of self-esteem, esteem of others, curiosity, or the need for success and personal adequacy. Interests are the active forces that direct our attention to activities or objects. They determine whether the child will read, how much he will read, and in what area he will read.

As teachers, we are concerned with two phases of interest. First, the interest of the child somehow must be captured if he is to learn to read, and second, we must help the child to make reading a habitual activity. Wheat [17] pointed out that as a person learns to read, reading enters his mental makeup as a permanent mode of behavior. He uses reading as a means of enjoyment, studying, and thinking. He will arrange his daily life in order to provide time for reading. He will make sacrifices to provide himself with books to read. He will use reading as a means of discovering new interests and of losing himself from the actualities of the external world. It is at this point that reading is a dominating interest within; indeed, it is at this point that reading acquires a motivational force of its own.

Our prime concern is that pupils do read. A reader is not a

pupil who *can* read; he is a pupil who *does* read. The kindergarten teacher, especially, is more interested in fostering interest in reading than in developing specific reading skills. Although children come to school with an attitude favorable to reading, this attitude is not necessarily self-perpetuating.

The sex of the pupil [18]

Teachers have always been concerned with the differences in achievement among boys and girls. One of the more obvious differences is in readiness for and achievement in reading. Girls as a group achieve better than boys in reading. They learn to read earlier, and fewer of them are significantly retarded in reading. They generally seem to perform better than boys in English usage, spelling, and handwriting.

Numerous attempts have been made to explain the differences in reading achievement. In general, the explanations have emphasized either hereditary or environmental factors. It has been suggested that girls have an inherited language advantage or that they reach maturity about a year and a half earlier than boys. Some writers suggest that today's schools are more fitted to the needs of girls. Most of the teachers are women and they adjust more easily to girls than to boys. Furthermore, teaching methods frequently may be more suited to the needs of girls than to those of boys. Studies also indicate that girls are promoted on a lower standard, and that both men and women teachers tend to overrate the achievement of girls and to underrate the achievement of boys.

The expectations of society require boys and girls to play distinctly different roles. Girls are supposed to be good, be feminine, and to achieve in school. On the other hand, boys are expected to be active and to excel in sports rather than in books. Girls, in addition, before coming to school engage in numerous activities that may better prepare them for reading. In their weaving, sewing, and doll playing they have more opportunity to develop near vision and motor coordination. Girls use reading more frequently than do boys for recreation. Reading materials generally are more in accordance with the interests of girls.

Certainly, not all reading disability cases are referred to the reading clinic. And of those who are referred not all of them may be referred for reading disability alone. It is quite possible that boys more frequently than girls tend to manifest their reading problems through aggressive tendencies, and as a result more of them are referred to the clinic. Girls who read poorly become quite inert in the classroom, but they rarely become aggressive. The reading problems of well-behaved girls may be undetected, or may be taken care of in the classroom.

A comparative study [19] of reading in Germany and the United States revealed that the mean reading scores of fourth- and sixth-grade German boys exceeded those of German girls and that the variability of scores was greater among the girls than among the boys. These findings are just the reverse of those in this country and suggest that sex differences may best be explained by cultural and environmental factors. It is interesting to note that the teaching staffs in Germany, even in elementary school, are predominantly male.

Instructional inadequacies

The instructional inadequacies sometimes evident in the teaching of reading are other variables of achievement that need to be evaluated. The child's readiness for reading and the level of achievement that he will attain in reading depend on his background of experience, his intellectual, physical, emotional, and social development, *and* the instructional program he receives. Reading disability is indeed at times the result of predispositions within the child, but more often perhaps the result of factors within the environment, factors for which good instruction may compensate or which poor instruction may aggravate. For some instructional programs, the child may not be ready until the age of seven; for others, he may be ready at the age of five.

Poor teaching may be a cause of reading disability or of lack of achievement in reading. Poor teaching is no less a handicap than is poor vision. It may even be true that reading disability cases are sometimes not understood because we have not looked in the right place. It is considerably easier to suggest multiple causality than to admit that our teaching has been inadequate. It is easier to seek the cause of reading disability in lack of experience or emotional upset than to take a hard look at the instructional program.

One of the most potent factors in preventing reading disability is to provide systematic instruction in the basic skills. Pupils from the beginning need to get meaning from the printed page. They need to acquire a sight vocabulary. They need to acquire ways of independently identifying words. They need to learn to avoid word calling, guessing at unknown words, or substituting words. They need to develop appropriate rate skills. They need practice in both silent and oral reading. Their reading needs to become smooth and rhythmical.

Reading disability is also related to numerous other factors that we might group under the general heading of institutional variables. The school environment is an important determinant of learning. Is the school achievement-oriented? Is the school environment unnatural? Children by nature have a need to behave aggressively, but in school may be confined almost completely to their little chairs. The book says, "Run, run, run," but the child must sit, sit, sit. Children by nature have a need to be active, but the emphasis in school may be to require them to be passive listeners. The type of control exercised in the classroom, the nature of the instructional materials, the library facilities, the expectations that the administration and staff have of the pupil, teacher shortages, grading practices, grouping practices, type of classroom organization, the types of measurement and evaluation, and the size of the instructional unit have a direct bearing on the rate of reading disability in a given school. Other things being equal, it is obvious that the child must have reached a more advanced developmental stage to be successful in a class of thirty-six pupils than in a class of twelve or thirteen pupils.[20]

Inadequacies in physical development

We have discussed various determinants of the child's achievement in reading which, if absent or lower than a given level, may cause or be related to reading disability. Let us look at another group of related conditions which, for want of a better term, we shall refer to as physical factors.

The child is both physical and physiological. Functions such as vision, hearing, and thought are possible only through the organs of the body, the eye, ear, or brain. If the organ is defective, the function is likely to be impaired. This may, especially in the case of vision, hearing, and thought, lead to serious reading difficulties. In general, good health is conducive to good reading, and poor health is often associated with reading deficiency.

Physical health

As noted earlier, reading is an act, a performance, or a response that the reader makes to the printed page. Unfortunately, certain factors may prohibit making the response. Glandular dysfunction, hemoglobin variations, vitamin deficiencies, nerve disorders, nutritional and circulatory problems, heart conditions, infected tonsils, poor teeth, rickets, asthmas, allergies, tuberculosis, rheumatic fever, or prolonged illness can lower or prevent reading achievement.

The teacher must be cautious in interpreting the relationship that these or similar factors seemingly have to reading deficiency. Generally, physical inadequacies are contributory factors rather than factors causing reading problems. Illness keeps the child from school and causes him to miss important phases of instruction. Any physical inadequacy makes it difficult to become enthusiastic about learning and may result in lowered vitality, in depletion of energy, in slower physical development, and hence in mental retardation. Physical inadequacies cause the child to center attention on them and away from learning. The child with a smashed finger, a broken hand, a headache, or poor eyesight may be unable to concentrate on a learning task. The malnourished child does not have the energy to be an effective learner.

Sometimes a lowering of the child's basic vitality is closely related to the functions required for successful reading. The basal metabolic rate, BMR, for example, affects the convergence of the eyes. If the rate is low, the child may not be able to aim his eyes properly in binocular vision, and thus may frequently regress, omit words, lose his place, and become fatigued. And, fatigue makes it difficult to become interested in a reading task. Attention suffers and comprehension is usually lowered. As nervous tension builds up, the pupil becomes disinterested, disgusted, and may even turn from reading completely.

Vision and reading

Visual defects are obvious causes of reading deficiency. They always cause discomfort and fatigue. They act as irritants and lower the efficiency of the individual. The teacher of reading thus needs to familiarize himself with the symptoms of eye disturbances, the types of visual defects, and the tests that might be used to detect more accurately the visual defects.

SYMPTOMS OF EYE DISTURBANCES

The symptoms of visual difficulty are many. Diskan [21] categorized them under three headings: complaints, appearance of the eye, and behavior of the child. Complaints include such problems as: headaches, dizziness, inability to see well, blurred vision, double vision, fatigue, inability to see the blackboard, or letters and lines running together.

Eye conditions that need attention are: red-rimmed, encrusted or swollen eyelids; recurring sties or lid inflammation; eyes or pupils unequal in size; drooping of one eyelid or both eyelids; eyes crossing inward or turning outward constantly or wandering occasionally; and eyes "shaking" or oscillating.

Behaviors that are indicative of visual problems are: difficulty in reading or in work requiring close vision; skipping of words or lines; rereading; losing of one's place; slow reading; frowning; excessive blinking; squinting; holding book too close; rubbing the eyes frequently; shutting one eye or tilting the head forward; stumbling over small objects; sensitivity to light; and inability to detect color.

It must be recognized that many of these signs and symptoms are common during colds and other illnesses, but any persistence of these complaints indicates the need for an eye examination.

Certainly the teacher should know these danger signs and look for them. Early detection of a child's visual difficulty may depend upon the teacher's alertness. Good vision will mean more comfortable reading, and a child who sees well tends to develop favorable attitudes toward reading.

Teachers frequently are appalled by the poor concentration of some of their students. Unfortunately, in some instances "poor concentration" is not the proper term. The pupil usually can concentrate, but it is on only one idea at a time.

His attempt to maintain single vision or to clear blurred vision may prevent concentration on the mental task at hand. His cortical powers are directed entirely to the maintenance of basic visual skills. This same need for conscious control of the ocular factors may keep the child from reading as rapidly as he might.

VISUAL DEFECTS

The teacher of reading needs also to become familiar with the various types of visual defects if for no other reason than that he needs to make different classroom adjustments for these defects.

Figure 3-2 illustrates the various visual defects commonly

Visual Defects

---

1. LACK OF VISUAL ACUITY

2. REFRACTIVE ERRORS

Myopia	*Astigmatism*	*Hyperopia*
(Nearsightedness)		(Farsightedness) (Hypermetropia)

3. BINOCULAR ERRORS

Lack of Fusion	*Strabismus*	*Aniseikonia*
	(Tendency of eyes to deviate) (Heterophoria)	Difference in size or shape of two visual images
Exophoria	*Esophoria*	*Hyperphoria*
(Outward deviation) (Wall eyes)	(Inward deviation) (Crossed eyes)	(One eye focuses higher than the other)

Figure 3-2

present among school children. We have grouped them under the headings, "Lack of Visual Acuity," "Refractive Errors," and "Binocular Errors."

Visual acuity does not seem to have the significance for reading achievement that some other visual factors have. First: Reading is a near-point task. One could fail the visual acuity test at 20 feet but possess good visual acuity at 16 inches. Second: To read the average book, one needs only 20/60 visual acuity.

Nevertheless, acuity is important. Each child should have at least 20/30 acuity at far point. The Snellen test letters should be used with the literate and the Snellen *E* letters with the illiterate.

Refractive errors are due to damage to, disease of, or weakness in the lens or other portion of one or both eyes. Generally refractive errors can be corrected by glasses. Glasses, however, do not increase the sensitivity of the eyes. They help the eye to focus and lower eye strain, but frequently fail to provide normal vision.

Myopia or nearsightedness is perhaps the most common among the refractive errors. The myopic eye is too long, with the result that the light rays come into focus in front of the retina. This forces the pupil to hold the book closer than the normal 16 inches or so. Distant vision generally is blurred. Usually concave lenses are prescribed for myopic conditions.

Hyperopia or hypermetropia generally is known as farsightedness. Where the myopic eye is too long, the hyperopic eye is too short. In this case, the image falls behind the retina. To remedy this condition, convex lenses are prescribed. In testing for farsightedness, if the child reads the 20/20 test line with + 2.00 diopter lenses, he should be referred.

Another type of refractive error, astigmatism, is the inability to bring the light rays to a single focal point. Vision is blurred. The underlying cause is an uneven curvature of the front or cornea of the eye. The cornea is spoon-shaped rather than spherical. Unless the distorted image is corrected by the use of cylindrical lens, the child fatigues easily and usually dislikes close work or prolonged distant vision.

The binocular difficulties have the commonality of giving the child a double image. Either the two eyes do not aim cor-

rectly or they give conflicting reports. When the ocular maladjustments are minor, the individual may compensate for them. If
the maladjustments are major, the child may see two of everything or the two images may be so badly blurred that he sees
neither image clearly. Somehow he needs to suppress one stimulus.
When he can suppress it only partly or only temporarily, he is
likely to lose his place, to omit words, or to regress.

Strabismus or muscular imbalance stems from an incoordina-
tion of the muscles that move the eyeball. The eyes actually are
aiming in different directions. One eye aims too far outward, too
far inward, or in a different direction from the other eye. A severe
case of strabismus may result in double vision; a less severe case,
in a general blurring of the image.

There are three types of strabismus or heterophoria. When
the deviation is outward, it is called exophoria (wall eyes); when
it is inward, esophoria (crossed eyes); and when one eye focuses
higher than the other, it is called hyperphoria.

Even a moderate amount of heterophoria or tendency of the
eye to deviate results in fatigue. As the reader tires, his eyes tend
to deviate even farther. Attempts to counteract this increase
fatigue. A vicious circle is set up. The pupil becomes inattentive
and irritable, loses his place, omits, and regresses. This incoordi-
nation is sometimes corrected by cutting some of the eye muscles.

Hyperphoria may lead to difficulty in reading, jumping of
lines, or misplacement of a word to a line above or below.

Two additional binocular defects are lack of fusion and
aniseikonia. To see clearly, the lenses of the two eyes must be in
focus. The images must fuse correctly, thus giving one mental
picture.

The light patterns focused on the retina generate nerve impulses that travel via the optic nerve and the visual pathways to
the visual centers of the brain. On the way, the impulses from the
nasal side of each eye cross, thus joining the impulses from the
temporal side of the opposite eye. Each cerebral hemisphere thus
receives impulses from both eyes. These impulses are then blended
into one picture.

An inability to fuse correctly or to form one picture is mani-
fested by mixing of letters and words, inability to follow lines
across a page, loss of place, and by slowness in reading.

Aniseikonia occurs whenever there is a difference in size or shape between the two ocular images. As a result fusion is difficult and the reader may become tense, experience fatigue, and have headaches.

Eye defects of one sort or another are rather common. These defects increase throughout the grades and may play an important role in reading inadequacy. Generally, the incidence of myopia does not distinguish the good reader from the poor reader. In fact, myopia may be associated with better-than-normal progress. Although hyperopia seems to occur somewhat more frequently among poor readers, Foote, former director of the National Society for the Prevention of Blindness, suggests that 10 to 15 per cent of first graders are so farsighted that they are unable to use their eyes in deciphering print without developing headaches, fatigue, or nervousness. There also is a lack of agreement concerning the effect that astigmatism has on reading. It may be a handicap to successful reading when the learner has a severe case.

Failure of the eyes to coordinate, as in strabismus and in lack of fusion, and failure of the eyes to give images of the same size seem to have more serious impact on reading development When the deviations are vertical, as when one eye focuses highe₁ (hyperophoria), the reader frequently loses his place and fixates at a point either below or above the line on which he should be reading. He frequently complains of not understanding what he is reading. This condition appears to occur with equal frequency among both good and poor readers. When the deviations are lateral in nature, the convergence may be insufficient as in exophoria or excessive as in cross eyes (esophoria). The former condition seems to occur more frequently among poor readers than does any other heterophoric condition. It leads to omissions, regressions, and loss of place.

Difficulties with fusion and aniseikonia also seem to be more common among poor readers than among good readers.

Deficiencies in binocular control lead to inadequate word perception and the consumption of an excessive amount of energy in maintaining single vision. The pupil will fatigue easily, experience distraction, poor comprehension, constant moving of the head, and difficulties in concentration.

Any interpretation of the relationship between visual defects and reading must consider the likelihood of multiple causation. Some children are more sensitive to visual problems than others. Some are able to perform well in short test periods and thus escape detection through the usual methods. In fact, some eye defects may not yet have been identified. We know far too little about the syndromes or patterns of reading defects generally. The simple fact is that some children with defective vision become good readers and that others without any visual difficulty do not learn to read. However, this does not indicate that good vision is unimportant to reading. Eye defects are a handicap to both good and poor readers.

Visual Screening Tests

Screening tests may be used by the classroom teacher to detect visual problems. They are useful in locating difficulties that require referral to a specialist.

In the past, the Snellen Chart test was the acceptable screening test. It consists of rows of letters or *Es* in varied positions. The pupil being examined stands twenty feet from the chart and names progressively smaller letters. The test identifies nearsightedness and measures visual acuity at a distance of twenty feet, but it fails to detect astigmatism and farsightedness. Since nearsightedness frequently is associated with good reading rather than with poor reading, the test is not too helpful in reading diagnosis.

The Snellen formula is $V = d/D$. V represents visual acuity; d is the distance at which the person is reading the letters; and D is the distance at which the person should be reading. Thus 20/60 means that the person sees at twenty feet what he should see at sixty feet. A 20/20 notation means that the pupil has 100 per cent visual efficiency at far point. Other ratios are: 20/35 . . . 88 per cent visual efficiency; 20/70 . . . 64 per cent visual efficiency; 20/100 . . . 49 per cent visual efficiency; and 20/200 . . . 20 per cent visual efficiency.

Here are some tests commonly used in visual screening:

- *A O Sight Screener*, American Optical Company, Kansas City, Missouri.

The A O Sight Screener is a portable vision screening instrument designed for rapid appraisal of seven visual functions. The Sight Screener utilizes polarized light, which permits a check of binocular vision without the need of prism lenses at the important near point. In addition, monocular acuity is measured in such a way that the subject is unaware of which eye is being checked.

The visual functions checked are:

1. Simultaneous binocular vision—to determine if the subject is using both eyes together, or is suppressing the image of one eye.
2. Visual acuity of both right and left eye.
3. Visual acuity of both eyes together.
4. Stereopsis—ability to judge depth binocularly.
5. Vertical phoria—the degree of neuro-muscular imbalance in the vertical plane (amount of hyperphoria).
6. Lateral phoria—the degree of neuro-muscular imbalance in the horizontal plane (amount of esophoria or exophoria).

The screening procedure consists of rotating one control knob to fourteen numbered positions and recording the subject's responses. Because of this simplicity, little time is needed for operator training.

- *Atlantic City Eye Test,* Freund Brothers, 1514 Pacific Avenue, Atlantic City, New Jersey.

This is an individual test usable in grades 1 and above. The test is designed to detect: defective visual acuity, excessive farsightedness, and abnormal eye muscle balance. The test is compact and portable and requires no technical knowledge to administer.

- *Keystone Visual Survey Telebinocular,* Keystone View Company.

This test uses stereoscopic slides to detect near and far point fusion difficulties, visual acuity difficulties, muscular imbalance, binocular efficiency, depth perception, nearsightedness, and farsightedness.

Available also is a Visual-Survey Short Test, a Preschool Test, Tests of Binocular Skill (tests binocular im-
pediments that interfere with reading), a Plus-Lens (for
Hyperopia), Ready-to-Read Tests (these test fusion, vertical posture, lateral posture, and usable vision of each eye
at near point), and a Periometer (ascertains the side vision
of the subject).

- *Massachusetts Eye Test*, Welch-Allyn Inc., Skaneateles
Falls, New York, or American Optical Company, 62 Me-
chanic St., Southbridge, Massachusetts.

This test contains a visual acuity test for distance, a
plus-sphere lens test for hyperopia, and Maddox-red test
lenses for vertical heterophoria testing at distance and for
horizontal heterophoria testing at distance and at near.

- *Master Ortho-Rater Visual Efficiency Test*, Bausch and
Lomb, Rochester, New York.

This test uses stereoscopic slides to detect difficulties
of visual acuity, binocular coordination, and depth perception. The test may be given in five minutes.

The test provides tests for vertical and lateral phorias,
acuity for both right and left eyes, stereopsis, and color.
Ortho-Rater scores are recorded on an easy-to-use card.
When these cards are placed underneath the transparent
standard, it is immediately evident if the person tested has
adequate, below-standard, or seriously lowered vision.

A Perimeter Attachment is available for the Master
Ortho-Rater. It provides a simplified technique for measuring lateral visual fields. A clearly marked dial indicates
the degrees of side vision.

- *New York School Vision Tester*, Bausch and Lomb, Inc.,
Rochester, New York.

This test, usable at kindergarten level and above,
measures acuity at far point and phoria at near or far
point. It requires about two minutes for administration.
It is an adaptation of the Ortho-Rater, only the slides being
different.

The test measures acuity, farsightedness, and muscular balance. It has easily manipulated Snellen tests of the well-known Massachusetts type. The child being tested does not have to read letters. The test distances of twenty feet and thirteen inches are produced optically, thus eliminating the need for a twenty-foot testing aisle.

- *Prism Reader,* Educational Developmental Laboratories, Huntington, New York. (McGraw-Hill Publishing Company.)

This instrument requires the eyes of the reader to diverge and converge to maintain binocular vision while reading.

Normal binocular vision requires the individual to coordinate the vergence function which enables him to maintain single vision with the focus mechanism which enables him to see clearly. The eyes thus must perform two acts simultaneously: posture themselves so as to produce a single image and accommodate so that they can produce a clear image.

The test permits the examiner to determine whether or not the individual will be able to maintain comfortable, single binocular vision under all conditions of seeing and accept whatever lenses may be required.

- *Reading Eye Camera,* Educational Developmental Laboratories, Huntington, New York. (McGraw-Hill Publishing Company.)

This camera measures the pupil's ability to use his eyes in reading.

After an oral pretest, the individual reads a test selection appropriate for his level of achievement. While he reads, small beads of light are reflected from his eyes and photographed onto a moving film. When he has finished, identifying initials are flashed onto the film. After a comprehension check, the filmed record is analyzed, and the reader's performance is compared with national norms derived from a study of 12,000 cases.

In addition to the standard test selections, an eye-

movement photography version of the Reading Versa-
tility Test is available. This test is used in measuring the
reader's ability to adjust his approach while reading for
varied purposes.

- *Spache Binocular Vision Test,* Keystone View Company,
  Meadville, Pennsylvania.

    This test measures eye preference in reading. It is
  usable at first-grade level and above and requires a stereo-
  scope to administer. Three levels are available: nonreaders and grade one, grade one and a half to two, and
  grade three and above.
    The test tells whether the pupil reads more with one
  eye than with the other and whether heterophoria or lack
  of good fusion at near point interferes with binocularity
  in the act of reading.

- *T/O Vision Testers,* Titmus Optical Company, Inc., Peters-
  burg, Virginia.

    These tests for ages three-adult measure acuity and
  vertical and lateral phoria (near and far) on the lower
  levels. On the seventh grade and above level they measure acuity, stereopsis, color discrimination, vertical phoria,
  and lateral phoria. These tests can be given at twenty
  foot approximations. Acuity and vertical and lateral phoria
  can be tested at reading distance. A perimeter attachment
  identifies individuals with restricted visual fields. A Plus-
  Lens attachment quickly identifies excessively farsighted
  children.

    Two simple tests which the teacher can use are the *Point of
Convergence Test* and the *Muscle Balance and Suppression Test.*[22]
The *Point of Convergence Test* is administered by holding a pen-
light or pencil in front of the pupil. The examiner gradually
moves the pencil horizontally toward the pupil's nose until the
student sees two pencils. The near point of convergence is the
distance in inches from that point on to the eye. Normal near-
point convergence is from one to three inches. In the *Muscle
Balance and Suppression Test,* a two- or three-foot string is held

by the pupil. One end of the string is held against the bridge of the nose by the index finger, being careful so as not to block the line of sight of either eye. A knot is then tied in the string sixteen inches away from the eyes. The student is instructed to look at the knot. Normally he will see the two strings touching each other at the knot, making a V shape. If the two strings seem to cross in front of the knot, the condition is esophoria. If they cross behind the knot, it is exophoria. Orthophoria or normal muscular balance is present if the strings cross at the knot. If only one string is seen, the child is suppressing one eye. If one string is higher than the other, the condition is termed hyperophoria.[23]

Since the vision tests described in this chapter are for screening purposes and frequently lack somewhat in reliability, in doubtful cases the child's welfare is better served if the teacher errs in referring him to the specialist than if he errs in not referring him.

THE EYE MOVEMENTS AND READING

In reading, the eyes do not make a continuous sweep across the page. They move in quick, short, saccadic movements with pauses interspersed. Eye movements are characterized by fixations, interfixation movements, regressions or refixations, and return sweeps. The time elements in reading are two: fixation time and movement time.

A fixation is the stop that the eye makes so that it can react to the graphic stimuli. It is the pause for reading. During fixations the intake process is suspended and the inner process of reading occurs. The length (in terms of words) and frequency of the fixation vary with the difficulty of the reading material, with the reader's facility in word recognition, with his vocabulary level, with his familiarity with the content, with his purpose, with his ability to assimilate ideas, and with the format of the printed page. For example, the more difficult the reading matter, the longer and more frequent the fixations tend to be.

A regression is a reverse movement. It is a return to a letter, syllable, word, or phrase for a refixation. It is a fixation in a right-to-left direction on the eye-movement photograph. Eye deficiencies that have prevented accurate sensation, inadequate directional attack, and improper coordination between vergence (permitting single vision) and focus (permitting clear vision) are frequent causes of regression. Sometimes the reader regresses out of habit. Such a pupil lacks confidence and feels the need for constant rereading.

Regressions also occur when the flow of thought is interrupted or when perceptions are recognized as inaccurate. Eye movements frequently overreach or underreach the limits of the reader's recognition span. Regressions for verification, for phrase analysis, and for re-examination of a previous sentence seem especially useful. The flow of thought may be broken in numerous ways, such as by failing to comprehend the basic meaning of a word, by failing to comprehend the meaning suggested by the context, or by failing to interrelate the meanings of all the words.

Upon completing a line the reader makes a return sweep to the beginning of the next line. The return sweep takes from fifty to fifty-four milliseconds. If the next line is missed entirely or if the eye lands on a point before or after the first word of the new line, the reader must locate the proper place and a refixation is required.

Eye movement skills develop rapidly during the first four grades, but after this relatively little improvement occurs. A slight improvement may occur between grades six and ten, after which a leveling process occurs.

Oculo-motor behavior has come to be regarded primarily as a symptom of the underlying perceptual and assimilative processes. Eye movements do not cause, but merely reflect efficient or poor reading performance. Generally, as the difficulty of the material increases and as the reader takes greater pains to read well, the pauses become more frequent and grow longer. The difficulty of the material rather than the nature of the subject is the crucial element.

The immature reader generally does not vary his eye movements with the difficulty of the reading matter or with a change of purpose. The good reader, on the other hand, is distinguished from the poor reader by his better word recognition, word analysis, and comprehension and these frequently are reflected in more efficient eye movements. Thus, eye movement patterns reflect the efficiency of the central processes of comprehension, and are generally symptomatic of the level of reading maturity the child has achieved. The poor reader makes extra fixations and regressions because he doesn't understand, and he needs training to improve word recognition and comprehension rather than eye movement.

Hearing and reading

Auditory adequacy is another important element in good reading. It means three things: auditory acuity, auditory comprehension, and auditory discrimination. The pupil must be able to transmit the sound waves from the external ear to the auditory centers in the brain. This is auditory acuity and may best be described as the recognition of the discrete units of sound. He also must comprehend and interpret what he has heard. And, he must be able to discriminate and retain what he has heard.

TYPES OF AUDITORY DEFICIENCY

Sound waves are described as wave frequencies rather than wave lengths. The shorter the wave length, the higher is the frequency. Wave frequency is equivalent to the number of complete waves that pass a given point per second and is reported in cycles per second (cps). Amplitude refers to the height of the wave. High frequencies give high pitch and low frequencies result in a low pitch. By increasing the amplitude, a low pitch becomes lower and a high pitch gets higher. Intensity of the sound is expressed in decibels. The human ear is sensitive to frequencies ranging from 20 to 20,000 cps.

There are two kinds of auditory deficiency: intensity deafness and tone deafness. A tone deaf person cannot discriminate between pitches. Intensity deafness is of three types. Central deafness is caused by damage to the auditory areas of the brain or by a neurotic conversion reaction (hysteria). A conductive loss stems from an impairment in the conductive process in the middle ear. Either the eardrum is punctured or there is a malfunction of the three small ossicles or bones in the middle ear. This reduces the person's hearing ability, but if the loudness of the sound is increased, he hears and understands. A person with a conductive loss can hear his own voice through bone conduction. Thus, the voices of others sound much softer than his own. To compensate, he frequently speaks softly so his voice conforms to the voices of others around him.

Nerve loss stems from an impairment of the auditory nerve. A person with such a loss hears the speech of others, but may not understand what he hears. The high-tone nerve loss prevents him from hearing and distinguishing certain speech sounds, especially such sounds as *f, v, s, z, sh, zh, th, t, d, p, b, k,* and *g.* Articulation generally is affected. The pupil may speak too loudly or may develop monotony in his voice. He shows signs of frequently misunderstanding the teacher. This type of hearing loss is common in old age. *Figure 3–3* categorizes the various types of auditory deficiency.

Types of Auditory Deficiency

Tone Deafness				Intensity Deafness
	Central Deafness	Conductive Loss	Nerve Loss	

Figure 3–3

Causes and Symptoms of Hearing Deficiencies

In more than 75 per cent of the cases of deafness, German measles, erythroblastosis fetalis, meningitis, bilateral ear infection, or a family history of deafness can be identified. In the remaining cases, the chief symptom is the inability to speak at the customary age.

Here are behaviors that may be indicative of hearing problems:

1. The pupil is inattentive during lectures in the classroom.
2. The pupil turns the head toward the speaker, cups the hands behind the ears, or tends to favor one ear.
3. The pupil complains of ringing or buzzing in the ears.

4. The pupil listens with a tense or blank facial expression.
5. The pupil confuses words with similar sounds.
6. The pupil hears the speech of others but may not understand what he hears.
7. The pupil has special difficulty with the sounds *f, v, s, z, sh, zh, th, t, d, p, g, k,* and *b.*
8. The pupil speaks in a monotone or the pitch is unnatural.
9. The pupil fails to respond to phonic instruction.
10. The pupil's pronunciation is faulty.
11. The pupil breathes through the mouth.

TESTS OF HEARING

The hearing of every child showing any of the above symptoms should be tested. Bond and Tinker [24] suggest a number of methods for doing this. A loud-ticking watch may be used as a simple test. Normally a child can hear the ticking up to a distance of about forty-eight inches. Anything below twenty inches probably indicates hearing deficiency. For a more accurate test an audiometer may be used. Audiometers produce sounds of different frequency and intensity levels for the purpose of measuring auditory sensitivity. They permit the audiologist to obtain an audiogram of an individual's hearing in terms of frequency and intensity.

The audiometer used in testing should provide for both air-conduction and bone-conduction testing and for introducing masking tones. There are two general types of audiometers: discrete frequency, providing tones in half- or full-octave steps; and sweep frequency, providing a continuous variation of frequencies. Hearing loss usually is measured in five-decibel steps. Some audiometers are similar to a portable phonograph with several connected telephone receivers that permit individual testing or the simultaneous testing of as many as ten children. For group testing with such an instrument children must be able to write numbers, although in individual testing a teacher could record a child's answers.

O'Connor and Streng [25] divide the hard of hearing into four groups. Those with an average loss of twenty decibels or less in the better ear require no special treatment, although it would be wise to seat them advantageously in the classroom. Children in the twenty-five to fifty-five decibel loss group may need speech training, and those with a loss of thirty-five decibels may need a hearing aid. A third group with losses ranging from fifty-five to seventy-five decibels usually cannot learn to speak without aid. The individuals in this group are considered educationally deaf. A fourth group consists of those who are suffering more than a seventy-five decibel loss. Members of this group cannot learn speech through sounds, and ordinarily the public school is unable to meet their needs. They require special treatment. Children with a forty decibel loss across the speech range will have particular difficulty with *ch, f, k, s, sh, th,* and *z.*

Although there may be little the teacher can do to improve auditory acuity, auditory discrimination at least in part may be learned. The teacher can train the child to become more aware of sound, to make gross discriminations such as between the sound of a bell and a horn, to discriminate among simple speech patterns such as differences between the vowels, and he can help him to recognize the phonetic elements of words. Furthermore, the teacher needs to make adjustments for the hard of hearing. With the hard of hearing he needs to minimize instruction that puts a premium on auditory factors. And, he must make sure that the pupil hears him when he does lecture.

Neural development

Research by neurologists and recent experiments with electrical stimulations of the brain have given us much information concerning the projection areas of the brain. *Figure 3–4* shows the auditory, visual, motor, somesthetic, and olfactory areas. The sense organs are connected with their special projection areas in the cortex, and the essential sensory processes occur there. An injury to the visual projection area, for example, may cause blindness.

The functions of the brain, however, are not restricted to the projection areas. More than three-fourths of the brain consists of association areas.

The visual projection area is surrounded by an association area known as the parastriate cortex. A second association area,

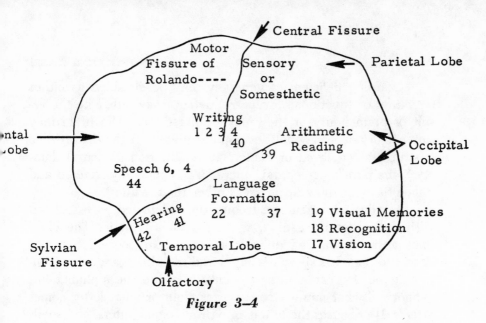

Figure 3-4

known as the peristriate cortex, surrounds the parastriate cortex. If the parastriate cortex is injured, the person cannot recognize or identify what he sees. If the peristriate cortex is injured, the person may be able to recognize what he sees, but he cannot recall the appearance of objects when they are not in view.

The nerve impulse travels from the retina along the optic nerve to visual area 17 in the occipital lobe. This area is concerned with seeing without recognition. In areas 18 and 19 recognition and visual memory occur. There the words are recognized as words. In area 39, the angular gyrus, the meaning of the word is comprehended. Eames [26] notes:

> This part of the brain has to do with the interpretation of symbols (letters, words, syllables) and combines the functions of recognition and visual memory for word forms. It is well known in neurology that a lesion here will interfere with the ability to read.

In the part of the brain lying between the hearing and reading areas, roughly areas 22 and 37, the association of sound and visual symbols occurs. Thus, since reading is commonly an association of a visual symbol with an auditory symbol, this part is of major importance in reading and is called the language-formation area. Injury here results in the inability to name one's concepts.

Learning deficiencies generally may be classified as either structural or functional. Structural defects may either be the result of brain injury or they may be hereditary. The brain may suffer injury or it may not develop adequately. If the disturbance is structural (delayed or inadequate maturation or neural damage), the pupil's perceptual functioning is generally affected and difficulties will show up in areas other than reading.

A mild brain damage, frequently undetected, is associated with difficulties in reading, writing, and arithmetic. The child finds abstract thinking difficult and has poor coordination and concentration. His speech is rapid and mumbled, and hence unintelligible. He can count to twenty or recite the alphabet but cannot tell what number comes after eight or what letter comes after *c*. He reverses the letters in writing, omits letters, and spells as though English were a completely phonetic language. The writing is cramped and angular. The letters vary in size and slant. Clumsiness in manipulation of small muscle groups (as in writing) is rather common. The execution in writing is jerky and arrhythmic. Frequently the jerkiness in writing is accompanied by jerky, stumbling, and explosive speech (cluttering). The writing looks the way the speech sounds. Finally, children with general language disabilities hear speech as an undifferentiated noise and see words on the printed page as an undifferentiated design. On more advanced levels (ten–fourteen age level) these children will usually have difficulty in organizing what they read or study. In explaining the language-disturbance syndrome, some suggest that the underlying cause may be delayed or disorganized maturation of the neural system.

Cerebral dominance

A condition thought to be dependent on the development of the brain is cerebral dominance. This implies that one cerebral hemisphere is more important in behavior or functionally more efficient than the other. The left hemisphere commonly is the language hemisphere and for most individuals, since most of us are right-handed, it also is the dominant hemisphere.

There are, however, exceptions to this general rule. Some persons are left-handed (right dominance), some are ambidextrous, with neither hemisphere being dominant (lack of dom-mance), and in others the dominance changes from activity to activity. The latter is termed crossed-dominance and is seen in individuals exhibiting left-eyedness and right-handedness. Do these conditions hinder reading proficiency?

There is little question but that poor readers, especially those showing up in reading clinics, frequently show a greater frequency of undeveloped dominance. Harris,[27] for example, reports a high proportion of reading disability cases develop preference for one hand later than the age of nine. In a later study [28] he suggests that if tests are sufficiently discriminative, genuine relationships between reading disability and laterality are found. Not all studies are so definitive.

In summary:

1. Learning occurs in an organism and whatever affects the nervous system of the organism may affect learning. Lack of neurological organization may be a key factor in reading difficulty.
2. The more we know about nerve excitation and brain functioning, the better we will understand the pupil's ease or difficulty of learning.
3. We may have two types of learners: those who have had appropriate neural development for learning and those who do not.

The pupil's preferred mode of learning

When some children read, they *see* the word, others *hear* it, and still others *feel* it. In other words, these learners are differentiated from one another by the way they characteristically react to stimuli. And it may well be that some children become reading disability cases because they are being taught by a method that they do not prefer and one which prohibits them from doing their best.

What is the evidence for differential modalities of learning? It would appear that the younger child, the slow learner, the corrective, retarded and reluctant reader, the child with visual defects, and boys generally have auditory preferences. The slow learner, the remedial reader, the reluctant reader who does not pay attention, and the child with both visual and auditory defects may have kinesthetic preferences. The older pupil, the gifted learner, the good and willing reader, and girls may tend to have visual preferences.

Remediation perhaps should emphasize teaching to the child's strength rather than to his weakness. It would seem reasonable also to utilize instructional materials which are congruent with each learner's particular strengths in perception, imagery, and recall. The end-goal of all diagnostic testing may well be to identify a pupil's preferred mode of learning.

How can one identify a pupil's preferred mode of learning? Let us look at some tests that can aid the teacher in doing this.

The Illinois Test of Psycholinguistic Abilities [29]

This test was developed for the purpose of identifying psycholinguistic abilities and disabilities in children of ages two and a half to nine. The test consists actually of nine tests which answer such questions as: Can the pupil interpret words auditorily? Will he profit from phonic instruction? Can the pupil learn through a "look and say" or a configuration method? Will he have difficulty with kinesthetic approaches?

Mills Learning Methods Test [30]

The purpose of this test is to determine the pupil's ability to learn new words under different teaching procedures. It seeks to determine by what method the child apparently learns most easily and remembers best.

The four methods used in this test are: the visual method; the phonic or auditory method; the kinesthetic or tracing method; and a combination method.

Four sets of picture word cards are used, containing primer to third grade level words: primer level (peach-colored); first grade (blue); second grade (green); and third grade (pink). A test record form is used to record pertinent test data and results.

The test begins with a pre-test to determine the forty unknown words that are later used in the four teaching methods test situations. The pretest should later be on the level on which there are forty words which the child does not know. The forty missed words are then recorded on the test record.

These forty words are then taught by each of the four methods suggested, each training session taking exactly fifteen minutes. On the first day only the pretest and one training session (perhaps with the kinesthetic method) is given. A twenty-four-hour interval is allowed before the child is tested on the first training session and a second training session (perhaps phonic) occurs. The total test interval is thus five days.

Screening Tests for Identifying Children with Specific Language Disability [31]

This test, by Beth Slingerland, is intended to identify children who have language difficulties. It consists of nine subtests and is designed for grades one to four, and identifies children who are unable to respond to even the best of configuration approaches. It measures visual copying, visual memory, visual discrimination, auditory perception, auditory memory, and auditory-visual association. It also gives clues to kinesthetic weaknesses.

Roswell-Chall Auditory Blending Test, Essay Press, P.O. Box 5, Planetarium Station, New York, New York.

This test measures the pupil's ability to blend sounds auditorily to form words. It is useful for judging the ease or difficulty that pupils will experience in phonics instruction. The test may be used routinely in grades one through four and with older children who have reading difficulties. It requires five minutes for administration.

It is an individual test and is presented orally. The tester says: "We are going to do some things with words and sounds. I will say the sounds in the words slowly and then you will tell me what the words are." The words to which the child must respond are: a-t, n-o, i-f, u-p, s-ay, m-y, b-e, t-oo, c-ow, h-e, st-ep, f-at, pl-ay, g-oat, ch-ain, b-ed, c-ake, r-an, r-ime, c-all, c-a-t, b-i-g, c-u-ff, s-a-d, g-o-t, m-a-p, d-e-sk, t-oa-st, and p-e-t.

Since poor blending may result from lack of instruction or unfamiliarity with sounds and from inadequate maturation and since the teacher will not know which is the significant factor, it is probably best to plan a step-by-step instructional program.

California Phonics Survey Test, California Test Bureau.

This group test, for ages seven–sixteen, requires about forty-five minutes for administration and uses seventy-five items to measure phonic adequacy. It uses listening and reading to reveal the most common reversals, confusions of blends and vowels, and other errors that reflect the inability to relate letter combinations to spoken sounds. The test may be administered by a specially prepared magnetic tape recording or be presented orally by the teacher.

Exercise 1 (twenty-five items) requires the pupil to find the printed form that corresponds to a spoken word or sound (the examiner reads *rog* and the pupil needs to find it in *rog, bot, pab, zen,* or indicate that it is none of them); exercise 2 (eleven items) requires the pupil to select the printed form that matches the end word of a spoken sentence (the teacher reads: "His little friend Susie said, 'No, she's not. She's a *ter'wit . . . ter-wit . . . ter-wit.'*" The pupil must select terwit from *twitter, trewett, wrerton, trempon,* or indicate that it is none of them); exercise 3 (ten items) requires the pupil to match real words with what the pupil hears; exercise 4 (fourteen items) requires the pupil to select the printed response that rhymes with the whole sound of the spoken stimulus word (mattle—parstle, fattle, dimply, sattling); and exercise 5 (fifteen items) requires a pupil to identify a group of letters when sounded that sound like a real word. The teacher can detect vowel, consonant, configuration, ending and sight word errors.

Scores on the test determine whether there is adequate phonic ability, some phonic disability, serious phonic difficulty, or gross phonic disability. There is an indication that pupils in the latter two groups need intensive or systematic retraining (or may simply have great difficulty learning through auditory means) and that speed reading courses may actually hurt them.

Auditory Discrimination Test, Language Research Associates, Box 95, 950 East 59th Street, Chicago, Illinois.

This auditory discrimination test for ages five–eight must be administered individually. The test contains forty items comprising three- to five-letter word pairs of the consonant-vowel-consonant variety. It requires from five to ten minutes for administration. It predicts articulatory speech defects and certain remedial reading problems.

Leavell Hand-Eye Coordination Tests, Keystone View Company.

These tests for ages eight–fourteen are used to determine the need for training on the Leavell Hand-Eye Coordinator. It provides scores for hand-foot preference, eye-ear preference, hand dexterity preference, and visual imagery.

Perceptual Forms Test, Winter Haven Lions Publication Committee, P.O. Box 1045, Winter Haven, Florida.

This test, for ages six–eight and a half, identifies the child who lacks adequate hand-eye coordination. The pupil is required to reproduce seven geometric forms—a circle, cross, square, triangle, divided triangle, horizontal diamond, and vertical diamond. A poor score suggests that the pupil should not be introduced to reading until hand-eye coordination has been improved through template training. Perceptual Testing Materials include: Perceptual Forms Teachers Manual, Perceptual Testing and Training Handbook, and Test Cards.

Phonics Knowledge Survey, Bureau of Publications, Columbia University.

This individual test for grades one–six takes from ten to thirty minutes to administer and measures the extent of the pupil's knowledge of phonics. Elements tested include: names of letters, consonant sounds, vowels, vowel generalizations, sounds of *c* and *g*, sounds of *y*, consonant blends, digraphs, vowel combinations, vowels followed by r, sounds of *qu*, sounds of *oo*, sounds of *x*, beginning consonant combinations, and syllabication.

Phonics Mastery Test, Follett Publishing Company.

This test is a part of the Botel Reading Inventory described in Chapter 2 and measures knowledge of consonants, vowels, syllabication, and nonsense words. The test takes fifteen to twenty-five minutes to administer. The test contains four subtests or levels. Level A requires the pupil to write the letter or letters representing the beginning consonant (batch—b), beginning consonant blend (plush—pl), and beginning consonant digraph (thence—th). The pupil next writes two or more words each rhyming with the words *ball, make, get,* and *will.* Level B requires the pupil to write the vowel sound heard in words and to indicate whether it is long or short. The pupil also must write vowel combinations (oo, ou, oi, au) and vowel-consonant combinations (ow, ar, ir, er, ur, or) heard in words. Level C requires the pupil to indicate the number of syllables in a word (excitement—three) and to indicate the accented syllable. Level D measures the ability to read nonsense words (ringtrape, pegflitting, fragmil, sloapclinger, tampillage, etc.).

Robbins Speech Sound Discrimination and Verbal Imagery Type Tests, Expression Company, Magnolia, Massachusetts.

This test for ages four and over is a speech sound discrimination and a verbal imagery test. It determines which types of speech sounds a child who manifests a phonetic speech defect of sensory origin is unable to differentiate and to help the pupil see, hear, and feel the differences between the individual speech sounds which compose these groups. This test thus has diagnostic and remedial value.

Younger children indicate their responses to an item by pointing to pictures while the other children indicate whether the three words read aloud to them sound alike and, if not, which differs from the other two.

The tests are based on the assumption that there are different and specific sound descriptions and different sense modalities. The test thus seeks to identify the eye-minded, ear-minded, and motor-minded.

McKee Inventory of Phonetic Skills, Houghton Mifflin Company.

This group test covers all of the phonetic and structural elements that are taught in the Houghton Mifflin basic reading series. Level three of the test identifies those children at grade three and above who have not mastered the basic word analysis skill.

Marianne Frostig Developmental Test of Visual Perception, Consulting Psychologists Press, Palo Alto, California.

This test, for pre-school and early school age children, was developed out of a need for an instrument which would furnish data for the normal growth of perceptual ability. The results suggest that the period of maximum visual perceptual development occurs between three and a half and seven and a half years, with many children experiencing a definite lag in their development. The test consists of fifty-four items divided into five sub-tests. Test A: *Visual motor coordination*—sixteen items—requires the pupil to draw lines within boundaries and connect points. Visual-motor coordination is important because well-directed eye-movements are a prerequisite for reading. Test B: *Constancy of Form*—eighteen items—requires the recognition of squares and circles drawn with a variety of shadings, sizes, grounds and positions in space. The perception of constancy of shape and size is essential if the pupil is to recognize words when they appear in unfamiliar context, color, size, or style of print. Test C: *Figure ground relationships*—five items—measures perception of intersecting and hidden figures. The analysis and synthesis of words, phrases, and paragraphs and the ability to locate specific information in a given place on a page require the ability to distinguish figure from ground. Test D: *Position in space*—eight items—requires the pupil to discriminate reversals or rotations in series of schematic figures. Test E: *Spatial relationships*—seven items— by connecting points the child is required to copy patterns involving a variety of angles and lengths of lines. The skill measured by this and the previous test is necessary if the pupil is to be able to discriminate between similar letters (b-d) and similar words (saw-was). Effective scoring depends upon the five judges who must be specifically trained in the administration of the test if the results of this test are to be valid and reliable.

What can the teacher do?

In this chapter we have looked at some of the major causes of reading disability. We identified and discussed such areas as inadequate experiential background, inadequate language background, inadequate maturation, inadequacies in intellectual-social-emotional development, lack of motivation, and instructional inadequacies. In addition we have examined the effects of visual and auditory inadequacy and of other physical-physiological factors on reading achievement. We also considered sensory modalities and their relationship to learning.

An important question is surely: "So what? You know the causes of reading disability, but what can you do about it?"

The teacher can do something about the causes of reading disability by:

1. Providing preparatory experiences necessary for learning.
2. Using and developing reading materials that present experiences familiar to the children being taught and that capitalize on the pupil's preferred modes of learning.
3. Helping children to develop their listening skills.
4. Helping children to articulate the sounds of the language.
5. Providing language training along with reading instruction.
6. Providing appropriate environmental stimulations so that maturational development may progress at an appropriate rate. Let instruction march slightly, but only slightly, ahead of the child's maturation process.
7. Using intelligence test scores to gear the instructional program to the ability level of the pupil.
8. Striving to expand the intelligence level of all children.
9. Checking the child for
   a. signs of illness or overall poor health
   b. visual problems
   c. hearing problems.
10. Looking for symptoms of neurological disturbances and referring the child to a specialist if this is indicated.
11. Teaching reading in such a way as to enhance the social-emotional development of the learner and so as to whet his appetite for reading.
12. Constantly evaluating his teaching.

But, even more important than the foregoing is the need to develop competency in identifying the actual cause from an accurate diagnosis of the symptoms. The special or remedial reading teacher is by definition an expert in tying together symptom and cause. The classroom teacher can become quite expert in doing the same thing.

It requires considerable skill and care to transfer the diagnostic data into an accurate prescription that can serve as the basis for remediation. In making the transfer we must recognize certain dangers. Sometimes the learner's symptoms may lead us to take faulty steps toward his remediation. What may appear to be the cause of his difficulty may be quite unrelated to it or may even be a result or symptom of his problems. But skill and experience in the translation of diagnostic data and an earnest desire to help each student attain the highest goals that his capabilities permit should serve as a firm foundation for remediation.

Look at the two symptoms tabulated in *Figure 3–5*. They are common symptoms of reading disability. But what is their cause? We have suggested four possible ones for symptom one (there are others) and three for symptom two and have suggested remediation in each instance. This is the type of skill needed by the classroom teacher.

Case study revisited

Let us return for a few moments to pupil 26. Why is he a retarded reader? What are the underlying causes of his retardation? You have just surveyed some of the more common causes of reading disability. We have agreed on two basic facts:

1. Reading disability rarely stems from a single cause; there commonly is a group of interacting factors, each in its own way contributing to the disability or preventing future growth.
2. The effect of inhibitory factors is multiplicative rather than additive. One factor by itself may keep a child from becoming a good reader.

As we examine symptoms that pupil 26 exhibits, the following causal factors emerge:

1. The pupil has not learned to articulate the individual phoneme, the vowels and consonants, is a poor oral reader, and cannot express himself in his own words. To remedy this, it is important that language training accompany reading instruction every step of the way. The cause probably is a deficiency in auditory discrimination. He

Symptom	Possible Cause	Possible Remedy
1. Inability to remember a letter visually or making frequent substitutions of words	a. Poor vision (p. 43) [32]	a. Check and remediate visual defect (p. 43); have pupil engage in exercises teaching discrimination of letters (pp. 158-160)
	b. Inability to tie letters together and remember them (c-a-t). Poor visual memory span (p. 43)	b. Provide tracing exercises to develop a "feel" for the word; stress training in visual discrimination of words (pp. 153-158)
	c. Reverses letters and so can't discriminate and remember them (b-d) (pp. 160-163)	c. Check if he also reverses nonsense syllables. Have pupil engage in exercises designed to change the pattern (pp. 160-163)
	d. Inattention, not wanting to learn (pp. 69-74)	d. Use language-experience approach discussed in Chapter 5 of this book
2. Inability to discriminate word sounds. For example, the teacher might say, "Now listen for the sound pig . . . big, dig, pig, pick." The child cannot deal with this problem	a. Poor hearing—poor auditory acuity (p. 51)	a. Check hearing and consult doctor (p. 51)
	b. Speech defects: (p. 114) "Father becomes fodder," "Shishter for sister," "Kool for School."	b. Training in articulation (pp. 114-120)
	c. Poor auditory discrimination (p. 51)	c. Seat child near teacher; check for high tone deafness and watch for sounds f, v, s, z, sh, zh, th, t, d, p, b, k, and g (p. 53); provide exercises in auditory discrimination (pp. 143-152)

Figure 3-5

needs special help in widening his eye-voice span if he is going to become a better oral reader.

2. The pupil cannot read for details, cannot read to learn, does not read critically, and does not organize what he reads. The cause may well be that he has not learned that reading is a thinking process. He must learn to think while reading.

3. The pupil exhibits a decided lack of interest in reading. The reasons for this may be:

   a. He may have been introduced to school and reading too early, with the result that he learned to dislike both school and reading. The interview with the stepmother certainly indicates as much. The pupil seems to have lost his natural enthusiasm for reading at an early age.

   b. Another causal factor is the inadequate memory and attention span. Adjustments must be made in reading instruction to compensate for these deficiencies. This pupil will fatigue more easily, and it is extremely difficult to be interested in reading when one is tired. Attention suffers and comprehension is usually lowered. As nervous tension builds up, the pupil becomes disinterested, disgusted, and may even turn from reading completely.

4. The self-image of the pupil seems to be another important cause of his reading disability. This is a discouraged boy. He has no confidence in being able to help himself. He feels inadequate and insecure in the school environment. The failure in reading only heightens these feelings. It threatens self-esteem and makes it almost impossible for him to be successful in school.

   The early painful experience, that of not wanting to go to kindergarten, has turned this pupil against school and probably against reading. The difficulties in adjusting to the school environment made it impossible for the pupil to expend the energies needed for learning. The poor start in school tended to make him feel "no good" and "bad inside."

Summary

As one completes this third step, the chances are that the following has been done:

1. A case history has been compiled.
2. The pupil's capacity has been analyzed, including, if possible, the results of hearing tests, visual screening tests, eye-movement data, hand and eye preference tests.
3. The level of oral and silent reading achievement has been determined.
4. The reading problem has been identified.
5. The factors that interfere with reading have been isolated.
6. The data have been collated and interpreted.

The written report of the diagnosis should include recommendations as to *how* the child should be taught and should suggest materials that may be used in teaching. It should outline specific weaknesses in word analysis and in comprehension. There might be statements about the child's spontaneity or lack of it in correcting his own errors; statements about the ease or lack of it with which the pupil develops insight into phonic generalizations; statements about the pupil's awareness or lack of awareness of phonetic differences in words; or statements about the reasons why the pupil substitutes words of similar meaning.

The teacher needs to become expert in reading the causes of reading disability.

Smith and Carrigan [33] note:

> Clinicians are like a small group standing beside a river full of drowning people. The victims are being swept seaward by the current of time. The clinicians can pull out a few, but the rest are lost. Few of the group are willing to go upstream to find out how the victims get into the river in the first place.

The teacher needs to know how the disabled reader gets into the river in the first place. To do this, he needs to be able to read the causes of reading disability. It is not enough to know the symptoms. The symptom has to be identified with the proper cause. Only in this way is remediation of reading disability possible.

---

[1] Smith, D. E. P., and Carrigan, Patricia M. *The Nature of Reading Disability.* Harcourt, Brace and Company, New York, 1959, p. 6.

[2] Henry, Jules. *Culture Against Man.* Random House, New York, 1963.

[3] Davis, Hallowell, ed. *Hearing and Deafness: A Guide for Laymen.* Holt, Rinehart and Winston, Inc., New York, 1947, p. 279.

[4] Van Riper, Charles, and Butler, Katherine. *Speech in the Elementary Classroom.* Harper and Row, Publishers, New York, 1955, p. 64.

[5] Artley, A. Sterl. "Oral Language Growth and Reading Ability," *Elementary School Journal,* 53 (February, 1953) 321-328, copyright 1953 by the University of Chicago, pp. 325-326.

[6] Tyack, David. "A Description of the Gillingham Method," pp. 87-88, in *Developing the Mature Reader,* Portland, Oregon, International Reading Association, 1966.

[7] Buswell, Guy T. "The Process of Reading," *The Reading Teacher,* 13 (December, 1959), pp. 108-114.

[8] Lefevre, Carl A. *Linguistics and the Teaching of Reading.* McGraw-Hill Book Company, New York, 1964, pp. 4-5. Reprinted by permission.

[9] Bateman, Barbara. *Reading as a Non-Meaningful Process,* Unpublished paper, University of Oregon.

[10] Baller, Warren R., and Charles, Don C. *The Psychology of Human Growth and Development.* Holt, Rinehart and Winston, New York, 1961, p. 22.

[11] Harris, Albert J. *Effective Teaching of Reading.* David McKay Company, Inc., New York, 1962, p. 3.

[12] Vygotsky, Lev Semenovich. *Thought and Language,* ed. and translated by Eugenia Haufmann and Gertrude Vakar. John Wiley and Sons, Inc., New York, © 1952, p. 104.

[13] Rousseau, Jean Jacques. *Emile.* Appleton-Century-Crofts, Inc., New York, 1899, p. 38.

[14] Bond, Guy L., and Tinker, Miles A. *Reading Difficulties: Their Diagnosis and Correction.* Appleton-Century-Crofts, Inc., New York, 1967, p. 140. Reprinted by permission.

[15] Bugelski, B. R. *The Psychology of Learning Applied to Teaching.* Bobbs-Merrill Company, Inc., Indianapolis, 1964, p. 59.

[16] Bond and Tinker, *ibid.,* p. 15.

[17] Wheat, H. G. *Foundations of School Learning.* Alfred A. Knopf, Inc., New York, 1955, pp. 57-58.

[18] For a recent summary and analysis of the data, see: Weintraub, Samuel. "Sex Differences in Reading Achievement." *The Reading Teacher,* 20 (November, 1966) pp. 155-165. For a discussion on viewpoints as to how to deal with sex differences, see: Wilson, E., Epstein, J., Feeney, E., and Wilson, T. "Sex Differences in the Elementary School," *National Elementary Principal,* 46 (November, 1966) pp. 8-12.

[19] Preston, Ralph C. "A Comparative Study of the Reading Achievement of German and American Children," *Changing Concepts of Reading Instruction*, International Reading Association, Scholastic Magazines, New York, 1961, pp. 109-112.

[20] Malmquist, Eve. "Organizing Instruction to Prevent Reading Disabilities." *Reading as an Intellectual Activity*, International Reading Association Conference Proceedings, Scholastic Magazines, New York, 1963, pp. 36-39.

[21] Diskan, Samuel M. "Eye Problems in Children," *Postgraduate Medicine*, 34 (August, 1963) pp. 168-178.

[22] Brungardt, Joe B., and Brungardt, Mike J. "Let's Stop the Prevailing Injustices to Children," *Kansas Teacher*, 73 (January, 1965) pp. 14-15, 50.

[23] *Ibid.*, pp. 14-15, 40.

[24] Bond, Guy L., and Tinker, Miles A. *Reading Difficulties: Their Diagnosis and Correction*. Appleton-Century-Crofts, Inc., New York, 1967, p. 113.

[25] O'Connor, Clarence D., and Streng, Alice. "Teaching the Acoustically Handicapped." *The Education of Exceptional Children*, Forty-ninth Yearbook of the National Society for the Study of Education, Part II, University of the Chicago Press, Chicago, 1950, pp. 152-176.

[26] Eames, Thomas H. "Visual Handicaps to Reading," *Journal of Education*, 141 (February, 1959) 1-36, p. 4. Reprinted by permission.

[27] Harris, A. J. *How to Increase Reading Ability*. David McKay Company, New York, 1956, p. 254.

[28] Harris, A. J. "Lateral Dominance, Directional Confusion, and Reading Disability," *Journal of Psychology*, 44 (October, 1957), pp. 283-294.

[29] Institute for Research on Exceptional Children, University of Illinois.

[30] Mills Center, Fort Lauderdale, Florida.

[31] Educators Publishing Service, Cambridge, Massachusetts.

[32] The pages refer to specific sections in Dechant, Emerald, *Improving the Teaching of Reading*. Prentice-Hall, Inc., Englewood Cliffs, 1964.

[33] Smith, D. E. P., and Carrigan, Patricia. *The Nature of Reading Disability*. Harcourt, Brace and Company, Inc., New York, 1959, p. 6. Reprinted with permission.

4

How to Organize and
Implement Remediation

Step IV of diagnostic procedure is actually the development of a plan for remediation. Identification of symptoms and causes is simply not enough. Diagnosis is meant to lead to remediation. It must serve as a blueprint from which remediation is structured. From a study of the diagnostic data, the teacher evolves a plan by and through which it is hoped the learner will improve in reading. The principles which we will discuss later in this chapter should help the teacher to formulate such a plan. They are basic procedures and principles that should guide all remedial instruction, irrespective of the type of reading disability.

Bond and Tinker [1] note:

> In studying a disabled reader, whether in the classroom or clinic, the diagnosis should be concerned with the collection of information necessary for planning a corrective program. There are two types of diagnosis—etiological and therapeutic. Etiological diagnosis is concerned with finding out what caused a child to get into difficulty. Such a search is often impossible and frequently useless for formulating a remedial program. It is of little use, for example, to search the records and find a child is in difficulty in reading in the fourth grade because he was absent from

school with the measles when he was in the first grade. Nothing can be done now to give him the help that should have been available when he returned to school after a month's absence during the first grade. A body of such information, collected and summarized for research purposes, would be most useful for the prevention of reading difficulties, but it is not useful now for the immediate job of correcting a reading disability that began several years earlier.

Therapeutic diagnosis is concerned with the conditions that are now present in the child in order to give direction to a program of re-education. The diagnostician concerned with therapeutic diagnosis searches for the reading strengths and limitations of a child and for any characteristics within this child's present environment or makeup that need to be corrected before this remedial instruction can be successful, or for conditions that need to be adjusted to before he can be expected to make maximum progress. The diagnostician would be more concerned about a current hearing loss, for example, than he would be about finding out that the child was in difficulty because he had had a temporary hearing loss several years ago.

The chapter thus deals with four questions: What decisions or what knowledge does the teacher of reading need before he can plan an effective remedial program? What principles should guide remedial instruction? What are the skills that must be developed in all remedial programs? And how can a corrective or remedial program be organized? Let us consider the first of these.

Decisions required of the teacher

Somehow, either on his own or with specially skilled help if it is available, the teacher must identify the child's problems and then plan and carry through the best possible corrective measures. This requires certain decisions based on particular information:

1. The teacher must decide whether the pupil actually is a retarded reader rather than a child of low ability. If he is a retarded reader, he must identify the nature of his retardation.

2. He must decide what type of teaching is needed.
3. He must determine whether the needed remedial work can best be done in the classroom or in separate facilities and, if in the classroom, whether individually or in a sub-group.
4. He must make an estimate of the proper length of the instructional period. The length will depend upon the skill being taught and on the physical well-being and social-emotional maturity of the child.
5. He must determine the most efficient methods and materials that can be used. He needs to determine what the difficulty level of the materials should be and whether the materials are interesting to the pupil. Bond and Tinker [2] emphasize ". . . there should be no compromise with difficulty even to get material of high interest."
6. He must be alert to and decide how to make adjustments for the child's special interests, for any emotional or physical defects, or conditions in the child's home and community environment that may block his reading growth.
7. He must be alert to and decide how to deal with the environmental factors, including the school, that might be keeping the pupil from progressing in reading.
8. He must decide how to interpret to the pupil the progress he might make.
9. He must plan independent work activities for the pupil.

Principles of remediation

Remedial teachers have developed certain principles that should guide all remedial or corrective instruction. A general observation might be that the principles underlying remedial or corrective reading instruction are basically the same that govern developmental reading instruction. Of these principles, the following seem most significant.

1. Develop a plan of remediation, put it on paper, and refer to it frequently as remediation progresses. Incidental teaching is simply inadequate with the retarded reader. Write flexibility into the plan. There needs to be flexibility in materials, methods, and attitudes.

2. Discover the child's area of confidence. Start where the pupil knows something. Nothing succeeds quite like success. One of the most therapeutic experiences for reading disability cases is success. Thus remedial instruction should begin at the level at which the pupil can be successful, probably about one grade-level below the pupil's ability. It should begin with short assignments, inspire confidence, and restore status to the child in the eyes of his peers, his parents, and teachers. In dealing with corrective or remedial cases it is necessary to remember that:

   a. The pupil is generally anxious and fearful of discussing his problem with an adult.

   b. His anxiety and guilt are especially high when he has experienced disapproval of his parents.

   c. The pupil's "don't care" attitude toward reading frequently is a "do care very much" attitude.[3] It is a safety valve that permits the pupil to save face. Both teacher and parent should permit the pupil to have this apparent attitude without developing a feeling of guilt on the part of the pupil.

3. The corrective or remedial methods are hardly distinct from developmental methods. One cannot "reteach" a pupil who never learned. One cannot remedy what was always lacking. Children receiving remedial education are distinct from normal readers in that they did not learn as a result of the educational procedures that were effective with most children. All the principles that apply to effective developmental instruction also apply to what is termed remedial teaching. The good teacher, whatever his title may be, starts at the child's present reading level, builds self-confidence in reading and uses a variety of reading methods. Perhaps the remedial teacher is somewhat more permissive, delves more precisely into the causes of the reading problem, uses a greater variety of materials and motivational devices, and individualizes the program to a greater degree. The methods and principles of remedial teaching and developmental teaching are distinguishable, if at all, by the emphasis on individualization. Remedial reading is not a magic hocus-pocus of special methods, but a more intense and personal application of the techniques used with all others. Consequently, it is the nature of the child rather than the nature

of the teaching that distinguishes the two procedures. Remedial measures are not cure-alls. They do not correct and eliminate all reading difficulties. But, of even greater significance is the fact that the classroom teacher can provide optimum remedial teaching.

4. Develop those skills and abilities which are most necessary for immediate successful reading.

5. Remediation should be based on and accompanied by continuous diagnosis. Teach, test, and reteach makes sense in the developmental phase. In remedial work the process is probably "test, teach, and retest." This identifies areas that need unteaching and helps to identify the pupil who is ready for regular classroom instruction.

6. No one symptom, error, or mistake of itself implies an ailment or a general deficiency. Even the best reader will err at times.

7. Perfect results on a test do not mean complete mastery. An average score of second-grade level, on any test, does not mean that all the pupil's reading skills are on a second-grade level. It is not uncommon to find children getting the correct answer through the use of an incorrect method. By incorrect method is meant any method that will hinder future progress (such as guessing).

8. The child's symptoms, if not correctly interpreted, may lead the teacher to provide the improper remediation. The so-called cause, upon careful analysis, frequently is found to be an effect of poor reading. The teacher thus expects from the expert psychological insight into why a given method is recommended.

9. The pattern of symptoms is usually more significant than the individual symptom.

10. Cures do not necessarily mean that the correct method of cure has been found. The intangibles of teacher–pupil motivations and teacher effectiveness generally play an important role. The good teacher may have good results regardless of method used. The poor teacher may experience only failure.

11. No remedial method has universal application. Methods of instruction should be selected which are in harmony with the best mode of learning for a given child.

12. The teacher's personality and his ability to enlist each child's active cooperation are often more important than the specific method used. "Learning occurs in a relationship. Rapport is a subtle thing." The pupil needs to develop a desire to learn.

In dealing with remedial cases, psychotherapeutic principles should be incorporated into the process. The teacher should:

   a. Develop a constructive relationship with the pupil (rapport). Drop the role of an authoritative teacher. Become an interested teacher.
   b. Be a genuine person.
   c. Give total and unequivocal acceptance to the pupil despite his frequent failures in school.
   d. Have complete faith in the pupil's improvableness and ability to read. It is a fact that if the significant adults in a pupil's life believe that he can succeed, his chances for success are appreciably improved.
   e. Develop a feeling of empathy—not sympathy. Objectivity must be maintained. If sympathy develops, the pupil feels that he has to please his teacher and that he cannot make mistakes. This often leads to tension.[4]
   f. Have a structured, well-defined program. The remedial program is more structured than the psychotherapeutic session.
   g. Arouse interest by judicious choice of materials.

   If the corrective or remedial teacher provides a relationship in which he is (a) genuine, internally consistent; (b) acceptant, prizing the learner as a person of worth; (c) empathically understanding of the learner's private world of feelings and attitudes, then certain changes are likely to occur in the learner. Some of these changes are: The learner becomes (a) more realistic in his self-perception; (b) more confident and self-directing; (c) more positively valued by himself; (d) less likely to repress elements of his experience; (e) more mature, socialized and adaptive in his behavior; (f) less upset by stress and quicker to recover from it; (g) more like the healthy, integrated well-functioning person in his personality structure; and (h) a better learner.[5]

13. No two reading disability cases probably stem from the same sources, have exactly the same pattern, or need the same instruction.

14. Select materials that the pupil can handle and in which he is interested. To do this, the teacher needs to know the pupil's instructional level. It is very important to remember that reading skills don't operate in a vacuum. The teacher needs proper materials, perhaps packets and kits; however, "packets and kits are fine for practice, tackling the dummy, but practice isn't to be confused with playing the game, of football or reading." [6] It is often not what materials that are used with retarded readers that is most significant, but rather what the teacher does with the materials.

15. Instill in the pupil a feeling of responsibility for his own progress. Progress charts should be developed. The units of improvement need to be small enough so that progress can be recorded at frequent intervals.

16. Some remedial approaches, if used flexibly, appear applicable to reading disability cases almost irrespective of cause.

17. Remedial sessions must be adapted to the pupil. Half-hour sessions are probably suitable for third and fourth graders; eighth graders might be able to handle hour-long sessions.

18. When we speak of remedial reading or reading disability, we often imply that there is a basic deficiency in the learner that impedes progress. It may be helpful to remind ourselves that the basic deficiency may be poor teaching.

    Improvement in reading is not necessarily brought about by spending more money, by bringing in consultants, by buying more gadgets and mechanical devices, or by resorting to newer approaches. Outstanding instructional programs in reading will be achieved "only through outstanding instruction." [7] This means, as Heilman notes, that "we must develop practices which are totally in accord with what we know about pupil-learning and what we know about reading and its relation to all school learning."

19. When the teacher and child meet, a major part of the teacher's armament must be knowledge of principles of learning. Many normal children learn readily in spite of repeated violations of learning principles. However, children with learning disabilities cannot do this.

    The following statements summarize learning principles particularly applicable in dealing with retarded readers:

    a. The pupil learns by doing, learning occurs under condiditions of practice, and overlearning is of crucial importance to poor readers. Retarded readers generally become better in word recognition the more frequently they see the word. However, practice or repetition *per se* does not cause learning. The pupil's practice must be both motivated and rewarded and it should be slightly varied from session to session.

b. The learner cannot learn without doing, but he won't do anything without being rewarded. The best rewards in the remedial setting are often pleasant pupil-teacher relationships, permissiveness on the part of the teacher, and feelings of success. The remedial teacher must divide the learning situation into numerous small steps and must reward the learning of each discrete step.

c. Learning is often a matter of present organization and reorganization, not simply past accretion. Perhaps no individual is ever completely free to behave on the basis of the present situation. Previous experiences have developed a set or pattern of behavior that is difficult to change. The retarded reader, even if he now sincerely wants to be a good reader, must live with his previous inapplication. But, each new situation has within it the potentiality for change. The pupil can usually make positive advances toward new goals and achievements. He has the potentiality for growth.

d. Letters might best be taught to most children as parts of a whole word, but the perceptual whole for the retarded reader often is the single letter. The size of the unit of instruction depends on the nature of the pupil and many retarded readers benefit greatly from a synthetic-phonetic approach.

e. The learner learns best when he is psychologically and physiologically ready to respond to the stimulus. The learner needs a proper attitude, should be ready to attend to the stimulus, and should have a felt need to learn. He needs also to have adequate maturity for learning. The learner will not respond unless he is motivated and he cannot learn unless he responds. The retarded reader's performance will improve only if he is interested in his work; if he is interested in improving himself; if the material to be learned has special significance for himself; and if he is attentive to the situation. Reduce motivations to zero and there is no performance and hence, no learning.

f. The teacher needs to ask himself whether he is trying to get the pupil to substitute one stimulus for another or whether he wants to elicit the correct response. In teaching the child to read, we obviously have a case of stimulus substitution. In essence we are asking the child to bring to the written word the same meanings that he previously attached to the spoken word.

Reading also involves response selection. A child who can read *the* and *there* may not be too sure of *their*. He makes provisional tries at the word and when he comes up with the correct pronunciational response the teacher reinforces this response, thus gradually stamping it in. Thus, from a series of possible responses the child gradually learns to select the correct response.

g. Each activity (reading of a sentence, for example) consists of a complex of individual movements, and improvement and learning are not necessarily attained by *much* reading but rather by increasing the number of correct movements in reading (moving from left to right, proper identification of the word, association of the proper meaning with the word, development of proper eye movements) and by reducing the number of incorrect movements (excessive regressions, improper word attack, etc.) in the total complex of movements comprising the total capacity. Improvement occurs because the learner gradually replaces the erroneous movements that he still is making with correct ones. Thus additional practice gives more opportunity to master the myriad of movements comprising a complex total performance.

This view of the learning of a skill certainly emphasizes the need for the teaching of specific habits. Telling a retarded reader "to read" is not specific enough. We need to teach specific habits in specific situations. This requires careful job analysis, leading to an identification of all specific movements. The curriculum, methods, and materials must be so specific that they will serve as proper stimuli to call forth appropriate responses.

h. The remedial teacher cannot be satisfied if the pupil comes up with the right answer. The remedial teacher must make sure that the pupil understands the process that is being taught. Guessing or accidental solutions are not enough. The teacher needs to take special note of such pupil reactions as: "I've got it, you just have to close your teeth every time you come to an *s* or your tongue will come out." There are levels of knowing. A pupil is said to know a sound when he can produce it; he may know it better when he can tell how he produced it.

The teacher thus needs to decide whether to reward the correct response, the correct process, or only the correct response when it is accompanied by the correct process.

It is important that the teacher not permit the learner to leave a learning situation without performing the response correctly. A pupil should read the word correctly before going on to another word. Bugelski [8] notes: "Here, teachers can also see the folly of allowing children to do homework without having the answers supplied. Such homework is not training or practice. It is a *test*."

The retarded reader should not "get by" with approximations of the correct answer.[9] The pupil should not be permitted simply to get a "general idea." Teachers frequently give partial credit for partially correct answers. Partially correct answers, such as reading *their* for *them* are in fact totally wrong. Bugelski [10] notes that "too many students are rated as 'knowing what to do' without being able to do."

It may well be that when the teacher says to the reader "read with care" that the pupil is not learning the molar response of reading but rather the micromolar response "when you read, read slowly."

i. The teacher should exercise great care, especially with the retarded reader, in not permitting extraneous materials to come between the stimulus and the response. The teacher must see to it that when the response is made, it is made to the proper stimulus and not to any of many other possible stimuli that may have intervened. Too frequently, in teaching, by the time the proper response occurs, the original stimulus situation has disappeared. The teacher must take great care that the necessary stimuli are so distinct for the pupil that he cannot help but see the connection between a given stimulus and the objective of teaching.

In reading, numerous errors arise because this is not done. The child who reverses, who sees *was* and reads *saw*, makes such an error. He has confused the stimulus. Reversals frequently may be simply stimuli that are not completely differentiated from all others.

j. The teacher will make fewer mistakes in teaching if he analyzes all the variables in behavior.

There are multiple causes of behavior. Some children do not read even though they profess a great desire to do so. Perhaps reading constantly conflicts with television and television may be the stronger stimulus, thus preventing reading.

Another factor that inhibits performance in reading is fatigue. As an organism continues to perform, as the retarded reader continues to read, for example, the tendency to read is gradually lessened. The pupil's tendency to perform may be lessened also by such factors as defective vision.

k. Learning retardation frequently results because the pupil cannot make the proper differentiations required for mastery of the learning task.

Differentiations take time and the teacher must constantly make adjustments for this. Thus the application of white paint at the choice points in an otherwise completely black maze leads to quicker and more accurate learning by the rat. In classroom learning, the method of teaching can be simplified or made unnecessarily difficult. The teacher can arrange the learning situation in such a way that the differentiations come easily or are more difficult. Teaching machines essentially strive to make each step to be learned so simple and small that it can be taken with great confidence and success. With the retarded reader, in particular, the learning task needs to be presented in structured, carefully planned steps.

The manner in which a problem is presented determines at least in some way whether past experience can be used appropriately or not. Some classroom arrangements are more conducive than others to the elicitation of insightful solutions. The evidence indicates that with

retarded readers, who often are weak in the visual association–memory area, materials should be presented through
the auditory and kinesthetic channels.

Individualization of instruction is the chief identifying mark
of good teaching and is totally dependent upon pupil diagnosis.
The wise teacher identifies individual differences and teaches
each pupil accordingly. The aim of remediation is to direct a
pupil into that set of learning experiences most appropriate for
him. The teacher thus must be extraordinarily sensitive to the
needs of the learner.

But what if the diagnosis is incorrect? This would obviously
result in wrong remediation; the greater the error in diagnosis,
the greater might be the harm.

We all realize that even the best diagnosis often is not totally
reliable. The diagnostic information is fallible, but this does not
make it worthless. It does mean that the degree of differentiation
in remediation that should be attempted is directly proportional
to the accuracy of the diagnosis. It would seem wise then to
begin remediation by using those principles, methods, and procedures that are developmentally sound. Only gradually and with
great care should the remediation depart from these.

The corrective or remedial teacher needs to avoid irreversible
decisions, at least as long as the cost of getting more information,
of making a better diagnosis, is lower than the cost of making
erroneous decisions.

The diagnostic-remediation process may be viewed as a matter of obtaining and transmitting information. Diagnosis brings
forth information about the pupil. We have suggested in this
book a positive and direct way of doing this by observation,
questionnaire, inventory, and test. Another approach is to begin
the remediation process with the problem as the pupil presents
it and to help the pupil rather immediately in solving it. This
latter approach consists of observing the pupil, working with
him, and studying, analyzing, and remediating during actual instruction and practice in reading. This approach calls for the use
of few tests.

The first teacher is narrowing the point where remediation
might be applied. He is confident that he can and that he ac-

tually has identified the significant areas of difficulty. The second teacher believes that it is not possible to predict what areas will be significant in the case before him. He prefers to risk some loss of time in order to avoid the risk of overlooking a significant area. The first teacher would thus at once plunge into a reading diagnosis. The second teacher would fear that such a direct attack might actually cause the pupil to fail to mention the real reason he hates reading.

Each teacher is gambling. It would appear that if the teacher strongly believes, because of his experience and knowledge, that the significant area is to be found in a limited area, he should study that area with maximum precision.[11] It would appear that experienced teachers would be safer in doing this than inexperienced teachers.

Systematic instruction of the basic reading skills

Today it is fashionable to assert that most reading failures are the result of faulty approaches in beginning reading. Delacato[12] notes that we have three types of biases in this regard. Those with an educational bias stress the importance of teaching techniques. We thus have the phoneticists, the configurationists, and myriads of other "experts" who advocate a given way of teaching. Those with a psychological bias suggest that if children were taught by highly specialized personnel using highly specialized remedial techniques under favorable emotional climates there would be no reading disabilities. Those with a psychiatric bias may suggest that emotional disturbance is at the root of all disability.

Delacato recommends that we go to the retarded readers themselves to find out what the disability is, what caused it, and how it may be remedied. Chall[13] notes that with regard to where the problem lies, whether in the initial reading approach, or in the deficiencies of the child, there probably is an interaction effect between the two. "Severe reading disability seems to require both—a predisposition in the child and an initial approach that ignores it."

As already suggested, we do not like the term "remedial reading program." Remediation along with diagnosis is an integral phase of the developmental program. Diagnosis and remediation must accompany all effective teaching. The developmental program is responsible for systematic reading instruction at all school levels. It includes developmental, corrective, and remedial instruction. We have used the phrase "corrective instruction of reading" to refer to the situation in which remedial activities are carried on in the regular classroom. When the remediation occurs outside of the regular classroom, we have termed it "remedial teaching." It seems clear that in an ideal situation or some sort of educational utopia, where there would be no retardation, the concept of and need for remedial teaching might disappear.

Corrective instruction usually occurs in the regular classroom. If a special teacher is available, the pupil might be assigned to him several times a week for forty-five to sixty minutes.

Corrective instruction stresses sequential development in word attack and comprehension skills, but uses special techniques and materials and concentrates on a particular reading deficiency. The corrective program is in addition to regular reading instruction.

Remedial teaching, because of its expensiveness, is necessarily limited. It is a slow process, on a one-to-one basis or at most on the basis of one teacher to three to eight pupils. Because of the expenses involved, "even when a special remedial teacher is available, it is likely that instruction will need to be individualized rather than strictly individual." [14]

The school thus needs to limit the number of pupils who will find themselves in a remedial classroom. As we have already noted, some poor readers—and in this group belong slow learners reading up to their ability, reluctant readers, and the disadvantaged readers—for the most part should be kept in the regular classroom. Some retarded readers need corrective reading, but will still stay in the regular classroom. Only the severely retarded readers need to be taken out of the classroom.

Remedial teaching or corrective teaching is not justified if it is not different from regular reading instruction. The instruction needs to be on a broader basis. *The corrective or remedial teacher needs to be completely familiar with the skills to be taught at all levels. He must be able to telescope, as it were, the total reading program into a relatively brief period of instruc-*

tion. He must appreciate and understand the continuity of the total reading program.

The remedial teacher must know how to teach (and must actually teach) the same basic skills that the classroom teacher teaches. We have thus reproduced here a list of the basic reading skills and have suggested books which the teacher might consult in teaching them.

The basic reading skills

I. Perception Skills

    A. Visual perception of form

    B. Visual perception of capital and lower-case letters and words

    C. Auditory perception of sounds

    D. Ability to move eyes from left to right and make accurate return sweeps

    E. Increased eye span

II. Comprehension Skills

    A. Word meaning

       1. Matching words with pictures

       2. Reacting to the sensory images (visual, auditory, kinesthetic, taste, smell) suggested by words

       3. Associating meaning and experiences with word symbols

       4. Inferring meanings from context clues and understanding words in context

       5. Inferring meaning from word clues—roots, suffixes, prefixes, compounds

       6. Matching words with definitions

       7. Recognizing antonyms and synonyms

       8. Associating printed word symbols with other symbols such as:

          a. musical notes, clef, sharp, flat, rest

          b. mathematical signs, plus, minus, half-dollar, cents, circle

          c. maps

          d. diacritical marks in the dictionary

    B. Phrase, sentence, and paragraph meaning
    C. Reading the context
    D. Reading for the main idea
    E. Reading for details
      1. Recognizing and organizing facts and details
      2. Reading and following directions

III. Word Attack Skills

    A. Using word configuration clues
    B. Using contextual clues
    C. Learning structural analysis clues
      1. Inflectional endings
      2. Words ending in *ing*
      3. Doubling the consonant before adding *ing*
      4. Compound words
      5. Prefixes and suffixes
      6. The apostrophe *s*
      7. The past tense with *ed*
      8. The plural with *es*
      9. The contractions
     10. Syllabication
    D. Learning phonic skills
      1. Auditory discrimination of speech sounds
      2. Teaching the initial consonant sounds and beginning consonant substitution
      3. Teaching the short vowel sounds
      4. Teaching the ending consonants
      5. Teaching median vowel substitution
      6. Introducing the various sounds of *a* and *u:*
        a. *a* as in "all"
        b. *a* as in "car"
        c. *a* as in "bass"
        d. *u* as in "full" or "dull"
      7. The consonant blends: bl, br, cl, cr, dr, fl, fr, etc.
      8. The letters k and q
      9. The long vowels
        a. a, e, i, o, u, y
        b. long vowel plus silent *e*
        c. ai, ay, ea, ee, oa, oe, ow

10. The ly ending
11. The le ending
12. S pronounced as *z*
13. Speech consonants ch, sh, th, wh, gh, ph
14. Soft sounds c and g
15. Three-letter consonant blends, scr, shr, spl, spr, squ, str, thr
16. The effect of r on a previous vowel, er ir, or, ur, and wa
17. The diphthongs, ei, ie, oi, oy, oo, ou, au, aw, ow, er, ue
18. Syllabication
19. Silent consonants
20. Foreign words
21. Special problems of two- and three-syllable words

IV. Reading–Study Skills

A. Dictionary skills
   1. Definitition—select correct meaning that fits the context
   2. Alphabetizing
   3. Syllabication
   4. Accent and guide words
   5. Use of the thumb index
   6. Pronunciation key
   7. Diacritical marks

B. Location and reference skills—use of encyclopedias, almanacs, magazines, card catalogues, etc.
   1. Locating specific information in a textbook
   2. Locating material in the index
   3. Ability to interpret cross references and to use the table of contents, glossary, and footnotes

C. Use of maps, charts, tables, and footnotes
D. Use of library resources: card catalogue, indexes
E. Organization skills
   1. Selecting main ideas
   2. Ability to follow directions
   3. Arranging events and items in sequence
   4. Putting together ideas from various sources

5. Answering questions that are answered in a printed passage
6. Summarizing
7. Outlining and underlining
8. Note taking
9. Ability to retain and apply what has been read
10. Ability to use study-methods, such as the SQRRR method—surveying, questioning, reading, recitation, review
11. Ability to read in specific content areas
12. Perceiving relationships: part-whole; cause-effect; general-specific; place, sequence, size, and time

V. Interpretative and Appreciative Skills

A. Evaluating what is read
B. Predicting and anticipating outcomes
C. Perceiving relationships or comparisons
D. Suspending judgment
E. Making inferences and drawing conclusions
F. Interpreting figurative expressions and picturesque language
G. Detecting bias
H. Detecting author's mood and purpose
I. Filtering facts
J. Differentiating between fact and opinion
K. Weighing facts as to their importance
L. Analyzing opinions
M. Recognizing literary form
N. Detecting and understanding the writer's purpose
O. Identifying and evaluating character traits, reactions, and motives
P. Recognizing literary and semantic devices and identifying the tone
Q. Determining whether the text affirms, denies, or fails to express an opinion about a supposed fact or condition

VI. Rate of Comprehension Skills

A. Left-to-right progression
B. Reduction of regressions

    C. Phrase reading

    D. Reduction of vocalization

    E. Ability to choose an appropriate reading technique—flexibility

    F. Scanning for specific information

    G. Skimming skills

VII. Oral Reading Skills

    A. Keeping eye ahead of the voice

    B. Enunciating clearly

    C. Pronouncing correctly

    D. Reading in thought units

    E. Varying pitch and volume of voice

    F. Adapting voice to size of room and audience

In the learning of these basic skills there obviously are differences among children in *rate* of learning. The retarded reader is simply a pupil who did not learn the skills at the rate that he is capable of learning them. The differences in learning *capacity* are just as great and as significant. Some children may never master all the skills. This again reinforces the need for individualization of each pupil's reading program. The teacher, whether in the classroom or in the remedial setting, must start the pupil at the point of success that he has attained and must permit him to advance as far as he can as rapidly as he can.

Even though we use grade level as a point of reference, it seems illogical to suggest that certain learnings are peculiar to first grade, second grade, or tenth grade. Learning to read is an individual process, and skill development does not come in capsule form. One cannot dish out a third-grade capsule to third graders and a fourth-grade capsule to fourth graders.

It is not our purpose here to outline in detail how to teach each of the broad groups of skills: Perception Skills, Comprehension Skills, Word-Attack Skills, Reading-Study Skills, Interpretative and Appreciative Skills, Rate of Comprehension Skills, and Oral Reading Skills. There are many fine books available that have this as their major goal. The following are representative of such books:

- Bond, Guy L., and Wagner, Eva B. *Teaching the Child to Read.* Macmillan, New York, 1966.
- Dawson, Mildred A., and Bamman, Henry A. *Fundamentals of Basic Reading Instruction.* David McKay Company, New York, 1963.
- DeBoer, John H., and Dallmann, Martha. *The Teaching of Reading.* Holt, Rinehart and Winston, New York, 1964.
- Dechant, Emerald V. *Improving the Teaching of Reading.* Prentice-Hall, Inc., Englewood Cliffs, 1963.
- Gray, Lillian. *Teaching Children to Read.* Ronald Press, New York, 1963.
- Harris, Albert J. *Effective Teaching of Reading.* David McKay Company, New York, 1962.
- Harris, Albert J. *How to Increase Reading Ability.* David McKay Company, 1961.
- Heilman, Arthur W. *Principles and Practices of Teaching Reading.* Charles Merrill Book Company, Columbus, 1961.
- Hester, Kathleen B. *Teaching Every Child to Read.* Harper and Row, New York, 1964.
- McKee, Paul, and Durr, William K. *Reading: A Program of Instruction for the Elementary School.* Houghton Mifflin, Boston, 1966.
- Monroe, Marion, and Rogers, Bernice. *Foundations for Reading.* Scott, Foresman and Company, Chicago, 1964.
- Russell, David H. *Children Learn to Read.* Ginn and Company, Boston, 1961.
- Smith, Nila B. *Reading Instruction for Today's Children.* Prentice-Hall, Inc., Englewood Cliffs, 1963.
- Spache, George D. *Reading in the Elementary School.* Allyn and Bacon, Boston, 1964.
- Strang, Ruth, McCullough, Constance, Traxler, Arthur. *The Improvement of Reading.* McGraw-Hill Publishing Company, New York, 1961.
- Tinker, Miles A., and McCullough, Constance M. *Teaching Elementary Reading.* Appleton-Century-Crofts, Inc., New York, 1962.

The two basic reading skills are still: identification of the word or sentence *and* association of meaning with it. Each of the books listed devotes a major section to the development of these skills. There are, in addition, numerous other commercial materials available to the teacher. Here is a list of some programs useful in developing word-attack skills. Each of these is described more fully in Chapter 7, which also lists other materials useful in teaching word-attack skills.

Basic Reading Series, J. B. Lippincott Company.

Basic Reading Skills, McCormick-Mathers Publishing Company.

Cordts Phonetic Books, Benefic Press.

Dialog I, Chester Electronics Laboratories.

Early to Read Series, Initial Teaching Alphabet Publications.

Eye and Ear Fun, Webster Publishing Company.

A First Course in Phonic Reading and A Second Course in Phonic Reading, Educators Publishing Service.

Happy Times with Sounds Series, Allyn and Bacon, Inc.

Hayes Mastery Phonics Workbooks, Beckley-Cardy Company.

I Learn to Read, Kenworthy Educational Service.

Instructor Basic Phonics Series, F. A. Owen Publishing Company.

Iroquois Phonics Series, Charles E. Merrill, Inc.

It's Time for Phonics, Webster Publishing Company.

Linguistic Readers, Harper and Row.

New Auditory Visual Response Phonics, Polyphone Company.

Phonetic Keys to Reading, Economy Company.

A Phonetic Reader Series, Educators Publishing Service.

Phonics Is Fun, Modern Curriculum Press.

Phonovisual Method, Phonovisual Products, Inc.

Reading Along with Me Series, Columbia University.

Reading Essential Series and Teaching Aids, Steck Company.

Reading with Phonics, J. B. Lippincott Company.

Rolling Phonics, Scott, Foresman & Company.

Sounds We Use, Wilcox and Follett.

Speech-to-Print Phonics, Harcourt, Brace and World.

Time for Phonics, Webster Publishing Company.

Words in Color, Learning Materials, Inc.

The following materials, and there is necessarily an overlap with the materials already listed, develop comprehension skill:

Reading Laboratories:

a. *EDL. Listen and Read Program.* Educational Developmental Laboratories.
b. *SRA Reading Laboratory*, Science Research Associates.
c. *Literature Samples*, Learning Materials, Inc.

    d. *Tactics in Reading*, Scott, Foresman & Company.
    e. *Webster Classroom Reading Clinic*, Webster Division, Mc-
      Graw-Hill Book Company.

Be a Better Reader Series, Prentice-Hall, Inc.
Building Reading Skills, McCormick-Mathers Publishing Com-
    pany.
Cowboy Sam Workbooks, Beckley-Cardy Company.
The Everyreader Series, Webster Publishing Company.
Gates-Peardon Practice Exercises in Reading, Bureau of Publi-
    cations.
Let's Read Series, Holt, Rinehart and Winston, Inc.
McCall-Crabbs Standard Test Lessons in Reading, Bureau of
    Publications.
New Practice Readers, Webster Publishing Company.
New Reading Skilltext Series, J. B. Lippincott Company.
Reading for Meaning Series, J. B. Lippincott Company.
Reading-Thinking Skills, Continental Press, Inc.
Specific Skill Series, Barnell Loft, Ltd.

This material is described more fully in Chapter 7, which
also lists other materials useful in teaching comprehension skills.

Our own book, *Improving the Teaching of Reading*, deals
with the development of the basic reading skills in the following
chapters:

I. *Perception Skills*

    a. Listening Skills, Chapter 5.
    b. Speaking Skills, Chapter 6.
    c. Auditory Discrimination Skills, Chapter 7.
    d. Visual Discrimination Skills, Chapter 7.
    e. Orientation Skills—Left-to-Right Progression, Chapter 7.

II. *Comprehension Skills*

    a. Chapter 7.
    b. Chapter 12.

III. *Word Attack Skills*, Chapters 10 and 11.
IV. *Reading Study Skills*, Chapter 11.
 V. *Reading in the Content Areas*, Chapter 11.
VI. *Interpretative and Appreciative Skills*, Chapter 11.

VII. *Rate of Comprehension Skills,* Chapter 9.
VIII. *Oral Reading Skills,* Chapter 2.

Organizing for corrective and remedial reading

Historically, classrooms have been organized into groups and the emphasis has been upon the development of a group organization that would permit the greatest amount of individual growth.

Unfortunately, the search for a happy balance between grouping and individualization is still in progress. It is our feeling that heterogeneous grouping with mobile, flexible subgrouping, rather than homogeneous grouping, has the most to offer in the regular classroom. Flexible subgrouping seems especially helpful in dealing with the problems of the pupil who needs corrective reading instruction. It permits the organization of clusters or subgroups of pupils with common reading needs.

CORRECTIVE READING IN THE CLASSROOM

As we have stated in previous chapters, corrective reading instruction should be reserved for the regular classroom. A few cautions are in order. Corrective instruction cannot be so organized as to embarrass the child and should certainly not be substituted for such pleasurable activities as recess or physical education. Neither should it give the appearance of simply being squeezed into the school day.

Because of the nature of the pupil needing corrective or remedial reading, drill sessions should necessarily be short. This means that on the lower elementary levels pupils may move from one group to another at fifteen, or even ten, minute intervals, if there are three groups.

The classroom teacher needs to spend some time with the entire class at the beginning of the class to introduce a new unit or topic or to give special assignments and directions. He may want to teach the entire class if he finds that all or most of the pupils are deficient in a particular skill such as the rules of punctuation. He probably needs to spend some time with the entire group at the end of the class to summarize and to make homework assignments. Between the beginning few moments and the end of the class the teacher frequently finds it necessary to group the youngsters according to their similarity of needs. The following organization of the reading period makes group instruction possible and permits greater individualization through the process of subgrouping.

THE READING HOUR

9:00–9:10   Common Activities
9:10–9:55   Subgrouping within the Classroom
9:55–10:00   Common Supgrouping Activities

Group I	Group II	Group III
9:10–9:25	9:10–9:25	9:10–9:25
Directed Reading	Free Reading	Reading Group with Teacher
(Practice on what has been taught)	(Application of what has been taught)	(Actual teaching)
1. Workbooks	1. Games	1. Basal reading instruction
2. Mimeographed seatwork	2. Free reading of library books— recreational reading	2. Specific skill instruction
3. Questions on the board to answer		
4. Use of programmed materials		
5. Use of listening stations		
9:25–9:40	9:25–9:40	9:25–9:40
Free Reading	Reading with Teacher	Directed Reading
9:40–9:55	9:40–9:55	9:40–9:55
Reading with Teacher	Directed Reading	Free Reading

Figure 4–1

The organization suggested in *Figure 4–1* permits the teacher to have simultaneously three groups, each at a different level of reading performance, each using its own set of materials, and each advancing at its own success level. Dividing the class into three groups according to reading levels or needs permits the teacher to use basal readers more closely approximating the individual pupil's achievement level. At another time, one group may be working on word recognition, another on comprehension, and a third on rate improvement, even though the youngsters composing a given group might be reading on different levels. Thus a child reading on third-grade level might be working with one reading on a fourth-grade level. Both of them may need help with diphthongs, consonants, or speech consonants.

If the situation prevails where all children on the same reading level are grouped together for reading instruction as in the Joplin plan, there still may be need of flexible subgrouping on a learning-activity basis in the classroom. There still might be three groups: those receiving actual instruction, those practicing what has been taught, and those applying what has been taught. Children also may be subgrouped on an interest basis. In the ungraded primary, the pupils move from level to level on the basis of their achievement.

Even with a reduction of the teacher–pupil ratio and with subgrouping, there is no easy solution to children's reading problems. The teacher may need outside help. One pattern of organization for corrective instruction may include the use of additional teachers or aides. The use of team teaching or of reserve or supplemental teachers to work with small groups has been found beneficial. Some schools assign a master teacher to work directly with the teacher during the regular reading period. The remedial reading teacher may help the classroom teacher by giving classroom demonstrations in the use of specific methods or materials. It may be possible to use parents or aides to help children listen to tapes, do workbook exercises, listen to children's oral reading, or make comprehension checks. The teacher may initiate team learning, in which pupils subgroup as a team and work together in the learning of new concepts, in applying skills, or in reviewing. Tutoring, a situation where one pupil works with one or more pupils who need help, has been used by many teachers.

Staggered scheduling is another organizational device useful in planning corrective reading instruction. Those youngsters who are to be kept in the regular classroom but who need special help in reading may be asked to report to school an hour early or leave an hour late. Perhaps the class can be so organized that half of the pupils report an hour early and leave an hour early; the other half comes an hour later, thus giving the teacher a smaller group to work with at each end of the day. Lunch periods could be staggered for similar effect.

REMEDIAL READING

Pupils who are seriously retarded may have to be taken out of the regular classroom and put into a special room where a remedial reading teacher or a special teacher will work with them.

A booklet entitled "A Guide for Establishing a Corrective Reading Program," published by McGraw-Hill Book Company, describes the physical layout of the remedial room (*see Figure 4–2*). Sometimes there is no classroom space available and the school may have to use mobile equipment. In another school the

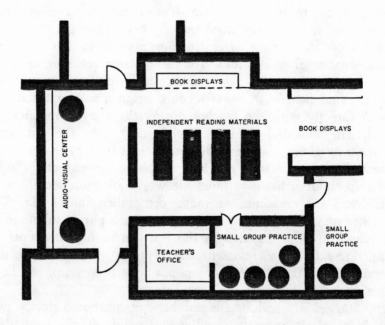

Figure 4–2

remedial teacher may function out of the reading materials center.[15]

Regardless of where the remedial room is, it should probably have two glass-partitioned offices: one for the remedial teacher and one for testing purposes. The glass partition permits the teacher to observe the testing from his own office. The room should also contain an audio-visual center, small group practice rooms, individual practice cubicles, desks, chairs, bookshelves, and office furniture. The reading room illustrated here does not make provision for a testing room and for individual practice cubicles.

Organizing for *remedial* instruction requires that pupils be dismissed from the regular classroom at scheduled times during the regular school day so that they can go to the remedial classroom for special instruction. The pupil reports to the remedial class for perhaps one lesson per day and then returns to his own classroom. It is important that we get the pupil back to the regular classroom as soon as possible. We recommend, therefore, that every nine weeks the following question should be asked and answered about every pupil: "Is he ready to be excused from the remedial class?"

Remedial instruction may be given during a regular study period or during a subject-matter class which requires reading for efficient performance. Sometimes the pupil is given remedial instruction before school begins or after school ends. In some schools remedial instruction is provided during the homeroom or the activity period. In other schools remedial instruction becomes a part of the English class.

The remedial room should be equipped with audio-visual materials of various types, filmstrip projector, tachistoscopes, accelerating devices, record players, children's records, tape recorder, listening stations, flashcards, and art supplies. It should contain books of all types, supplementary readers, programmed reading materials, multilevel reading laboratories, testing and diagnostic materials, magazines, games, and all kinds of word recognition and comprehension development materials.

Case study revisited

As we look again at pupil 26, we ask: "What has this chapter to offer us?" How might we plan the pupil's corrective program?

We have decided that he is indeed a retarded reader rather than simply a slow learner. All indications are that he can improve in reading with the help of corrective instruction. We have also decided that he is an example of general retardation, even though he exhibits characteristics of pupils having a specific retardation. Corrective instruction for him is probably best done in the regular classroom, sometimes in the total group and sometimes on a subgroup basis.

The materials to be used with him should be on about fifth-grade level of difficulty. Corrective education begins with success. The teacher needs to identify the pupil's level of confidence —the level at which the pupil can be most successful. Since this pupil's problem is intimately related to lack of interest and motivation, the teacher will need to use interesting materials. He will need to be both an interested and an interesting teacher. He will have to change the pupil's attitude.

If at all possible, the pupil should take an active part in selecting the materials for reading. He should be given the opportunity to share his reading experience with other pupils. The teacher may want to capitalize on sports magazines, comics, and on pupil-prepared materials. The pupil should be encouraged to keep a record of his own progress and of the books that he has read. The teacher may want to develop progress charts. In Chapter 6 we list sources of books designed to encourage the reluctant reader. Perhaps, the most important lesson to be applied in this particular case is that lack of interest and motivation is a continuing block to his reading growth. The retarded reader's performance will improve only if he is interested in his work, if he is interested in improving himself, if the materials have special significance to him, and if he is attentive.

Incidental teaching simply is not enough in dealing with a retarded reader. There is a need for teaching of specifics. Telling a pupil to "read" is inadequate. The specifics that need emphasis with pupil 26 are:

1. Learning to infer meanings from context clues
2. Matching words with definitions
3. Inferring meanings from word clues—roots, suffixes, prefixes

4. Learning to read for details
5. Learning to read critically
6. Learning to use word configuration clues
7. Expansion of eye–voice span
8. Learning skills in auditory discrimination
9. Learning to phrase correctly and to read smoothly
10. Learning to enunciate, pronounce, and articulate
11. Learning to read without excessive regressions and vocalization
12. Learning to use the dictionary and to select the correct meaning that fits the context
13. Learning adequate reference and locating skills, use of the library, and ability to organize data
14. Learning better rate skills

This pupil needs to be helped to develop those skills and abilities which are most necessary for immediate success in school. He is an eighth grader and as such has to cope with problems of content reading. The teacher should help him first and foremost to read and master the textbooks that he has to use. If this is not possible, textbooks must be found that are written on his level of comprehension. Sometimes this means the teacher must resort to a textbook designed for a lower grade level, or he may have to develop his own materials.

In teaching pupil 26, it is important for the teacher to realize that retarded pupils are generally anxious and fearful of discussing their problem with an adult. Their anxiety is especially high when they have experienced the disapproval of their parents. Often such a pupil will act as though he doesn't care, but beneath it all he cares very much.

The teacher must develop a constructive relationship with the pupil. He needs to give the pupil a feeling of total and unequivocal acceptance despite his frequent failures in school.

Pupil 26 has a short memory and attention span. It thus is indicated that the remedial sessions cannot be too long. An eighth grader might normally be able to handle hour-long sessions; for this eighth grader, half-hour sessions might be long enough. This pupil will fatigue intellectually very easily. The teacher needs to exercise great care that extraneous materials do not come between the presentation of the stimulus and the response. When the retarded reader makes a response, it must be made to the proper stimulus. When he says *saw*, make sure that the word actually is *saw* and not *was*.

A retarded reader learns by doing. There needs to be a lot of meaningful practice. If you think he knows it, practice some more.

Many of the techniques suggested in Chapter 5 for working with retarded readers should be used. You may want to refer to those in Chapter 6 under the heading, "The Dyslexiac Reader."

Summary

This chapter dealt with key questions that the teacher needs to ask about each pupil, with the principles that should guide reading instruction, and with the composition of a developmental reading program, and therefore indirectly of a remedial program. It also offered suggestions on how to organize for corrective and remedial instruction. Before discussing remedial methods, it seems that the reading teacher should first take a look at those methods generally recommended for the regular classroom. This is in agreement with the view, previously outlined, that remedial instruction must be founded on a sound developmental approach. Chapter 5 thus takes a close look at reading methods.

---

[1] Bond, Guy L., and Tinker, Miles A. *Reading Difficulties: Their Diagnosis and Correction.* Appleton-Century-Crofts, New York, 1967, p. 153.

[2] *Ibid.,* p. 454.

[3] Ibid., p. 183.

[4] Roswell, Florence. "Psychotherapeutic Principles Applied to Remedial Reading." *Improvement of Reading Through Classroom Practice,* International Reading Association Conference Proceedings, Newark, 1964, pp. 145-7; also Klausner, Dorothy C.: "Screening and Development of the Remedial Reading Teacher." *Journal of Reading,* 10 (May, 1967) 552-559.

[5] Rogers, Carl R. "The Place of the Person in the New World of the Behavioral Sciences." *Personnel and Guidance Journal,* 39 (February, 1961) 442-451.

[6] Baldwin, Maurine. "Effective Reading as Springboard for a High School Reading Program." *Developing the Mature Reader,* 1966 Proceedings, Portland Oregon Council of International Reading Association, 1966.

[7] Heilman, Arthur W. "Moving Faster Toward Outstanding Instructional Problems." *Vistas in Reading,* Proceedings of the Eleventh Annual Convention, International Reading Association, Newark, 1967, pp. 273-276.

[8] Bugelski, B. R. *The Psychology of Learning Applied to Teaching.* Bobbs-Merrill Company, Inc., Indianapolis, 1964, p. 104.

[9] *Ibid.,* p. 103.

[10] *Ibid.,* p. 103.

[11] Cronbach, Lee J. "The Counselor's Problems from the Perspective of Communication Theory," *New Perspectives in Counseling,* University of Minnesota Press, 1955.

[12] Delacato, Carl H. *The Treatment and Prevention of Reading Problems,* Charles C. Thomas, Springfield, 1959.

[13] Chall, Jeanne. "How They Learn and Why They Fail." *Improvement of Reading Through Classroom Practice,* International Reading Association Conference Proceedings, Newark, 1964, pp. 147-148.

[14] Otto, Wayne and McMenemy, Richard A. *Corrective and Remedial Teaching of Reading.* Houghton Mifflin Company, Boston, 1966, p. 73.

[15] Reprinted by permission from *A Guide to Establishing a Corrective Reading Program,* published by Webster Division, McGraw-Hill Book Company.

5

A Survey of
Reading Methods

A basic thesis formulated in the previous chapter is that corrective or remedial methods are in reality developmental and that remedial reading is not a hocus-pocus of special methods, but a more intense and personal application of those methods that are effective in the regular classroom.

If these principles are true, it is not enough for the teacher of reading to know what skills to develop. He must know how one learns to read and what methods are most appropriate for a given child. He must be well versed in reading method. This chapter thus deals with some of the newer methods of teaching reading.[1]

Stimulus approaches

Today, and rightfully so, we are seeing the proliferation of methods, theories, approaches, and programs. Apart from configuration and phonic approaches, there have recently been presented to educators models of various types that have sought to alter the stimulus situation in reading or that have sought to provide more penetrating analysis of the reading process.

We might divide these varieties of newer approaches then into (1) those that emphasize method, that which the teacher does—hence the stimulus aspects—and (2) those that emphasize

the pupil's capacities, potentials, and behavior, or the organism—
especially the mediational aspects. Let us begin with stimulus
approaches.

ALPHABET SYSTEMS

The relationship between the sounds of the English language
and the way these are represented is not entirely consistent.
Many approaches have been made to this problem. One approach
is to change the word form. The printed symbols themselves are
modified so as to make the relationship more consistent. Approaches which do this we have labeled stimulus approaches,
because they emphasize the stimulus variables. The emphasis in
these approaches is simply this. Change the nature of the stimulus
in a given way, such as by changing the alphabet, and it will lead
to easier and improved learning.

The Initial Teaching Alphabet (ITA)

Perhaps the most discussed stimulus model in the literature
today is the Initial Teaching Alphabet Model. Pitman,[2] its modern originator, spoke of the Augmented Roman Alphabet (ARA);
the name has now been changed to Initial Teaching Alphabet
(ITA). It is said to make reading easier because of the following:

1. Coding of the basic sound units of English is regularized.
   There is one symbol for each single sound.
2. The number of characters is reduced by using only lower-
   case letters.

The ITA model presents a total of forty-four symbols. The
basic thesis is that children should use a more reliable alphabet
until they have acquired proficiency in it, at which point they
should switch to the traditional alphabet and spelling.

Systems similar to the ITA system began as early as 1551.
In that year John Hart suggested a new set of principles of spelling and in 1569 in *Orthographie* he proposed to teach reading by
using an alphabet that has as many letters as there are sounds
or voices in speech. Alexander Ellis noted that by 1845 there
were twenty-six "phonetic alphabets" for teaching reading, including those of Benjamin Franklin and Brigham Young.

In each of these early efforts there was an attempt to simplify

materials or stimulus aspects by presenting a one-to-one correspondence between letters and sounds. *Figure 5–1* illustrates the
ITA alphabet.[3]

Figure 5–1

The ten-vowel modification model

A model with import similar to ITA is the "ten-vowel" modification of the alphabet by Leo G. Davis in *k-a-t spelz cat*[4] and
Davis's transliteration of *McGuffey's First Reader*. Its basic change
is the use of small capitals A-E-I-O-U to designate long vowels
and lower case a-e-i-o-u to designate short vowels. It is based on

a thirty-one-letter alphabet. Davis maintains that there are no reading problems; only spelling problems.

The Unifon System

John Malone designed the Unifon System. It uses a different symbol for every phoneme. The system consists of forty capital letters.

In the May, 1962, issue of *Elementary English* Malone wrote:

> . . . the orthography for a language has one powerful and overriding need, that of isomorphism. In classic concept, the alphabet of a language should be such that there is one unique symbol for each phoneme, and one unique phoneme for each symbol; this quality is the means by which a language is made readily accessible. . . .

The Unifon System has been used in some school districts in Illinois, Washington, D. C., and Michigan.

The diacritical marking system

Edward Fry [5] suggests the use of diacritical markings to indicate how each of the traditional letters should be pronounced. The diacritical markings are introduced to regularize the phoneme-grapheme relationship. Fry refers to this as the Diacritical Marking System or DMS. The diacritical markings are temporary, soon to be replaced by normal spelling and writing.

The value of the system is said to lie in (1) the greater regularity of the phoneme-grapheme relationship (than, for example, in the ITA system); (2) the ease with which the child can transfer his learning to regular orthography because the basic word form is preserved; and (3) the difficulty with spelling is not increased.

Words in Color

Gattegno,[6] in *Words in Color*, proposes a synthetic phonic approach using color. Each of the forty-eight sounds is represented by a color, even though it is written in numerous ways. For example, the sound of short *i* may be written as *a* (senate), *ai* (mountain), *ay* (always), *e* (pretty), *ea* (guinea), *ee* (been), *ei* (forfeit), *eo* (pigeon), *ey* (money), *i* (sit), *ia* (carriage), *ie* (sieve), *o* (women), *u* (busy), *ui* (build), or *y* (hymnal), but in Gattegno's system these letters would all be in red. Color thus is used to unify English even though it does not alter the spelling. Gattegno has found that forty-eight colors are sufficient to account for almost all the sounds in English.

The letter *a* colored white represents the *a* in *bat;* when colored blue-green, it is the *a* in *lane.* The *u* as in *but* is yellow, the *i* as in *pin* is red, the *e* as in *pet* is blue, and the *o* as in *pot* is orange. The consonant *p* is brown, the *t* is purple, *s* is dark lilac, and so on.

Words in color comes with colored charts, phonic code, word cards, *Word Building Book,* a *Book of Stories,* and three *Words in Color books.*

Gattegno notes that in the following sentences all the italicized letters would have the same color since they have the same sound: "My fri*e*nd s*ay*s I s*ai*d that my p*e*t l*e*opard did not eat *a*ny of the d*ea*d h*ei*fer that we are to b*u*ry." The italicized a's in the following sentences would all be colored differently: "*a*ll w*a*s dark; the m*a*re left the vill*a*ge land and, *a*s m*a*ny forecast, this led to her fat*a*l accident." [7]

The color approach is based upon a definition of reading as the decoding of writing into speech. Meaning comes as the pupil discovers that the sounds of written words are like those of words he has both heard and spoken.

LINGUISTIC APPROACHES [8]

A stimulus approach with different emphasis is the linguistic approach. The linguists, especially Bloomfield, Soffietti, and Fries, suggest that the inconsistencies of the English writing system should be delayed and that in initial reading experiences only letter combinations or graphemes that represent regular and consistent relationships between sounds and printed symbols should be introduced. Linguists emphasize that reading is primarily a language process and that the major task facing the child is the mastery of the graphic system that reflects the spoken language system. The linguist claims he has more to offer than a retreat back to either a phonemic alphabet or to phonics. The linguist is not so much concerned with the representation of a single grapheme as with a pattern of graphemes. He emphasizes the relationship between patterns of phonemes and patterns of graphemes. He admits that the correspondence between written and spoken English is weak if one relates individual letters and sounds. However, the correspondence between letter patterns and word groups is high.

Lefevre [9] (pp. 247-278) has adapted linguistic ideas to meaningful reading. He suggests an analytical method to teaching reading emphasizing language patterns. He emphasizes that meaning comes only through the grasping of the language structures exemplified in a sentence. Meaning thus depends on the intonation, the word and sentence order, the grammatical inflections, and certain key function words. Intonation, or the pauses and stresses in oral language, are represented by (1) capital letters, periods, semicolons, and question marks, (2) by the order of the words, (3) by grammatical inflections signaling tense, number, and possession, and (4) by such function words as *the, when, nevertheless,* or *because.* Only by reading structures can full meaning be attained. Or to put it another way, unless the reader translates correctly the printed text into the intonation pattern of the writer, he may not be getting the meaning intended.[10]

Bloomfield and Barnhart [11] presented in 1961 a linguistic approach in *Let's Read: A Linguistic Approach.* Its emphasis was that English writing is alphabetic and that reading is merely the act of responding vocally to the printed letter as it functions with other letters. Reading is the making of the appropriate sounds for letters. Bloomfield felt that initial teaching of reading for meaning is incorrect and that meaning will come quite naturally as the alphabetic code or principle is discovered. Emphasis thus is put on beginning with letters and sounds as they function in monosyllabic regular words. The linguistic approach stressed by Bloomfield and Barnhart is very similar to analytic or whole-word phonics. The stress is on the consistencies in the language, and the child is exposed initially only to these consistencies. And, the letter is not sounded alone; it is sounded only in the context of other letters or the word.

Soffietti's system,[12] that of Daniels and Diack,[13] proposed in the *Royal Road Readers,* and Fries's system [14] are basically linguistic systems. Daniels and Diack call their system "the phonic

word method." They teach letter meanings functionally in words
and do not isolate speech sounds. Soffietti stresses the importance
of beginning with words in which each letter has only one phonetic value.

Linguists thus are not in agreement on their point of emphasis. Bloomfield associates individual letter and sound in the
context of the total word; Fries associates syllable and sound;
and Lefevre notes: ". . . what reading requires is recognition
and interpretation of the graphic counterparts of entire spoken
utterances as unitary meaning-bearing patterns; this is *reading
comprehension.*" [15]

Linguistics likewise is not a new approach. Teachers have
always used a linguistic approach when they have said: "Read
this the way you would say it." By this simple statement, they
were paying attention to structural linguistics and intonation
patterns.

Programmed Learning Model

Today numerous materials designed to teach reading are
being presented in programmed form. Programmed materials are
an innovation emphasizing self-instruction, increased pupil partic-
ipation, and almost immediate feedback of results.

Programmed materials have the following obvious advantages:

1. They provide immediate knowledge of success or failure.
2. They permit each pupil to advance at his own success
   rate.
3. They require the pupil to progress through a logical
   sequence of steps of increasing difficulty, each step being so small that it can be met successfully and yet lead
   the pupil closer to full mastery.
4. They prohibit the bypassing of any step without mastery.
5. They bring the pupil into contact with the best minds—
   those who prepared the materials.
6. They require the pupil to be constantly active and alert
   and to construct his own response.
7. They provide for readiness by presenting material of
   appropriate difficulty.

8. They provide the teacher with a rather accurate measure of where the pupil is and thus may lead to more meaningful homework and study.
9. They involve the gradual removal of the stimulus. This has been described as fading.
10. They require the pupil to listen or read carefully and to give his full attention. Unlike in the classroom, the teaching material does not flow on without the pupil's attention. The machine sits idle if the learner is not concentrating on the task at hand.
11. The materials are actually pupil-made. The programming is continuously evaluated and corrected until ambiguities and gaps are removed.
12. They permit the teacher to help individual pupils because all the pupils are working in their own workbooks.
13. The pupil actually has a longer reading period.

In the last few years numerous programmed materials designed to teach reading skills have appeared. A mechanical programmed learning device is the Edison Responsive Environment or Edison Talking Typewriter.[16] The pupil sits in front of the E.R.E. (talking typewriter). He can reach only the typewriter keyboard. All other parts are behind a transparent shield. When he presses a key, the letter is printed in large size and a pre-recorded voice names the letter. As soon as each of the letters is learned, more complicated programming is introduced. The pupil progresses from the alphabet to words, sentences, and stories. At more advanced levels he can type complete stories and read them aloud to be recorded and played back.

Initially, an electric typewriter was used. The fingernails of the child were painted in different colors to match colors on the keyboard. When the fingernail–keyboard colors matched, the machine worked; if they did not match, the typewriter did not work. In teaching reading, a picture of a cow with the letters c-o-w is flashed on a screen. The letters c-o-w are illuminated on the typewriter permitting the child to practice the letters and word. The illumination on the keyboard and the letters c-o-w on the screen gradually fade, and when the picture of the cow reappears the child is expected to type c-o-w.

Here are some published programmed materials:

- Brogan, Andrews, and Hotchkiss, Emily. *Dialogue I: An Aural-Oral Course in Phonics.* Chester Electronic Laboratories, Inc., 1963.

  The thirty-one tapes, accompanied by sixty-two booklets, provide a programmed phonics course for first-grade or remedial groups.

- Brown, James. *Programmed Vocabulary.* Appleton-Century-Crofts.

  This is a packet of 320 printed originals containing a step-by-step lesson plan to improve word power and reading ability.

- *Building Reading Power,* Charles E. Merrill Books, Inc.

  This programmed course for improving reading techniques is designed for students who read on or about the fifth-grade level. There are fifteen different booklets, covering such topics as picture and verbal context, visual clues, definitions, synonyms, antonyms, context, prefixes, suffixes, main ideas, central thought of a paragraph, and details of a paragraph.

- Deighton, Lee C., and Sanford, Adrian B., *et al., The Macmillan Reading Spectrum.* Macmillan, 1964.

  This is a nongraded, multilevel program for building the vital reading skills. It consists of six word-analysis booklets, six vocabulary development booklets, and six reading comprehension booklets. Placement tests are provided. The lessons in the skill booklets are self-directing and self-correcting. Included also are two sets of books, sixty in all, ranging from a second-grade reading level to eighth-grade.

- Fry, Edward B. *Lessons for Self-Instruction in Basic Skills.* California Test Bureau, 1963.

  This is designed for grades three–nine and teaches reference skills, following directions, levels of interpretation and vocabulary development.

- *Honor Products Programmed Materials,* Honor Products, Inc.

  These materials consist of a pushbutton teaching machine and the following programs:
  1. *A Guide to Efficient Study* (ninth grade)
  2. *Building Words* (seventh grade)
  3. *Fun with Words–Homonyms* (second grade)

4. *Persuasive Words—Effective Word Usage* (eighth grade)
5. *Reading Comprehension* (ninth grade)
6. *Synonyms and Antonyms* (ninth grade)
7. *Vocabulary Building* (ninth grade)
8. *Word Clues* (seventh grade)

- *Imperial Primary Reading Program,* Imperial Productions, Inc., Kankakee, Illinois.

This is a self-teaching program for grades one–three on forty tapes.

- *Michigan Successive Discrimination Language Program,* Ann Arbor Publishers, 711 North University, Ann Arbor, Michigan, 1964.

This programmed basal reading series covers auditory, visual, and space discrimination, letters, words, phrases, sentences, paragraphs, manuscript writing, phonemic analysis, spelling, oral composition, and comprehension.

- *Peabody Rebus Reading Program,* American Guidance Service, Inc., Circle Pines, Minnesota.

This is a programmed approach to readiness and beginning reading instruction. It consists of two workbooks, using a vocabulary of picture words (rebuses).

- *Programmed Phonics,* Educators Publishing Service.

These two books, for grades four–six, are designed for remedial teaching of phonics. There are three general objectives: (1) to train the student to attribute the proper sound to each letter in a word or syllable; (2) to train the student to perceive aurally and visually, and to respond vocally to each letter in a syllable and each syllable in a word in a left-to-right sequential order; and (3) to train the student to read whole words accurately and quickly.

Assuming a fair understanding of initial and final consonant sounds, Books 1 and 2 teach a basic phonic repertory, including a review of difficult consonants and of all consonant blends. In addition, the student is trained to use principles of structural analysis and basic rules of pronunciation.

An aural-visual approach is used involving a workbook and either a tape or a script which may be read by the teacher. Each lesson presents several phonic elements through a series of auditory discriminations and dictations. The tape or script gives directions, prompts examples, and works through each frame and each page with the student. Having written a response, the student is informed immediately of the correctness or incorrectness of his answer. Correct answers are uncovered by moving a plastic mask down the page as the lesson progresses.

- *Reading.* M. W. Sullivan, Behavioral Research Laboratories, Box 577, Palo Alto, California.

  This is a two-series program of eight books designed to develop basic alphabetic, phonic, and structural skills.

- *Sullivan Programmed Reading,* Webster Division, McGraw-Hill Book Company.

  This is a fully developed phonic reading program consisting of a pre-reading series and series I, II, and III. In all, twenty-one programmed books are available.

- Taylor, S., Frackenpohl, H., McDonald, A., and Jolene, N. *EDL Word Clues,* Educational Developmental Laboratories, 1962.

  These are programmed workbooks, with seven–twelve reading level. Each *Word Clues* book consists of thirty lessons of ten words each.

LANGUAGE-EXPERIENCE APPROACH [17]

A fourth stimulus approach is the language–experience approach. It teaches beginners to read through associating print with meaningful personal experiences. The experience approach began some sixty years ago when Flora J. Cooke at the Chicago Institute and later at the Francis Parker School began putting on the blackboard children's oral expressions. It grew and developed as a part of the Progressive Education Movement. The latter deemphasized the importance of systematic and sequential presentation of materials in favor of purpose, interest, and meaning. In 1934 Nila Smith termed this approach the "experience method," and recently it has been termed the language–experience approach.

The experience approach, advocated in *Learning to Read Through Experience* by R. Van Allen and Doris M. Lee,[18] and presented in the *Language-Experiences in Reading* (Roach Van Allen and Claryce Allen),[19] illustrates the language-experience approach in beginning reading. *Language Arts for Beginners,* A

Portfolio of Charts [20] provides the teacher with help in the use of experience charts. The personalized reading program as described in *Educator's Guide to Personalized Reading Instruction* [21] is a classroom organizational pattern which permits the language-experience approach to operate.

TEXTFILM READING PROGRAM

The textfilm reading program, originated by Glen McCracken in the New Castle Experiment, features the use of correlated filmstrips to accompany each page of printed text.

The textfilm frame contains the same image as in the textbook. Each lesson begins at the screen and ends in the textbook. This approach has demonstrated its usefulness in motivating children and in addition permits reading to begin at a far-point. It takes cognizance of the fact that at age six many children are farsighted and thus might more sensibly be taught to read at a distance.

The mediational approaches

Let us now turn our attention to the mediational approaches. The mediational approaches emphasize the neurological, physiological, and chemical changes that accompany reading. They note that learning and indeed reading occur in a cranium. Some children do not learn to read because internal events have gone awry. Specialists in remedial reading are aware that faulty teaching methods *per se* are not always the cause of reading failure. The conditions limiting learning often appear to be not in the method but in the learner.

Some today lean toward a biological-neurological explanation of reading disability rather than on an emotional or multicausal approach. Reading difficulties thus often are said to have been caused by damage to or dysfunction of certain localized areas of the brain or of other physiological mechanisms.

Let's take a look at one of these approaches. Orton [22] suggested that in learning to read the pupil develops memory traces from words both in the dominant (left for the average individual) and the nondominant (right) hemisphere, but that those in the nondominant hemisphere normally are mirror images of the former and thus are suppressed. He adds that if cerebral dominance is well developed by the time reading begins, reading proficiency is not affected. If, however, no special dominance is developed or if the engrams or memory traces in the right hemisphere (left dominance) become active, reading difficulties occur, and the child will read once with a left, and then with a right orientation.

Delacato [23] has revived this mixed-dominance theory with some changes. He believes that neurological development and organization of the human organism are the key to language and reading development and to language and reading difficulties. It is suggested that the basic difference between man and the animal world is that man has achieved cortical dominance, rather than cellular quantity. When the dominant hemisphere experiences certain trauma, loss of language skills results.

Delacato recommends that:

1. Children should be encouraged to engage in unified one-sided activity (e. g., do not allow children to have double-holster gun sets). Until preference for one side is evidenced, naturally both sides should be given equal opportunity to become dominant.

2. Children should not be allowed to suck the thumb of the dominant hand.

3. Parents should be sensitized to anoxia and head injuries as possible causes of language disturbance. Since crying and breath-holding may reduce cortical oxygen supply, they should be reduced to the minimum level.

4. All tonal activity, listening to music or singing, should be deleted in remedial teaching. Oral reading should be done in whispers, thus activating the dominant hemisphere and developing unilaterality.

5. Since poor readers lack cortical organization (they exhibit faulty posturalization in sleep) mothers should be taught to posturalize their children. From the age of nine weeks on children should be posturalized on their stomachs when put to bed.

6. The reading activity should originate at the word sight level—learn words at sight through configuration. The language—experience approach is encouraged. Children are

taught reading by wholes at the outset. To begin they are given common experiences as a class group, such as going on a trip. Upon their return to the classroom the teacher and children discuss what they did and saw, and the teacher writes an "experience chart" which is dictated by the children. The experience chart is made in sentence and story form. After the sentences are recorded and read, they are broken down into meaningful phrases. Having learned to recognize sentences and phrases containing between 100 to 150 words via this method, the children are given books which, through proper teacher planning, will contain most of the words met via the experience charts.

7. Later a dualistic system of recognizing new words as wholes is used: recognizing them through small familiar words which make up the large words and through the sound components of words. No child should be taught the letter-sound method until he has established complete unilaterality, has complete mastery of left to right progression (this usually takes more time and effort for the left-handed children), and does not reverse letters or words.

8. Finally the teacher should evaluate how each child masters reading skills most efficiently, and should teach the child via the method which best meets his needs. No "one" method will be the most efficient for all children. At this point an eclectic approach to methods is ideal. If neurological organization has been achieved, method is secondary.

9. Peripheral activity . . . such as vision, dexterity, skills, phonetics, various reading techniques, is meaningless in remediation if the total neurological organization is defective. The prerequisite to peripheral therapy is central neurological organization.

An evaluation of reading methods

Obviously, when one speaks of reading methods, there are many divergent points of view, and it is just as obvious that one's point of view is the result of one's own, perhaps biased, interpretations. We believe in an eclectic point of view.[24]

Eclecticism generally is defined as "the selection and orderly combination of compatible features from diverse sources," the combination of valid elements from various theories into an harmonious whole. Few teachers have arrived at such a synthesis. Few teachers can honestly say that the approach which they are using is a systematic and orderly synthesis of data from various theories. And yet, eclecticism of some kind seems necessary.

We thus propose an eclecticism for the *teacher* that encourages him to select from the great variety of approaches that one or combination of approaches which best meets the needs of the pupil. We propose that the selection of method or approach in teaching reading should be based on the individual differences of the learner. Perhaps instead of the word, eclecticism, we should borrow the phrase of Elizabeth Vazquez, a principal of Homestead School in Garden City, New York. She speaks of an "All-Method Method" of teaching reading.

THE RATIONALE FOR ECLECTICISM

We believe eclecticism makes sense because: (1) children do in fact learn to read through a variety of approaches; (2) children are different; and (3) teachers are different. Let's look at each of these.

As one scans the literature, listens to experts in the field, or observes practices in the classroom, one is amazed by the many methods of teaching reading. Each method is proposed as an answer to a reading problem; perhaps not *the* answer, but nevertheless an answer. There is not one advocate of a method who submits that his method does not work or who is unable to adduce evidence as to its effectiveness. And the fact is that children have become readers, indeed good readers, through analytic, synthetic, or combination approaches.

Thus, unless one is willing to call every researcher or practitioner who claims to have success with a given method a cheat, one has to accept that success may come by many paths. Since many different roads can and do eventually lead to reading proficiency, we are unwilling to accept that only one method, one approach, or one technique is successful with *all* children. There simply is not sufficient evidence in support of one approach that warrants universal allegiance to it as the supposedly best or only way of teaching reading.

A second argument for eclecticism is the fact that children are different and learn differently. Eclecticism is based on the assumption that until it is possible to standardize youth, it seems unwise to standardize reading method. If children were all alike, we might look for *the* method. Indeed, we would have found it long ago. If all children were identical twins, with identical experiences, we would not notice individual differences among them. And, without the individual differences, we would have no need for a variety of methods. If there were no differences, there would be no need to differentiate. But, the simple fact is that children are different from one another intellectually, physically, emotionally, socially, and perceptually, and they seem to be differentiated on the basis of the method that is beneficial to them.

We have gone through a period in which there has been frequent debate over phonics. Today, this debate has generally subsided, and the reason for this is that we have come to accept that children react differently perceptually. Each child reacts to a "perceptual whole," but for some the perceptual whole is a word; for others, a part of the word. The whole child reacts, but he is not necessarily best stimulated holistically. What constitutes a whole is different from individual to individual and is determined by the meaningfulness of that unit and the ability, experiences, purposes, maturation, and perceptual skill of the learner.

The really successful teacher is one who has developed an extraordinary sensitivity to the differences among children in the classroom and makes adjustments for them.

Teacher differences are a third reason for eclecticism. The teacher's preferred mode of reaction may be as significant as the method of teaching that he is using. Two equally competent teachers may not be able to use the same method with equal effectiveness. It may be as significant in the education of future teachers (and in your own personal success in teaching) that you and prospective teachers develop competency in method in line with your own natural style of responding and communication. Some one of you, because of your personal make-up, may do a beautiful job with individualized reading; another, because of his personal characteristics, may be doomed to failure.

THE CONSEQUENCES OF ECLECTICISM

What does the acceptance of eclecticism imply? It implies, among other things: (1) that the teacher understand the differences in children; and (2) that the teacher become familiar with a host of reading methods.

We have already discussed the importance of the teacher's knowledge of the pupil that he is trying to teach. The effectiveness of the teacher's knowledge with a specific method depends to a great degree on his understanding of the pupil whom he wants to teach. This differential in knowledge of the learner quite frequently accounts for the fact that one teacher is successful with a particular method and another teacher fails. A method of teaching is adequate only if the teacher knows enough about the child so that he can adapt the method to the specific child. In addition to an understanding of the pupil's maturational, experiential, intellectual, neural, physical, social, emotional, motivational, language, and sensory characteristics, knowing the pupil means knowing his *preferred mode of learning*. Identification of the child's preferred mode (or modes) of learning may well be the ultimate goal of all classroom diagnosis.

It is quite possible that a child might not be ready for reading, he might not be mature enough, because we are asking him to use a sensory modality which is less developed than another. Some children are more ready to learn through a phonic approach; others through a visual approach; and again others through a kinesthetic approach. We need to identify the child's differential ability to learn by ear, eye, or touch before choosing a given reading method to use with him.

A second major consequence of accepting a position of eclecticism is a need to become more familiar with a great variety of methods of teaching reading. The teacher of reading today needs to be able to provide proper remediation all along the way. This means he needs to know what is best or probably best for a given child. It is not enough to know *a* method of teaching. It is necessary to know *the* method that is best for a *given* child. This means he must become familiar with a host of methods.

Teachers with the most novel of approaches to teaching reading often claim to be unusually successful with their method. It may be, and indeed often is so, that these teachers work harder or are more enthusiastic than the average teacher. But, it may also be true that their novel approach may be especially effective with some child because it meets his need in a special way. There are methods or specific approaches to teaching that make a world of difference for the individual child. One child benefits from one type of instruction, another may not.

There probably is some good in every approach. The Initial Teaching Alphabet (ITA) approach has already demonstrated its usefulness by simplifying the alphabet. Whether it is better over-all than some other approaches has not been put to sufficient test. Davis's system, as propounded in *K-at spelz cat*, the Diacritical Marking System of Fry, and Gattegno's color approach may each help some child to learn and remember better.

A child who has difficulty associating meaning with what is read may be especially helped by a linguistic approach such as Lefevre's.[25] It may help the reader to translate the printed text into the intonation pattern of the writer. Another child may be aided by linguistic approaches such as those proposed by Bloom-field, Soffietti, Daniels and Diack, or by Fries, which stress the phonetic consistencies of the language.

The teaching machine approach, originally proposed by Pressey, or programmed learning approaches generally may help a child who has special need for a detailed step-by-step sequential presentation of learning tasks and who needs a constant and continual confirmation of his own progress.

Another pupil who has a special need to be interested and who learns best when the reading materials describe meaningful personal experiences may learn best through the language—experience approach or the textfilm approach.

Some children, and we do not know how many, may not learn so readily because certain internal events have gone awry. We cannot emphasize enough that all learning, including how to read, occurs in a cranium. Children think and learn differently because of differences in neural development. Neurological factors are key factors in language and reading development. Delacato summarizes the thinking on this subject when he notes that "peripheral activity . . . such as . . . various reading techniques are meaningless in remediation if the neurological organization is defective." We can learn from each of these people and from the methods they are advocating.

When the teacher is acceptant of the student, when he respects the individuality of the pupil, shows understanding and empathy, has deep faith in the improvableness of the pupil, and identifies the pupil's area of confidence, we find that that teacher's pupils generally are successful. Because learning occurs in a relationship, the teacher's personality and his ability to enlist the child's active cooperation are often more important than the specific method used.

The simple fact is that other factors that make for disability in reading frequently pale into insignificance when the teacher is an interesting and an interested teacher. The teacher must be something of an expert in reading method, but he also must care for the pupil. Teaching method is not the final answer. The superiority of one method over another resides in such factors as teacher knowledge of and teacher enthusiasm for the method. Reading disability seems to require a predisposition in the pupil and an initial approach or method that ignores it.

Summary

Chapter 5 considered various methods of identifying the *word* and ended with a discussion of eclecticism. In conclusion, one might add:

1. A high percentage of children learn to read regardless of the method. Many different methods can and do eventually lead to reading proficiency. This principle applies also to remedial instruction.
2. There are methods or specific teaching approaches that make a world of difference for a specific child.
3. The method that works best for a given child depends on the individual child.
4. Some teachers may not make use of the best that is available, but if the teacher is a good and an interested teacher, other factors often pale into insignificance.

In evaluating the trend in reading method, we should like

to quote from our book, *Improving the Teaching of Reading*, p. 195:

> In reading, good teaching seems to mean that the teacher must devise techniques of instruction which help the pupil to construct a generic code or a coding system that has wider applicability in reading than would the rote identification of individual words. The code has wider application than in the situation in which it was learned. The child learns to "read off" from this generic code information that permits him to attack other words. . . . The child, in a sense, must be taught to be a better guesser by knowing the language system and the phonogram-phoneme interrelationships.

The newer approaches in reading, in one way or another, seem to be carrying out the implications of that statement.

---

[1] For a discussion of the basal reader method, the individualized reading method, and the phonic and word methods, as well as other synthetic and analytical methods, see: Dechant, Emerald. *Improving the Teaching of Reading*, Chapters 8 and 9.

[2] Pitman, I. J. "Learning to Read: An Experiment." *Journal of the Royal Society of Arts*, 190 (February, 1961) 149-180.

Downing, John. "The ITA (Initial Teaching Alphabet) Reading Experiment." *The Reading Teacher*, 18 (November, 1964), 105-110.

Downing, J. A. *The Initial Teaching Alphabet Explained and Illustrated*. The Macmillan Company, New York, 1964.

Downing, J. A. *The ITA Reading Experiment*. Evans Brothers, London, 1964. The *Early-to-Read Series* consists of 8 readers, 5 workbooks, and teacher's manuals. The Resource Kit for teacher training consists of Alphabet Sheet, The Story of i/t/a, i/t/a Bulletin, brochure about i/t/a's Early-to-Read Stories, and magazine reprints. These are available from i/t/a Initial Teaching Alphabet Publications, Inc., 20 East 46th Street, New York, N.Y.

[3] Reproduced with permission of Initial Teaching Alphabet Publications, Inc.

[4] This is available through Carlton Press, Inc., 84 Fifth Avenue, New York.

[5] Fry, Edward. "A Diacritical Marking System to Aid Beginning Reading Instruction," *Elementary English*, 41 (May, 1964) 526-529, 537.

[6] Gattegno, Caleb. "Teaching Reading: An Indefinitely Renewable Problem." *Spelling Progress Bulletin*, 4 (Fall, 1964) 15-17.

Gattegno, Caleb. "Words in Color," pp. 175-191, in *The Disabled Reader*, ed. by John Money. Johns Hopkins Press, Baltimore, 1966.

Gattegno, Caleb. *Words in Color: Background and Principles*. Learning Materials, Inc., of Encyclopaedia Britannica Press, 1962. The program contains a *Background and Principles Book,* charts 1 to 21 (colored), *Phonic Code* (8 charts in color), *Word Cards, Word Building Book, Books 1, 2,* and *3, Book of Stories,* and Worksheets.

7 Gattegno, Caleb. "Teaching Reading, An Indefinitely Renewable Problem," *Spelling Progress Bulletin,* 4 (Fall, 1964) 15-17.

8 For a fuller discussion see: Bartkowiak, Deanna. "Linguistics and Reading: Four Views." *Elementary English,* 44 (April, 1967) 386-391.

9 Lefevre, Carl A. "Reading Our Language Patterns: A Linguistic View—Contributions to a Theory of Reading," *Challenge and Experiment in Reading,* International Reading Association Conference Proceedings, 7 (1962) 66-70.

10 Lefevre, Carl A. *Linguistics and the Teaching of Reading.* McGraw-Hill, New York, 1964, pp. 247-278.

11 Bloomfield, L. "Linguistics and Reading," *Elementary English,* 19 (1942) 125-30, 183-6. Bloomfield, L., and Barnhart, C. L. *Let's Read: A Linguistic Approach.* Wayne State University Press. Detroit, 1961.

See also the Linguistic materials and reading series coauthored by Leonard Bloomfield and Clarence Barnhart: *Let's Read* (grades 1-9) and workbooks: *Let's Work* (1-9).

12 Soffietti, J. P. "Why Children Fail to Read." *Harvard Educational Review,* 25 (1955) 63-84.

13 Daniels, J. C., and Diack, H. *Royal Road Readers.* Chatto and Windus, London, 1954; Educators Publishing Service, Cambridge.

Daniels, J. C., and Diack, H. "The Phonic Word Method." *Reading Teacher,* 13 (1959) 14-21.

Daniels, J. C., and Diack, Hunter. *Progress in Reading in the Infant School.* Institute of Education, University of Nottingham, 1960.

14 Fries, Charles C. *Linguistics and Reading.* Holt, Rinehart and Winston, New York, 1963.

15 Lefevre, Carl A. "A Comprehensive Linguistic Approach to Reading." *Elementary English,* 42 (October, 1965) 651-9.

16 Talking Typewriter (Edison Responsive Environment System). Responsive Environments Corporation, 21 East 40th Street, New York, New York.

Johnson, Dorothy K. "Experimenting with the Talking Typewriter." *New Directions in Reading,* ed. by Ralph Staiger and David A. Sohn. Bantam Books Inc., New York, 1967, pp. 32-36.

17 Crutchfield, Marjorie A. "In Practice: The Language—Experience Approach to Reading." *Elementary English,* 43 (March, 1966) 285-297.

18 Allen, R. V. and Lee, Doris M. *Learning to Read Through Experience.* Appleton-Century-Crofts, New York, 1963.

19 Allen, R. V., and Allen, Claryce. *Language Experiences in Reading.* Encyclopaedia Britannica Press, Chicago, 1966.

20 Sartain, Harry W. *Language Arts for Beginners.* Fourteen chart activities for use in teaching kindergarten and first graders. D. C. Heath and Company, Boston.

21 Barbe, Walter B. *Educator's Guide to Personalized Reading Instruction.* Prentice-Hall, Inc., Englewood Cliffs, New Jersey, 1961.

22 Orton, S. T. "Specific Reading Disability—Strephosymbolia," *Journal of American Medical Association* (April, 1928) 1094-1099.

Orton, S. T. *Reading, Writing, and Speech Problems in Children,* W. H. Norton, New York, 1937.

Orton, June L. "The Orton-Gillingham Approach." *The Disabled Reader,* ed. by John Money, John Hopkins Press, Baltimore, 1966, pp. 119-145.

For a method based on Orton's thesis see: Spalding, Romalda Bishop and Spalding, Walter T. *The Writing Road to Reading.* Whiteside, Inc., New York, 1962.

[23] Delacato, Carl H. *The Treatment and Prevention of Reading Problems.* Charles C. Thomas, Springfield, 1959.

Delacato, Carl H. *Diagnosis and Treatment of Speech and Reading Problems.* Charles C. Thomas, Springfield, 1963.

Doman-Delacato Reading Development Program for preschool children: *Child's Word Builder Book, Giant Symbol Card Set, Giant Word Card Set, Child's Reading Book, Parent's Teaching Book.* Systems for Education, Inc., 612 North Michigan Avenue, Chicago, Ill.

[24] For a more complete discussion of this position, see: Dechant, Emerald. "Why an Eclectic Approach in Reading Instruction." *Vistas in Reading,* Proceedings of the Eleventh Annual Convention, International Reading Association, Newark, 1967, pp. 28-32.

[25] Lefevre, Carl A. "A Comprehensive Linguistic Approach to Reading." *Elementary English,* 43 (October) 1965, pp. 651-659.

6

Meeting Individual Needs

Chapter 6 concerns itself with those pupils who need even more individualized attention than the average retarded reader; with reading methods that are specifically labeled remedial methods; and with the evaluation of remedial methods. Let us begin first with a discussion of the needs of each of the following groups of learners:

1. Slow Learners
2. Disadvantaged Readers
3. Reluctant Learners
4. Severely Emotionally Disturbed Retarded Readers
5. Dyslexiac Readers

Each of these groups needs a slightly different reading program and remediation must be adapted to individual needs. For example, we need to present different stimuli and to present them in a different way for the learner who is deficient because of inadequate capacity than for the one who is deficient because of a verbally impoverished environment. Let us first look at the slow learner.

The slow learner

The slow learner may or may not be retarded in terms of his ability level, but he is almost always retarded as to grade level.

He generally has an IQ of between 70 and 90. This pupil begins to read at age seven or later, will read slowly and haltingly, and is achieving below grade level in areas other than reading, such as spelling or arithmetic. He does not need a remedial program. In fact, pushing him may only hurt him. He may interpret it as dissatisfaction with his wholehearted efforts.

Certainly major adjustments must be made for the slow learner in the context of the developmental reading program and in the rate at which he is expected to progress through it. He requires a longer readiness program than does the average child. To begin formal reading instruction before the slow learner has attained a mental age of six or more is often to waste the time of both teacher and pupil and will result in pupil discouragement. The extended readiness program of the slow learner should emphasize social interaction, story-telling, arts and crafts, dramatizing, music, and recreational activities. Reading charts built from the direct experiences of the children are especially useful. These charts will be read and reread with pride and satisfaction by mentally retarded pupils at chronological ages considerably beyond those at which they can be used with normal children. In the early stages of learning, listening will need to be stressed more than reading.

The teacher needs to give detailed and simplified directions for all work, providing concrete illustrations and short-range projects resulting in frequent rewards. There must be frequent rereading of materials, more use of oral reading, and an emphasis on physical activity and specific, concrete projects in connection with the learning experiences.

In the slow learner's reading program, it is necessary to spend considerable time on phonetic and structural analysis and, frequently, to encourage lip movements, vocalization, and pointing at the word. The emphasis should be on word knowledge and the mastery of simple comprehension skills. The slow learner cannot use context clues so well as children of average intelligence. He makes more vowel errors and omits more sounds.

The slow learner appears to have little need for rapid reading skills. He will not read many different materials. He has a difficult time reading for practical purposes. The reading of the slow learner, especially when he is about ready to leave school, should be functional in nature. He needs to learn the working vocabulary required to function effectively as an American citizen.

From his experience with slow learners, Kirk[1] suggests that the teacher should keep the following in mind:

1. It should not be expected that the slow learner should learn to read at the life age of six when he enters the first grade . . .
2. His rate of learning to read is slower than that of other children . . .
3. Throughout his school career the slow learner has not been able to succeed in reading like other children . . .
4. Health and environmental handicaps have been found more frequently in the slow learner, thus contributing to his reading retardation.
5. Other school subjects, like history, geography, and even arithmetic computation, are difficult for him since they require efficient reading habits.
6. Due to difficulties in reading, lack of interest in recreational reading, and avoidance of an unpleasant task, reading does not become a part of the life of a slow learner.

The teacher can help this pupil in the regular classroom:

1. By providing a friendly, accepting, and encouraging relationship. Teacher attitudes substantially affect the performance of the slow learner. The teacher must believe in the improvableness of the learner.
2. By creating a learning environment where simple reading is important. Teach him to read road signs, city directories, a letter from a friend, want ads, newspapers, an application blank, a menu.
3. By pacing the learning according to the pupil's ability.
   a. Introduce only a few materials at any given time.
   b. Review daily.
   c. Introduce materials in varied contexts.
   d. Simplify materials, explanations, and techniques.

   The basic vocabulary needs to be carefully controlled. Instead of using many different primers or readers, build many reading situations which require the pupil to use his limited vocabulary over and over again. The use of workbooks is especially recommended.

4. By coordinating all the language arts. Reading orally to the pupil is very beneficial. Let the pupil do oral reading. Sometimes he needs to hear himself say the word to understand what he is reading.

5. By not underestimating the slow learner's ability to learn. Don't simply let him do busy work, draw aimlessly, trace and copy words and sentences.

6. By having the pupil see his progress every day. Nothing succeeds like observed and tangible success.

   a. Have him keep a card file of words that he has learned to spell or read.

   b. Have him construct a picture dictionary, perhaps of shop tools. The teacher needs to provide opportunities for the pupil to "shine" in some area.

7. By providing drill on new words:

   a. Let the pupil write, pronounce, and read the word.
   b. Use all the sense avenues.

8. By providing ample opportunity for review and repetition. The slow learner profits greatly from repetition. He may get the gist of a story only in spurts. Each rereading adds more to his understanding.

9. By giving special attention to eye movements and line-to-line sequence.

10. By individualizing instruction. The teacher needs to give as much individual help as possible.

11. By not putting him into a remedial program simply because he is reading below grade level.

12. By using concrete illustrations to develop concepts and generalizations.

13. By providing short-range goals. Projects should not be too long.

14. By emphasizing the visual and auditory characteristics of words. Word analysis is very helpful. The teacher needs to emphasize sound symbols.

15. By breaking complex learning tasks into small steps. The use of programmed materials and teaching machines is

especially recommended for slow learners. They divide
the task into small steps and use frequent repetition and
other supportive cues to make the correct response dominant.

16. By employing a variety of teaching techniques.
17. By familiarizing himself with methods of teaching specifically designed for the slow learner. In addition to
those discussed in the last part of the chapter are the
following:

> Kirk: *Teaching Reading to Slow-Learning Children,*
> Houghton Mifflin.
>
> Bruechner and Bond: *Diagnosis and Treatment of
> Learning Difficulties,* Appleton-Century-Crofts.
>
> Featherstone: *Teaching the Slow Learner,* Colum-
> bia University.
>
> Monroe and Backus: *Remedial Reading,* Houghton
> Mifflin.
>
> Kephart, N. C. *The Slow Learner in the Classroom.*
> Charles W. Merrill Books, Inc.

The disadvantaged reader

With four of our fourteen largest cities having one deprived
child for every two of their populace and with it being estimated
that by 1970 the other ten cities will have the same ratio,[2] and
since many of these children are poor readers and are thus educationally handicapped, there is need to look closely at the reading needs of these children. The problem is even more acute if,
as some social scientists contend, one of three youngsters in the
country as a whole is educationally deprived.

The disadvantaged child or the experientially deprived child
belongs to no single race or color. People of varied colors and
national origins are poor and fail to achieve the goals established
by the main stream of society.[3]

What characterizes the disadvantaged child?

1. He lacks a proper self-image. He feels alienated from the
larger social structure.
2. He expects little from life and has little academic drive.

He has a weak sense of the future and seems to lack ambition.

3. He tends to be afflicted with more health and physical difficulties.
4. He is deficient in language development, has a limited vocabulary, and even though he uses short sentences, these are sprinkled with grammatical errors. Sentence structure is faulty.
5. He has mastered the public language (this uses simple declaratory sentences) but cannot deal with the formal language. His language contains few clauses or structural complexities. He does not use the school language.
6. He has more perceptual difficulties. He recognizes fewer objects than most children. He is deficient in auditory attention and interpretation skills. He learns less from what he hears than does the middle-class child.
7. He tends to perform poorly on tests and his achievement in school is low. He is slow at cognitive tasks. He is unaware of the ground rules for success in school.
8. His reading achievement tends to be substantially below his ability level.
9. He learns more readily through a physical and concrete approach.
10. If he is a boy, he values masculinity and views intellectual activities as unmasculine.
11. His attention span is short and he is not motivated by long-range goals.
12. His experiential background is meager. He does not have the experience to make words meaningful.

The need for concerted effort to improve the language and reading skills of the disadvantaged child is apparent. The following techniques might prove helpful.[4]

1. Make every effort to obtain a true estimate of the pupil's potential. The *Wechsler Intelligence Scale for Children,* the *Stanford-Binet Intelligence Scale,* the *I. P. A. T. Culture Fair Intelligence Test,* or a similar test should be used to obtain an IQ or mental age score. Do not use

tests which only hammer home the point that the pupil is stupid.

2. Teach disadvantaged children to "learn how to learn." They do not know what it means to be taught.

3. Build on oral language as a prerequisite to dealing with printed language. This child will not know a word like steeple although a dozen steeples may be visible from the classroom window. Develop experiential and oral meanings for words. The Peabody Language Development Kit and the Ginn Language Kit A provide a systematic program of language experiences on the first-grade level.

4. Develop speaking-reading-writing relationships through the use of experience stories, audio-visual devices and concrete illustrations. Many visual stimuli should be presented together with the verbal stimuli. Make tapes of the pupil's oral reading.

5. Teach reading as a life-related process. When saying: "We wash our hands," have the children do it and write the sentences on the blackboard for them to read. Experientially deprived children perhaps more so than any other group learn by doing. In the middle and upper grades the pupil needs to develop an awareness that reading is important. Too often, the fact that he cannot read causes him little concern.

6. Make frequent use of experience charts. Permit children to verbalize and to communicate orally. Reading assignments should be brief and concrete.

7. Display books strategically and attractively for personal and group examination. Show a filmstrip about a book; read from a book. Make available materials that present his own ethnic group in a good light. Instead of trying to get him to adopt a new culture, help him to improve within the framework of his own culture.

8. Only gradually introduce books as readers, moving back and forth from charts to books as the situation demands.

9. Give special attention to readiness for reading and for learning. Be reasonably certain that pupils have a chance of understanding the materials.

10. Do not limit the approach in reading to any one method or one approach.
11. Teach phonics and structural analysis as means of figuring out the pronunciation of words. Few disadvantaged children know either the alphabet of letters or the alphabet of sounds. Emphasize visual and auditory discrimination, but especially auditory discrimination.

    Disadvantaged children profit from a great deal of auditory and visual perception activities. The *Michigan Successive Discrimination Listening Program* and the *Frostig Program for the Development of Visual Perception* stress such activities. A new program with similar emphasis is *Readiness for Learning: A Program for Visual and Auditory Perceptual-Motor Training*, by J. B. Lippincott. It is designed for kindergarten–first grade level.
12. Provide an atmosphere of trust where the pupil can learn self-assurance and self-direction; raise his aspirational level; help him develop pride in himself. For example, choral reading may be used to great advantage. This permits the pupil to respond and yet it does not single him out if he makes an error. Programmed materials give him all the time he wants or needs without pressuring him for an answer. They permit him to check on his own answer without subjecting him to embarrassment because the teacher or another pupil saw his error or deficiency. The teacher must proceed on the assumption that the pupil can improve.
13. Make use of materials that are specifically designed for culturally deprived children. The Detroit city schools have been using multicultural readers. Some recommend the use of the Montessori approach. *The Progressive Choice Reading Program*, described later in this chapter, is designed specifically for the disadvantaged child. Another program on junior high–senior high school level for disadvantaged children is *Reading in High Gear* by Science Research Associates. The *Miami Linguistic Readers*, D. C. Heath and Company, form a two-year beginning reading program for bilingual and culturally disadvantaged pupils. Books available are: *Biff and Tiff, Kid Kit*

and the Catfish, Nat the Rat, Tug Duck and Buzz Bug, The Sack Hut, On the Rock in the Pond, The Picnic Ship, Hot Corn Muffins, The Camping Trip, and *The Magic Bean.*

A new brochure, *A Reading List for Disadvantaged Youth,* is available through the American Library Association. Another source of books is: Ornstein, Allan C. "101 Books for Teaching the Disadvantaged." *Journal of Reading,* 10 (May, 1967) 546-551.

Dandy Dog's Early Learning Program, American Book Company, is a combination book–record program useful with slow learners and non-English speaking children.

The teacher of experientially deprived children will want to become familiar with:

Bloom, B. S., Allison Davis, and Robert Hess. *Compensatory Education for Cultural Deprivation.* Holt, Rinehart and Winston, Inc. 1965.

Frost, Joe L., and Glenn R. Hawkes. *The Disadvantaged Child: Issues and Innovations.* Houghton Mifflin Co., 1966.

Gowan, John C. and Demos, George D., *ed. The Disadvantaged and Potential Dropout.* Charles C. Thomas, 1966.

Bereiter, Carl and Englemann, Siegfried. *Teaching Disadvantaged Children in the Preschool.* Prentice-Hall, 1966.

Ansara, Alice. *A Guide to the Teaching of Reading* (for teachers of the disadvantaged). Educators Publishing Service.

Taba, Hilda and Elkins, Deborah. *Teaching Strategies for the Culturally Disadvantaged.* Rand McNally, Skokie, Illinois, 1966.

Strom, Robert D. *Teaching in the Slum School.* Charles E. Merrill, Columbus, 1965.

Webster, S. W., *ed. The Disadvantaged Learner: Knowing, Understanding, Educating.* Chandler Publishing Company, 1966.

14. Greatly expand the amount of time that is devoted to reading instruction. On the upper-grade levels put special emphasis on study skills.

15. Structure the reading program in such a way that the pupil thinks of reading as the process of bringing meaning to the page.[5] Don't ask the child, "What does this word mean?" His answer will probably be wrong. Rather, ask him: "What does this word make you think of?" Such a question preserves his self-concept and allows the teacher to develop new or additional meanings.

16. Take an attitude of "positive expectancy"[6] toward the pupil, focusing on his assets rather than his weaknesses. As Niemeyer, president of Bank Street College, notes: "A major reason for low achievement among children in poor neighborhoods is the low expectation as to their learning capacity held by teachers."

The following suggestions might prove helpful in organizing the reading program for the disadvantaged pupil:

1. Use team teaching, permitting the grouping of children into very small groups when needed. Disadvantaged children might be assigned to small classrooms or subgrouped for specific teaching.

2. Have half of the children report an hour early and leave an hour early; the other half comes an hour later, providing the teacher with a smaller group at both ends of the day. Reading and related language arts may be taught in these periods of reduced class size. Lunch periods might also be staggered with similar effect.

3. Reduce the teacher-pupil ratio.

4. Use "reserve teachers" or "supplemental teachers" to work with groups of eight to twelve for one hour each day to help the lowest reading groups.

5. Assign "master teachers" on the basis of one master teacher to six to ten less experienced teachers to help them and to work with small groups.

6. Use "remedial reading teachers" to give demonstrations for classroom teachers, and to secure needed materials for teaching reading.

7. Use parents in the classroom as aides to help children listen to tapes and to use the library and to help the teacher with record keeping.
8. Use counselors, psychiatric social workers, psychologists, nurses, secretaries, speech specialists, etc., as consultants in dealing with the more severe cases.

The disadvantaged learner is essentially inexperienced in language. He knows too few words and too few meanings. The teacher must accept his manner of expression, but must guide the learner toward using complete sentences. This learner's language, while quite adequate away from school, is not adequate for success in school. Engaging the learner in conversation, fostering language development through role playing and dramatic representation, and reading aloud to him each day are all good procedures to use in developing language competency.

The reluctant reader

The root of the reading difficulties of a given pupil often is the mental attitude of the pupil. He may not like school and he may like reading less. In such a case, there may be no genuine disability. The pupil is disinterested and therefore has not developed competency.

Motivation flows from interest. Without interest there is usually no will to do, no drive to learn. Without motivation, the pupil simply will not develop into a mature reader.

The solution to this pupil's reading problem begins then with a change of attitude. This pupil will not be an adequate reader until he wants to read. How do you get him to want to read? The teacher can promote interest in reading in numerous ways:

1. Read to children.
2. Develop charts to be placed on the reading table containing pupil-made jokes, riddles, statements, and stories. Other charts may contain famous sayings, a poem, or a list of words.
3. Provide a wide selection of easy reading materials—materials which pupils *may* read, not *must* read. As

Murphy [7] notes, when we say to children, "You must read this," we may be creating nonreaders. The pupil should not feel depraved because he doesn't like "As You Like It."

4. Help each child to find materials of appropriate content and difficulty. Do not emphasize literary content only. Generally, the content should provide adventure, action humor, romance (for girls), and surprise. The stories should be about children and heroes. The teacher should take special interest in the pupil's independent reading.

5. Use book exhibits, book fairs, book advertisements, periodicals, and bulletins to stimulate interest in reading. Provide books to fit children's immediate interests.

6. Give children an opportunity to share their reading experiences through book reports, panels, or round-table discussions.

7. Develop a book club or hobby club. Choose a "Book of the Week." Devote an assembly to a particular author or invite a favorite author to school.

8. Introduce children to the reading topic by illustrating the content with TV, films, recordings, and other audio-visual aids. Give an introduction to the book to create interest. Whet their curiosity.

9. Provide class time for library reading.

10. Let children read more than one version of a biography.

11. Stay in the background. The pupil's recommendation of a book carries more weight than the recommendations of ten teachers.

12. Recommend the sports page, magazines, or even the comics to children who do not read.

13. Let the pupil keep a record of his own progress, of the books he has read, of the books he would like to read, and of the movies he has seen that are based on books. There is nothing so discouraging as a teacher who is concerned more with errors than with successes. The teacher should be an exciter rather than an examiner or tester.

14. Have reading materials parallel the pupil's interests. The teacher needs to identify the pupil's interest and to introduce the pupil to books dealing with topics of special

interest to him. Dunn, Anita E.; Jackman, Mabel E.; and Newton, J. Roy in *Fare for the Reluctant Reader*, Argus-Greenwood, Inc., Albany, 1964, provide an annotated bibliography for children in grades seven through twelve. The books are listed alphabetically by author under categories that represent these teen-age interests: adventure, sports, love, careers, tips for teens, and mystery. Other book lists are the following:

Adams, Ruth. *Books to Encourage the Reluctant Reader*. Scholastic Book Services, Englewood Cliffs, New Jersey.

Bush, Bernice. *Fare for the Reluctant Reader: Books, Magazines, and Audio-Visual Aids for the Slow Learner in Grades 7-10*. New York State University, Albany, 1964.

Martin, Marvin. "Fifty Books They Can't Resist." *Elementary English*, 39 (May, 1962) 415-416. (for sixth graders)

Books for Reluctant Readers, Doubleday and Company, Inc., Garden City, New York. This annotated book samples English classics, poetry, music, science, social studies, teen-age interests, and novels. Each book is accompanied by a designation of interest level and of reading level.

Here are some low vocabulary–high interest materials:

Basic Vocabulary Series, Garrard Press.

Cowboy Sam Series, Benefic Press.

Everyreader Series, Webster Publishing Company.

Folklore of the World Series, Garrard Press.

The Frontiers of America Books, Children's Press, Inc.

High Interest Easy-to-Read Books, Follett Publishing Company.

Jim Forest Readers, Harr Wagner Publishing Company.

Gateways to Reading Treasures, Laidlaw Brothers.

Junior Everyreader Series, Webster Publishing Company.

Morgan Bay Mystery Series, Harr Wagner Publishing Company.

Pleasure Reading Series, Garrard Press.

Reading Caravan Series, D. C. Heath and Company.

Reading Incentive Series, Webster Division, Mc-Graw-Hill Book Company.

Reading-Motivated Series, Harr Wagner Publishing Company.

Stories for Teenagers, Globe Book Company.

Target Series, Mafex Associates.

Teen-Age Tales, D. C. Heath and Company.

Webster's New Practice Readers, Webster Publishing Company.

The severely emotionally disturbed retarded reader

Good methodology and techniques of teaching reading do not necessarily lead to the removal of reading retardation. Some reading problems, especially those of an emotional nature, may have their roots outside of the reading situation and a frontal attack on the reading problem may have little effect. The situation might be visualized thus:

1	2	3	4
Serious reading deficiency	Pupil receives remedial instruction	No noticeable sign of improvement	A new method (x) is attempted

5	6	7	8
No positive results	Try method (y)	No positive results	Solution may be in removing emotional inhibitors

In such a situation remediation begins with an attack on the emotional factors that prohibit the child from making the responses required for successful learning to read.

Psychological problems at times are the sources of a reading problem. Eisenberg [8] notes:

> No single pattern of psychopathology is characteristic: among the more common patterns are anxiety states that preclude attention to academic tasks, preoccupation with fantasy such that the child is psychologically absent from class, passive-aggressive syndromes in which resistance to parental coercion is subtly executed by a hapless failure to learn, low self-esteem based upon identification with an inadequate parent, and schizophrenic thought pathology in which letters and words become invested with idiosyncratic meanings. Reading failure is a final common pathway for the expression of a multiplicity of antecedent disruptions in learning.
>
> At the same time, it must be recognized that the reading difficulty is in itself a potent source of emotional distress. Embarrassed by fumbling recitations before his peers, cajoled, implored, or bullied by his parents and his teachers to do what he cannot, the retarded reader is first disturbed and finally despondent about himself. His ineptness in reading penalizes him in all subjects and leads to his misidentification as a dullard. With class exercises conducted in what for him is a foreign language, he turns to other diversions, only to be chastised for disruptive behavior. However begun, the psychiatric disturbances and the reading disability are mutually reinforcing in the absence of effective intervention. For such children, psychiatric treatment may be necessary before response to remedial techniques can be expected.

Great care, however, must be taken that the emotional symptoms which result from reading failure are not immediately advanced as the cause of the reading problem. The first assumption that should be made is that the emotional disturbances are the result of, rather than the cause of, reading failure. One of the really great rationalizations in the classroom for doing nothing or giving up is that the child is emotionally disturbed.

In these cases a thorough study of the pupil's physical, mental, social, and emotional development is needed, an investigation which is not usually possible by one person alone. Psychiatrist, psychologist, teacher, social worker, pediatrician, neurologist, and others need to cooperate in resolving this pupil's learning and emotional disorders.

Holmes [9] points out that in discussing reading and personality difficulties with children and their parents phrases such as "reading diagnosis and treatment" are often more acceptable than "personality maladjustment and therapy."

In dealing with the severely emotionally disturbed pupil who is also a reading disability case, therapy and remedial reading often must be combined. The greater the intensity of the emotional problem, the greater tends to be the need for both therapy and individual instruction. Various therapeutic techniques: play therapy, group interview therapy, and individual interview therapy have been used successfully.

Therapy removes pressures and tension and clears the way for attentive concentration on the reading material. In most cases it removes a fear of reading and allows the child to develop attitudes favorable to reading.

The dyslexiac reader

Dyslexia [10] (specific reading disability, congenital word-blindness, or developmental dyslexia) is a massive unreadiness for reading. It is a failure to learn to read even though the child has had appropriate instruction, comes from a culturally adequate home, is properly motivated, has adequate sensory equipment, has normal intelligence, and shows no gross neurological defect.[11] Perhaps 2 per cent of the poor readers are dyslexiac.

The following characteristics identify the dyslexiac:

1. The dyslexiac reader is usually a boy.
2. His IQ is usually in the normal range.
3. There is persistent and frequent left-right confusion.

    a. There is a reversal of concepts: floor for ceiling, go for stop, east for west.

    b. Penmanship is characterized by poorly formed and irregular characters. Drawing and copying are poor.

    c. He comes from families in which there is left-handed-
ness or language disorders or both.

    d. He shows evidence of delayed or incomplete estab-
lishment of one-sided motor preferences. He tends to
be left-handed, ambidextrous, or shows mixed dominance. These orientational problems may not be present in the older dyslexiac. On earlier age levels, lack
of form perception and of directional sense and dyslexia may go hand in hand.

4. He often has speech difficulties and poor auditory discrimination. Stuttering, lisping, stammering, and cluttering often are quite noticeable.

5. He is more likely to have been premature or to have sur-
vived some complication of pregnancy.

6. He is generally an underachiever.

7. He is hyperactive, distractable, impulsive, shows poor
motor coordination, has a short attention span, and per-
severates excessively.

8. He is weak in visual imagery and has poor visual memory.

The following reading characteristics are usually present:

1. There is difficulty in associating sounds with visual symbols.

2. The pupil ignores details within words, basing word recognition on initial letters, length of word, etc.

3. He frequently reverses letters (*b* and *d*) and words (*was*
for *saw*).

The following principles are useful in trying to teach the
dyslexiac case: [12]

1. Focus on the simplest, most basic perceptual-associa-
tional elements within a total word or Gestalt. Introduce
only one association at a time (*m* as distinct from *n,* so
he can distinguish *map* from *nap*). Emphasize details
by having the pupil fill in missing letters in words.

2. Associate sound with this element. Practice with a single
sound for the specific letter being learned. Gradually
move to blending and the total word.

3. Always pronounce the word.
4. Write or trace the word.

   a. This uses the kinesthetic sense.
   b. It makes the child pay attention to detail.

5. With the severely retarded it is useful to use all sensory pathways. Have the pupil look at the letter, hear and say it, sound, and trace it simultaneously. When working on comprehension, have him try to get the main idea of a paragraph from hearing it read aloud to him, from reading it aloud, reading it silently, and expressing his ideas both orally and in writing. He may draw or chart, if possible, the ideas presented. There seems to be no one approach that works with all reading disabilities. The teacher might want to try any of the methods suggested in Chapter 5 or any of the methods suggested later in this chapter.

   The evidence tends to indicate that severe reading disabilities of a neurological origin need to use methods other than the configuration method to develop a memory for words. Many authorities recommend that the child form letters and words from modeling clay, etch the letters in a tray whose bottom has been lined with clay, write letters in wet sand, paint letters with a brush on butcher paper, or write the letter with finger paints. Even though attention may be the most basic result of kinesthetic training, this is a worthwhile goal.

6. Overteach the responses—without laborious sounding out.
7. Minimize interference in the classroom.
8. Arrange the situation so the child is usually correct, thereby improving his motivation and confidence.
9. Provide the proper materials. Here are some booklists directed at the retarded reader:

   Books for Slow Readers, Holiday House.

   Darling, Richard L. "Lists of Books for Retarded Readers." *School Life,* July, 1962.

   Roswell, Florence and Chall, Jeanne. *Selected Materials for Children with Reading Disabilities.* City College Educational Clinic, New York, 1959.

Spache, George D. *Good Reading for Poor Readers*. Garrard Press, Champaign, Illinois.

Sometimes severe reading disability is neurological in origin, either following brain injury or degeneration of the nervous system. It is not always possible to distinguish between developmental dyslexia and dyslexia of a neurological nature. In fact, there is no foolproof way of diagnosing specific dyslexia, but whatever the etiology of reading retardation may be, the principles of remediation seem the same or at least are very similar.

Remedial methods

We have already indicated that there is no one best method for teaching reading and there is no one best remedial or corrective method. There may be a best method for a given learner. There may even be a best method for a special segment of the learner population. There may even be a best method for a given teacher because he is most comfortable with it. The teacher of reading thus has to look at many methods. Because he doesn't know whose brand of reading method is the best buy, he has to consider a variety of possibilities, each of which might have some merit and validity in a specific teaching situation.

It is not possible to survey all remedial methods, but let's look at some key ones.

THE VISUAL METHOD

Every method of teaching reading relies on vision and the visual skills of the learner. Children learn to identify words through:

1. The word's general configuration—its length, its general appearance, its contour.
2. The word's identifying characteristics—its more subtle features, the double letter (moon), the long tail at the end (key), a special letter.
3. The detection of small words or known parts in words—the *cow* and *boy* in *cowboy*.
4. Syllabication and structural analysis.
5. Picture representation—as by showing a picture with the word.

Gates,[13] a strong advocate of the sight, word-configuration approach, believes that normally the same methods, procedures, and techniques should be used with the retarded reader that work with most children in the regular classroom. He emphasizes the need for greater enrichment and more careful management of the reading diet of the retarded reader. So-called remedial methods are employed only as a last resort.

The basic task facing the child in this approach is to associate a sound and a meaning with a printed form. Most teachers, in introducing the pupil to reading, use a visual configuration approach, but experience has amply demonstrated that not all pupils learn to read through this approach. There thus have arisen other methods to help those pupils who do not learn through the sight-configuration method. Many of these have been described in Chapter 5. There are other methods that have been associated most frequently with remedial instruction. These commonly put greater emphasis on the use of sound and kinesthetic sense avenues. Let's look at a few of them.

MONROE METHOD

Numerous writers have advocated phonetic methods both for remedial work and as a general portion of the developmental program. Monroe [14] in 1932 evolved a synthetic phonetic approach using considerable repetition and drill. The basic emphasis was the development of auditory discrimination. Pictures are mounted on cards and the child is taught to identify initial consonants and consonants followed by a vowel. After a few of these phonetic elements are known, blending is begun. Gradually, the child is initiated into the reading of specially written stories. Tracing is used in this method as the need arises, but the child uses a pencil rather than the forefinger for tracing. Monroe found her method to be highly successful with serious reading disability cases and with children who have great difficulty in making visual associations.

FERNALD METHOD [15]

The steps in the Fernald method vary from word tracing to word analysis and are determined somewhat by the ability and progress of the child. At the lower ranges of achievement, the child selects a word that he wishes to learn. The teacher writes the word on paper in large script or print. The child may even dictate a sentence such as, "I like my mother." The teacher records this on paper. There is little or no control of the vocabulary. The child then traces each word with the forefinger, saying each part of the word as he does the tracing. The process continues until the child can write the word without the benefit of the copy. The child's fingers must make contact with the paper as he traces. Words thus learned are later typewritten and then included in stories for the child to read. As new words are learned, they are collected by the pupil in an alphabetical file. As the child advances, tracing may cease entirely, but pronouncing the word while writing it is always an essential feature.

The kinesthetic method develops through four stages:

a. *Tracing, calling, and writing the word*
   1. The teacher writes the word for the pupil in large print, perhaps on the chalkboard.
   2. The pupil traces the word, pronouncing the word in syllables as he traces.
   3. The pupil tries to write the word, repeating steps one and two if he is unable to do so.
b. *Writing without tracing*
   Gradually the pupil attempts to write new words without having to trace them.
c. *Recognizing the word*
   The pupil gradually comes to recognize the word on sight. He learns the printed word by saying it to himself before writing.
d. *Word analysis*
   The pupil is taught to break the word into smaller parts. He now recognizes words by their similarity to words that he already knows.

The kinesthetic method is time-consuming, but it has many advantages. It teaches left-to-right orientation, and the sound of the word is associated with the visual stimulus. The child seems to acquire phonic skills without having formal training and he develops skills in syllabication. The method is designed especially for clinical use and requires almost constant direction from the teacher.

Harris [16] lists the strong points of this method:

1. It enforces careful and systematic observation and study of words.
2. It makes necessary a consistent left-to-right direction in reading.
3. It provides adequate repetition.
4. Errors are immediately noted and corrected.
5. Progress can be noted by the child at practically every lesson.
6. The sensory impressions from tracing, writing, and saying the words reinforce the visual impressions and seem to be of definite value to children whose visual memory is very poor.

The Hegge, Kirk, and Kirk Grapho-Vocal Method [17] requires the pupil to sound out and write each word. The pupil pronounces the word entirely phonetically (synthetic phonics) and later writes the word from dictation. The steps thus are:

1. Sound the words letter by letter.
2. Blend the sounds together.
3. Pronounce the words.
4. Write the words.

Fernald's method is a VAKT (visual, auditory, kinesthetic, and tactile) method. There are similar methods labeled only VAK. In these, the pupil does not do any tracing of the word.

The Unified Phonics Method

The Unified Phonics Method [18] by Spalding and Spalding is a phonics method which teaches reading through a spelling-writing approach and through a study of about seventy phonograms in the English language. These are single letters or letter combinations which represent forty-five basic sounds. The authors recommend their program as a beginning reading program and suggest that through the use of this program remedial reading will not be needed later. The steps in teaching are the following (pp. 40-42):

1. Teach the phonograms by having pupils say in unison the one or more sounds of each phonogram.
2. The pupil writes each phonogram. The letters are not named.
3. Any phonogram of two or more letters is called by its sound. Thus *eigh* is *a*.
4. Have children write words from the Ayres list.
5. Teach the basic laws of spelling.
6. Reading is begun only when the pupils have learned enough words to comprehend instantly the meaning of a sentence.

Here are the seventy phonograms:

b	s	ur	ew	ie
c	t	wor	ui	igh
d	v	ear	oo	eigh
f	w	sh	ch	kn
g	x	ee	ug	gn
h	y	th	ea	wr
j	z	ay	ar	ph
k	a	ai	ck	dge
l	e	ow	ed	oe
m	i	ou	or	gh
n	o	oy	wh	ti
p	u	oi	oa	si
qu	er	aw	ey	ci
r	ir	au	ei	ough

THE COLOR PHONICS SYSTEM

The Color Phonics System [19] presents the letters in color in such a way that once the principle of coding has been mastered the pupil can immediately identify the sound. It is an outgrowth of the method used by Edith Norrie at the Ordblinde Institute in Copenhagen. The method is designed to be used with the dyslexiac reader. It is not to be used with the color blind or with the brain injured suffering from color agnosia. The system is based, among others, on the following assumptions:

1. The most successful techniques for teaching dyslexiacs are founded on a phonetic basis.
2. Each letter should be taught separately or in given combinations which can be arranged and rearranged again and again in various order. Bannatyne believes that the fundamental neuropsychological deficit of the dyslexiac child is the inability to sequence correctly, especially auditorily. The pupil must vocalize constantly, sounding out the successive phonemes which make up a word.
3. The dyslexiac child has difficulty mastering the irregular orthography of the English language, but replacing the irregular phonetic structure of the language with a regular one requires the child to transfer to the traditional orthography at a later date. As the dyslexiac child finds it extremely difficult to memorize a set of sound-symbol associations, an additional set of symbols for the same sounds is scarcely likely to solve his problems. Color coding permits the child to identify the sound in a direct way.
4. The pupil must overlearn sound-symbol associations through a variety of stimuli and sensory pathways.

Bannatyne believes that the Color Phonics System is quite compatible and can be used in conjunction with the Fernald Method, the Gillingham Method, or Daniels' and Diack's systems as developed through the Royal Road Readers. For teaching with this system the following points are emphasized by Bannatyne:

1. The vowels are printed in red. The pupil learns that there must never be a word or syllable without a red letter (the letter *y* has a red band under it because it can be used as a vowel).
2. If the child suffers from severe dyslexia, the teacher usually begins with the phonetically regular words and short sentences.
3. Broad developmental stages are discernible in the Color Phonics System: If the child does not know the shapes of the letters, obviously he will have to be taught them, and the best way to do this is to select the single letters which have the largest number of single-sound associations in lan-

guage usage. These will be an azure *a*, a yellow *e*, a pink *i*, an orange *o*, and a rust *u*. The child will have to copy the letters many times, and if he does not know the names of the letters, the vowel sounds should be the ones associated with them (p. 208).

4. After the child knows the shapes of the letters of the alphabet, he begins the second stage, namely, building up a knowledge of simple phonics by a process of gradual introduction to the sounds of both consonants and vowels. The program starts with a few frequently occurring sounds, which are built into simple little words and sentences, using the common vowels mentioned above. It is necessary at this stage that the child have every opportunity to overlearn the color coding for each vowel phoneme as it is introduced (pp. 208-209).

5. The purpose of Stage 3 is to extend the range of color-sound associations and to build up rapidly a reasonable vocabulary using those associations.

6. At all times, with the help of the teacher, words will be broken up into syllables whenever the individual letters are used. One technique which helps the child with breaking a word into syllables, memorizing colors, and spelling generally is the use of rhymes and rhyming (p. 209).

7. A problem frequently encountered during Stages 2 and 3 is that of blending phonemes. Frequently, the inability to blend is a direct result of faulty teaching, inasmuch as the pupil has learned to voice unvoiced consonants by adding unwanted vowels. In other words, the individual phonemes are not being correctly pronounced by the child, so a correct blending is impossible. The word *lit* cannot be blended if the *l* is pronounced *luh*. More often than not, this inability to synthesize sounds into meaningful speech is an aspect of the primary inability of the dyslexiac to sequence auditory material in the absence of auditory sounds, whether these be in the form of environmental stimuli (e.g., heard words, color cues) or neurological engrams, that is, permanent thought-word associations available on demand.

8. There are only two methods for facilitating blending. The first is to tell the child to form his mouth in preparation for saying the initial consonant of a syllable but then to say the following vowel instead. This technique is useful when the initial consonants are unvoiced ones anyway. The second technique consists of demonstrating a single syllable in two

parts, namely, the initial consonant and the remainder of the syllable as a whole. Thus cat is taught not as *c a t*, but as *c at*, the number of "breakdown units" being kept to a manageable minimum. At the same time, the word *cat*, as a *gestalt*, is presented in both its written and spoken forms, and these are simultaneously analyzed into their component letters and phonemes. If this intensive analytic-synthetic simultaneous approach is thoroughly taught during the first few weeks and months, the dyslexiac child will be prevented from forming many of the poor blending habits that such children so often acquire. The individual letters of the Color Phonics System are eminently suited to this analytic-synthetic method of teaching blending because they can very easily be physically separated or drawn together. Before leaving the problem of blending, it is worth re-emphasizing the importance of teaching the phonemes correctly in the first place. Probably more damage is done to dyslexiac children by slovenly teaching of phonics than by any large amount of precise speech training (pp. 209-210).

9. At some time toward the end of the third stage, the child should be introduced to the twenty or so spelling rules, one by one. He should be given plenty of practice in applying the rules, and although this should take up no more than a few minutes at a time, during the remainder of the lesson he should constantly be reminded when he contravenes any rule he has learned. In the long run, it is easiest for a dyslexiac, with his weak verbal memory, to remember a few set principles than thousands of those arbitrary letter-sound sequences called (printed) words.

10. This third stage takes the pupil from the point where he vaguely realizes what reading is technically all about to the point where he has attained a recall vocabulary of one hundred to two hundred words and an immediate recognition vocabulary of three hundred to five hundred words. In addition, the pupil should have learned most of the common phonetically irregular words which are linguistically necessary for structuring the language. These irregularly spelled words, which are the bane of the dyslexiac child's life, are much less of a problem when he learns them initially by using the color coding cues.

11. In Stage 4 the black vowels replace the colored ones. It is necessary to ensure that the pupil pronounce clearly and in

an overly precise way each phoneme in every word he speaks or writes. It may even be necessary to train the child to speak clearly, and in such a case a speech therapist should be called in and briefed. The teacher herself must be careful to avoid sloppy or rapid speech, and at all times she must realize that clear vocalization and auditory sequencing of words are the most important requisites for successful remediation.

12. It is by iterated sound-symbol association (with emphasis on sound) that the dyslexiac child obtains that intuitive appreciation of language skills and usage which provides the basis for an automatic, instantaneous recognition or recall of the written word, and it is the acquisition of this associative fluency which is the objective of the fifth stage (pp. 211-212).

Bannatyne believes that by the time the pupil has finished Stage 5 he is reading up to the level of the average eight- or nine-year-old.

THE PROGRESSIVE CHOICE READING METHOD

The Progressive Choice Reading Method [20] is an outgrowth of studies by Myron Woolman. Two programs based on Woolman's ideas are available today. The first of these, entitled *Lift Off to Reading*,[21] is useful with educable and trainable mental retardates, culturally disadvantaged, the emotionally disturbed, bilinguals, and dyslexiacs. *Reading in High Gear* [22] is designed for older, underachieving, culturally disadvantaged readers at the adolescent level. Woolman emphasizes elements in words. He begins with a "target word" by discussing its meaning. The learner then must differentiate the linear and curvilinear components which compose the letters of the target word. These components are then combined into individual letters and discrimination of the letters is stressed. The pupil next writes the letter by tracing it, finally writing the letter without tracing. The third step consists of learning the sound that is most commonly associated with the letter. Woolman teaches the g, for example, as *guh*, noting that this is a necessary crutch in the beginning and that the pupil quickly gets rid of it when he has mastered a "feeling" for the consonant. The pupil must utter the sound when he sees the printed form of the letter and he must write the letter when he hears it pronounced for him. Fourthly, the reader must learn to combine various vowels and consonants into single sounds. Finally, the pupil must read and write the "target words."

GILLINGHAM METHOD

The Gillingham Method [23] is a multisensory approach emphasizing the linguistic and graphic regularities of English words. It is termed an alpha-phonetic method and begins by teaching the child a few short vowels and consonants that have only one sound. It does not use letters that, if reversed, become new letters. Thus initially it steers clear of letters such as *b* and *d*. It is a combination method, using the auditory, visual, and kinesthetic sense avenues (pp. 40-42). It is a synthetic phonics system rather than an analytical phonics approach. The teaching processes that result in the association of the visual, auditory, and kinesthetic processes are called linkages. The method consists of eight such linkages.

Linkage 1. The name of the letter is associated with the printed symbol; then the sound of the letter is associated with the symbol.

Linkage 2. The teacher makes the letter and explains its form. The pupil traces it, copies it, and writes it from memory. The teacher directs the pupil to move in the right direction and to begin in the right place when making the letters.

Linkage 3. The phonogram is shown to the pupil and he names it. The child learns to associate the letter with its "look" and its "feel." He learns to form the symbol without looking at the paper as he writes.

Linkage 4. The teacher says the phoneme and the child writes it.

Linkage 5. The child is shown the letter and asked to sound it. The teacher moves the child's hand to form the letter and the child sounds it.

Linkage 6. The teacher gives the name of the phonogram and the pupil gives the sound.

Linkage 7. The teacher makes the sound and the pupil gives the name of the letter.

Linkage 8. The teacher makes the sound and the pupil writes the phonogram. Sometimes the pupil writes without looking at the paper, and also names the letter.

Using the multisensory approach, the Gillingham Method introduces the linguistic and graphically regular words first. Only gradually is the pupil introduced to exceptions.

Evaluating remedial methods

The teacher of reading also needs to determine the effectiveness of various procedures in terms of the gains in reading achievement. Over the course of years, many quite different procedures have been suggested for evaluating remedial methods, but too few data actually are available concerning their relative effectiveness. And for that matter, some writers actually challenge the effectiveness of special methods of remediation. Young,[24] for example, suggests that the personality of the teacher and his ability to enlist each child's active cooperation are more important than the specific method used. On the other hand, numerous studies on remedial and diagnostic methods indicate that reading difficulties can be either entirely or at least largely eliminated.

Rankin and Tracy [25] list three methods of measuring and evaluating individual differences in reading improvement.

1. *Crude gain.* In this situation comparable tests are given before (the pretest) and after (the post-test) a remedial program. The score at the start of the program is subtracted from the score at the end of the program and the difference is considered as improvement. Children will naturally show improvement if a difficult test is given in the beginning and if an easier test is administered after the completion of the program.
2. *Percent gain.* In this approach the gain between the pre- and post-test is expressed as a percentage of the initial score. The formula then is: percent of gain $= \dfrac{\text{post-test} - \text{pretest}}{\text{pretest}}$
3. *Residual gain.* This is the difference between the actual post-test score that was predictable from the pretest score. For a discussion of this third procedure the reader may want to consult the articles by Rankin and Tracy in the *Journal of Reading,* March, 1965, and March, 1967.

Many faulty conclusions apparently have been drawn from reading research because residual gain was not considered. As Sommerfield [26] points out, there is a natural tendency for those people who score at the extremes of a distribution on the first test to score closer to the mean of the distribution on the second test. The scores tend to regress toward the mean.

Although the research worker can use control groups or make statistical corrections to eliminate regression effects, frequently this is not done.

Dolch [27] has cautioned that research can come up with the wrong answer unless it is carefully planned and watched. He recommends vigilance in these areas:

1. Compare equal teachers working equally hard.
2. Compare pupils of equal ability and equal home influences.
3. Compare equal school time and emphasis.
4. Watch carefully the size of the class.
5. Beware of misleading averages.
6. Watch for unmeasured results.

In discussing these points, Dolch emphasizes that the teacher using the method frequently is far more important than the method used. Numerous variables enter into any experiment. Sommerfield [28] indicates that the reported results of experimental reading programs may be influenced by the subjects involved, the techniques and materials used, the conditions under which the study was done, the tests that were employed, the statistical devices used, and perhaps the bias or misinterpretations of the investigator.

Studies often do not make allowance for the differences in both skill and motivation among teachers. Control groups are taught by the "regular" teachers; experimental groups are taught by teachers who have a special interest in the project and can give more time to their students. Brownell [29] notes that the critical determinant of achievement is teaching competency rather than the system of instruction. He also notes that results frequently are evaluated by means of test scores, but this is not necessarily what is educationally significant. The measurable is not necessarily the significant and the significant is not necessarily measurable. Achievement at the moment is evaluated; the transfer value of what has been learned is rarely evaluated. There may also be differences in motivation between the pupils in a control group using the regular methods and the experimental group using a new method.

Summary

This chapter has looked at the special problems of the slow learner, the reluctant learner, the disadvantaged reader, the severely emotionally disturbed retarded reader, and the dyslexiac reader. It has surveyed remedial methods and has considered the problems in evaluating improvement from remedial teaching.

---

[1] Kirk, Samuel A. "Characteristics of Slow Learners and Needed Adjustments in Reading," *Classroom Techniques in Improving Reading*, Supplementary Educational Monographs, No. 69, University of Chicago Press, Chicago, 1949, pp. 172-176.

[2] National Education Association. *Schools for the 60's*. McGraw-Hill Book Company, New York, 1963.

[3] Black, Millard H. "Characteristics of the Culturally Disadvantaged Child," *The Reading Teacher*, 18 (March, 1965) pp. 465-470.

[4] Mackintosh, Helen K., Gore, Lillian, Lewis, Gertrude M. *Educating Disadvantaged Children in the Primary Grades*. U.S. Department of Health, Education, and Welfare. U.S. Office of Education, 1965.

See also: Whipple, Gertrude and Black, Millard H. *Reading for Children Without—Our Disadvantaged Youth*. International Reading Association, 1966; Olson, Arthur V. "Teaching Culturally Disadvantaged Children." *Education*, 87 (March, 1967) 423-425; and Rauch, Sidney J. "Ten Guidelines for Teaching the Disadvantaged." *Journal of Reading*, 10 (May, 1967), 536-541.

[5] Kincaid, Gerald L. "A Title I Short Course for Reading Teachers." *The Reading Teacher*, 20 (January, 1967) pp. 307-312.

[6] Strang, Ruth. "Teaching Reading to the Culturally Disadvantaged in Secondary Schools." *Journal of Reading*, 10 (May, 1967) 527-535.

[7] Murphy, George E. "And Now—The Package Deal." *The Reading Teacher*, 20 (April, 1967) 615-620.

[8] Eisenberg, Leon. "Epidemiology of Reading Retardation," pp. 3-19, in *The Disabled Reader*, by John Money, Johns Hopkins Press, Baltimore, 1966. Reprinted with permission.

[9] Holmes, J. A. "Emotional Factors and Reading Disabilities." *The Reading Teacher*, 9 (October, 1955), pp. 11-17.

[10] Money, John, ed. *Reading Disability*. Johns Hopkins Press, Baltimore, 1962.

[11] Eisenberg, *op. cit.*, p. 14.

[12] Bryant, N. Dale. "Some Principles of Remedial Instruction for Dyslexia." *The Reading Teacher*, 18 (April, 1965) 567-572.

[13] Gates, A. I. *The Improvement of Reading*. The Macmillan Company, New York, 1947.

[14] Monroe, Marion. *Children Who Cannot Read*. University of Chicago Press, Chicago, 1932, pp. 111-136.

[15] Fernald, Grace M. *Remedial Techniques in Basic School Subjects*. McGraw-Hill Book Company, Inc., New York, 1966.

[16] Harris, Albert J. *How to Increase Reading Ability*, 3rd edition. Longmans, Green and Company, New York, 1956, p. 386. By permission David McKay Company, Inc.

[17] Hegge, T., Kirk, Samuel, and Kirk, Winifred. *Remedial Reading Drills*. George Wahr, Publisher, Ann Arbor, 1955.

[18] Spalding, Romalda Bishop and Spalding, Walter T. *The Writing Road to Reading*. Whiteside, Inc., William Morrow and Company, New York, 1962.

[19] *Color Phonics System*, Educators Publishing Service, 301 Vassar Street, Cambridge, Massachusetts.

Bannatyne, Alex D. "The Color Phonics System," pp. 193-214 in Money, John, ed. *The Disabled Readers*. Johns Hopkins Press, Baltimore, 1966.

[20] Woolman, Myron, *The Progressive Choice Reading Program*. Institute of Educational Research, Inc., Washington, D.C., 1962.

[21] Woolman, Myron, *Lift Off to Reading*. Science Research Associates, Chicago, 1966.

[22] Woolman, Myron, *Reading in High Gear*. Science Research Associates, Chicago, 1965.

[23] Gillingham, Anna and Stillman, Bessie W. *Remedial Training for Children With Specific Disability in Reading, Spelling, and Penmanship*. Educators Publishing Service, Cambridge, 1966. Available also are: *Phonetic Drill Cards, Phonetic Word Cards, Syllable Concept, Little Stories*, and *Introduction of Diphthongs*.

[24] Young, Robert A. "Case Studies in Reading Disability." *American Journal of Orthopsychiatry*, 8 (April, 1938) pp. 230-254.

[25] Rankin, Earl F., Jr., and Tracy, Robert J. "Residual Gain as a Measure of Individual Differences in Reading Improvement," *Journal of Reading* (March, 1965) pp. 224-233; also Tracy, Robert J., and Rankin, Earl F., Jr., "Methods of Computing and Evaluating Residual Gain Scores in the Reading Program." *Journal of Reading*, 10 (March, 1967) pp. 363-371.

[26] Sommerfield, Roy E. "Some Recent Research in College Reading." *Techniques and Procedures in College and Adult Reading Programs*, Sixth Yearbook of the Southwest Reading Conference, Texas Christian University Press, Fort Worth, 1957, p. 24.

[27] Dolch, E. W. "School Research in Reading." *Elementary English*, 33 (February, 1956) pp. 76-80.

[28] Sommerfield, *op. cit.*, p. 56.

[29] Brownell, W. A. "The Evaluation of Learning Under Dissimilar Systems of Instruction." *California Journal of Educational Research*, 17 (March, 1966) pp. 80-90.

Materials for Teaching
Reading

The materials surveyed in this chapter include those for both developmental and remedial instruction. It would obviously be desirable if we could offer an evaluation of all the materials listed. Perhaps this might be possible if we were talking about five to ten items of material and if we were recommending for a given pupil. It is clearly impossible when dealing with the numerous materials on the market today.

To provide for the specific needs of slow learners, disadvantaged children, the reluctant readers, and the retarded readers a great variety of remedial and special help programs ranging from elementary school through high school has been developed. There is no panacea for reading problems, but the newer media can help. It is most important that the materials used with a given pupil are suited to his needs. Incorrect materials or the incorrect use of appropriate materials can actually cause or intensify reading problems. In selecting materials, the teacher needs to make sure that they are on the appropriate difficulty level, on an appropriate interest level, and that they take into account the pupil's deficiencies and problems.[1] It makes sense to vary materials from time to time and to use in remedial instruction materials that are normally not used in the classroom.

Here are additional guidelines that might help the teacher to make appropriate choices: [2]

1. The program should provide a multiple approach to learning.
2. The program should give guidance in developing the thinking skills of the pupils.
3. The materials should elicit active responses on the part of the pupil.
4. The program should provide for diagnostic teaching, extensive diagnostic measures for assessing pupil needs, and activities designed to meet individual differences.
5. The program should provide guidance and materials for structuring flexible instructional groups.
6. The program should be easy to use, should be keyed to specific objectives, and needs to have been tested prior to public distribution. It should actually instruct, allow for independent learning, and pace learning to individual differences. It should be able to be used to review instruction given by the teacher, thus facilitating the teacher's efforts.

It is impossible to list here all the materials, even all the good materials, that are available to the teacher of reading. We will thus limit ourselves to some of the more used and newer materials designed to develop comprehension and word recognition skills, audio-visual materials, mechanical devices, and professional books.

Skill-improvement materials

THE BASAL READING SERIES

In the greatest number of schools the basal reader is still the most important material used in the reading program. Its importance seems especially significant in the primary years.

The basal reading program leads the pupil by logical and sequential steps to the mastery of the basic reading skills. It is perhaps true that basal readers in their attempt to provide systematic instruction, controlled vocabularies, and mastery of the basic reading skills have failed to some degree in providing purposeful reading. Be that as it may, they have been shown to be helpful in developing reading proficiency in most children. They represent what many people believe to be the "best" materials available for leading the child from the prereading stage to actual reading.

All basal series provide a series of workbooks. These are especially useful in meeting individual needs, in stimulating interest in reading, in providing opportunities for practice, in varying instructional procedures, and in making optimum use of pupil and teacher time.

In some workbooks today there is an attempt to apply the same principles as do the best programmed learning materials. The pupil is introduced to word recognition and comprehension skills in small steps, and advances to higher levels only after successful completion of the simpler task. The workbooks provide the repetition, self-competition, and day-to-day records that make it possible for the pupil to grow and for the teacher to diagnose and to remediate the pupil's inadequacies.

Here is a list of the major reading series:

- *The Alice and Jerry Basic Reading Program,* Harper and Row, Publishers.
- *Bank Street Readers,* The Macmillan Company.
- *Basic Reading Series,* J. B. Lippincott Company.
- *Betts Basic Readers,* American Book Company.
- *Building Reading Skills Series,* McCormick-Mathers.
- *Catholic University of America Faith and Freedom Series,* Ginn and Company.
- *Chandler Language-Experience Readers,* Chandler Publishing Company.
- *City Schools Reading Program,* Follett Publishing Company.
- *Developmental Reading Text-Workbooks,* Bobbs-Merrill.
- *Developmental Reading Series,* Lyons and Carnahan.
- *Easy Growth in Reading Series,* Holt, Rinehart, and Winston, Inc.
- *Economy Reading Workbooks,* Economy Company.
- *Gateway to Reading Treasure Series,* Laidlaw Brothers.
- *Get Ready to Read Series,* Bobbs-Merrill.
- *Ginn Basic Readers,* Ginn and Company.
- *Harper and Row Basic Reading Program,* Harper and Row, Publishers.

- *Learning to Read Series*, Silver Burdett Company.
- *The Macmillan Readers*, The Macmillan Company.
- *Merrill Linguistic Readers*, Charles E. Merrill Books, Inc.
- *The New Basic Readers*, Scott, Foresman and Company.
- *Open Court Basic Readers*, Open Court Publishing Company.
- *Prose and Poetry Series*, L. W. Singer Company.
- *The Quinlan Basic Readers*, Allyn and Bacon, Inc.
- *Reading Essentials Series*, Steck Vaughn Company.
- *Reading for Interest Series*, Revised. D. C. Heath and Company.
- *Reading for Meaning Series*, Revised Edition, Houghton Mifflin Company.
- *Royal Road Readers*, Educators Publishing Service.
- *Scott, Foresman Basic Reading Program*, Scott, Foresman and Company.
- *Sheldon's Basic Reading Series*, Allyn and Bacon, Inc.
- *Sounds of Language Series*, Holt, Rinehart, and Winston, Inc.
- *SRA Basic Reading Series*, Science Research Associates.
- *Winston Basic Readers*, Holt, Rinehart, and Winston, Inc.

READING LABORATORIES

Reading kits or laboratories are possibly the most used materials to supplement the basal reading series. They have individualized the teaching-learning process. They have made it possible to teach the individual pupil on his own level of competency.

The laboratory or kit usually consists of a number of separate cards, sheets, or booklets which are graduated in difficulty. The pupil works with the materials on his own level, advancing through them at his own success rate. He reads, answers questions independently, corrects his work, and keeps his own progress chart. The teacher provides him help when needed.

Here are some common laboratories:

- *EDL. Listen and Read Program*, Educational Developmental Laboratories, Inc. (McGraw-Hill Publishing Company).

    This junior–senior high program is designed to develop listening and reading skills. The pupil listens to tapes and works in individual workbooks. Thirty tapes are available.

- *EDL. Study Skills Library*, Educational Developmental Laboratories.

    This series of materials is designed for grades four through nine, and teaches interpretation, evaluation, organization, content area reading, and reference skills. There are three kits at each level: one on research skills, one in which these skills are applied to social studies, and one in which they are applied to science problems.

- *Hoffman Gold Series,* Hoffman Information Systems, Inc., 2626 South Peck Road, Monrovia, California.

    This program is composed of six achievement units, each containing ten study units. The ten albums each contain four filmstrips and two records. The first filmstrip and one side of the first record contains the "story." The pupil both sees and hears the story and reads it with the narrator. The second filmstrip and the opposite side of record 1 test recall and comprehension. The pupil records his answer in an answer book at his own rate. The third filmstrip and side one of record 2 measure vocabulary. The fourth filmstrip and the second side of record 2 develop word attack skills. A Mark IV Audio-Visual Projector that handles filmstrips and records comes with the program. The pupils use headphones. The program is designed for three through nine grade levels.

- *Listen: Hear,* Paul S. Amidon & Associates, Inc.

    This is a complete tape-recorded series on how to listen for upper elementary and junior high. The ten tapes are on: what is listening, purposive listening, retentive listening, perceptive listening, critical listening, evaluative listening, attentive listening, deductive listening, stabilization of listening skills, and keeping your listening alive. Response booklets are available for the pupils.

- *Literature Sampler,* Learning Materials, Inc.

    This laboratory previews 144 books from reading grade levels four through nine. There are *how* and *why* questions and explanations of why answers are adequate and inadequate.

- *Peabody Language Development Kits,* American Guidance Service, Inc.

    These kits are designed to stimulate oral language development. They emphasize reception (auditory, tactual, visual), conceptualization (divergent thinking, convergent thinking and associative thinking), and expression (vocal-motor). The materials are for mental age levels of four and one half to eight. The kits consist of a manual of lessons, stimulus cards, "story" and "I Wonder" posters, tapes containing tales, teletalk (two-way intercom set), and two puppets.

- *The Reading Spectrum,* Macmillan Company.

This is a nongraded, multilevel program for building the vital reading skills. It consists of six word analysis booklets, six vocabulary development booklets, and six reading comprehension booklets. Placement tests are provided. The lessons in the skill booklets are self-directing and self-correcting. Included also are two sets of books, sixty in all, ranging from a second-grade reading level to eighth-grade.

- *Reading Improvement Skill File,* The Reading Laboratory, Inc.

This laboratory is an illustrated, graded, color-keyed, multilevel program consisting of 180 exercises for grades six through thirteen in literature, history, natural sciences, social sciences, art, music, humor, sports, and adventure. Both comprehension and vocabulary development are stressed.

- *SRA Advanced Reading Skills Program,* Science Research Associates.

This program for high school level is a series of twenty-four lessons developing speed and flexibility, comprehension, vocabulary, and critical reading.

- *SRA Graph & Picture Study Skills Kit,* Science Research Associates.

This kit for intermediate grades teaches interpretation of graphic forms, charts, diagrams, photographs, and editorial cartoons.

- *SRA Reading for Understanding Laboratory,* Science Research Associates.

These four thousand selections are useful in grades three through twelve for developing critical comprehension. The paragraphs are graduated in difficulty, and cover comprehension, reasoning, inference, interpretation, and meaning. There is a Junior Edition kit (grades three through eight) and a Senior Edition Kit (grades eight through twelve). Each kit contains 400 lesson cards, one placement test, a student record book, forty answer key booklets, and teacher's handbook.

- *SRA Reading Laboratory,* Science Research Associates.

The laboratory consists of a series of graded and skill development materials for grades one through twelve. The primary laboratory includes a phonics program. The elementary laboratory, generally used in grades four through six, consists of materials designed to develop comprehension, vocabulary, rate, and attention span. The laboratory contains power builders (reading selections with comprehension questions), rate builders, and listening skill builders. Following the power builders is a "Learn About Words" section which teaches phonics and structural analysis. Labs available are: Lab IIa (levels two through seven); Lab IIb (levels three through eight); Lab IIc (levels four through nine); Lab IIIa (levels three through twelve); Lab IIIb (levels five through twelve); Lab IVa (levels eight through fourteen). Listening–Note Taking Skill Builders begin at grades eight and nine. Reading Laboratory I: Word Games is the phonics portion of the laboratory. It is a separate laboratory, containing 44 Word Games, a *Phonics Survey* test, a *Teacher's Handbook,* and *My Own Book for Word Building.*

- *Sullivan Reading Materials,* Webster Division, McGraw-Hill Book Company and Behavioral Research Laboratories.

  Series I, II, and III of the Sullivan programmed materials are available through Webster Division. Available in the remedial program are sixteen programmed textbooks, plus a number of correlated readers. Reading readiness books *A, B, C,* and *D* are also available.

- *Tactics in Reading,* I and II, Scott, Foresman and Company.

  These Ready-Skill, Box Exercises include practice on use of context, structural and phonetic analysis, use of the dictionary, imagery, sequence, inferences, and vocabulary building. One kit is for ninth grade; another, for tenth grade. The exercises are printed on fifty cards.

- *Webster Classroom Reading Clinic,* Webster Division, McGraw-Hill Book Company.

  This laboratory, for reading levels two through eight, includes: a set of 224 reading skill cards, each with comprehension questions; one set of sixty-three word wheels for teaching phonics and structural analysis; twenty copies of *Conquests in Reading;* basic sight vocabulary cards; group word teaching game; twenty copies of *The Magic World of Dr. Spello;* and the book *Teachers Guide to Remedial Reading.* Each of the skill cards is color-keyed and filed according to reading difficulty.

COMPREHENSION DEVELOPMENT MATERIALS

In addition to the basal reading series and the reading laboratories there are numerous other materials designed specifically to develop comprehension skills. The following materials are illustrative of the materials available:

- *Activities for Reading Improvement Series*, Steck-Vaughn Company.

    This three-volume series for junior high school students develops reading comprehension, skimming and following directions, vocabulary and word building, and reading for enjoyment.

- *Advanced Skills in Reading*, Macmillan Company.

    These three books for junior high develop paragraph and sentence meaning, context clues, word analysis, skimming, details, following directions, making inferences, locating information, perceiving relationships, using the dictionary and studying, organizing, and remembering.

- *Barnell Loft's Specific Skill Series*, Barnell Loft, Inc.

    These books on levels one through six contain the following titles: *Using the Context, Getting the Facts, Following Directions, Locating the Answer,* and *Working with Sounds.*

- *Basic Reading Skills for Junior High School*, Scott, Foresman and Company.

    This workbook and its companion for the high school cover main ideas, word-form meaning, relationships, context clues, word analysis, phrase and sentence meaning, sensory imagery, dictionary, plot structure, author's purpose, summarizing and organizing, and reference materials.

- *Be a Better Reader Series*, Prentice-Hall, Inc.

    These books for grades four through twelve develop phonics, use and meaning of prefixes and suffixes, syllabication, rapid and critical reading, location of information, and vocabulary development. The emphasis is on content area reading, especially literature, social studies, physical and biological sciences, and the new mathematics.

- *Better Reading*, Globe Book Company.

    These exercises in skimming for main ideas, finding the key thought, in making inferences, in outlining, in detailed reading, in study skills, in organizing, phonetic analysis, and vocabulary improvement are for grades five through eight.

- *Building Reading Confidence,* C. S. Hammond and Company.

    This textbook for grades five and six teaches: recognizing words through taking them apart, how to pronounce words correctly, adding to your vocabulary, getting the facts, understanding paragraphs, reading between the lines, how to read and understand arithmetic problems, how to skim, finding words in the dictionary, following directions, and how to outline, organize, and remember.

- *Building Reading Skills,* McCormick-Mathers Publishing Company.

    These books for grades one through six emphasize word recognition and word, phrase and sentence meanings.

- *Cenco Reading Program—Child Edition,* Cenco Educational Aids.

    This program, for culturally-deprived children who are unable to comprehend basic words beyond the third and fourth grade level, includes a reading pacer, fourteen lesson rolls, student workbook, and a dictionary.

- *Cenco Reading Improvement-Course for Pre-High School,* Cenco Educational Aids.

    This program is similar in nature to the one above. It has eight lesson rolls and is geared to an initial reading speed of one hundred words per minute.

- *Conquests in Reading,* Webster Division, McGraw-Hill Book Company.

    This remedial workbook teaches basic relationships between consonant sounds and symbols, short vowel sounds, sound blending, Dolch words, difficult vowel and consonant sounds, silent letters, compound words, syllabication, prefixes and suffixes.

- *Cowboy Sam Series,* Benefic Press.

    This high-interest series has fifteen titles, including *Cowboy Sam and Big Bill, Cowboy Sam and Miss Lily, Cowboy Sam and the Rustlers,* and *Cowboy Sam and the Rodeo.* Difficulty level ranges from pre-primer to third grade. Workbooks to accompany the readers are available. The following titles are offered: *Workbook for Cowboy Sam and the Fair, Workbook for Cowboy Sam and the Indians, Cowboy Sam and Porky,* and *Workbook for Cowboy Sam and Shorty.* They range from primer to third grade level.

- *Easy Road to Reading Improvement Series,* Marand Publishing Company.

    This is a two-volume remedial reading series, entitled *Pat,*

Lad and the Sleepy Pig and *Rednose the Elf*, for grades one through four, combining look-say and phonic method. Two correlated workbooks accompany the series.

- *The Everyreader Series*, Webster Publishing Company.

    This is a corrective reading program for middle- and upper-grade pupils. These eleven high-interest, low-difficulty readers (fourth-grade difficulty) include such titles as: *The Gold Bug and Other Stories, Cases of Sherlock Holmes, Ivanhoe,* and *Ben Hur.*

- *Gates-Peardon Reading Exercises,* Teachers College Press.

    These materials for grades one through seven develop the ability to read for general significance, to predict outcomes, to understand directions, and to note details. For remedial readers they are useful in grades seven through nine.

- *Language Experiences in Reading,* Level 1, Encyclopaedia Britannica Press, Inc.

    This series, consisting of three books, contains six units and develops oral and written language skills, word recognition and vocabulary skills, oral reading, and writing skills. The series is on kindergarten–first grade level.

- *Maintaining Reading Efficiency,* Developmental Reading Distributors.

    This manual, for junior high to adult level, provides exercises in the application of reading skills.

- *McCall-Crabbs Standard Test Lessons in Reading,* Teachers College Press.

    These paperback materials are designed for grades two to twelve and stress rate of reading and comprehension. Each booklet contains seventy-eight lessons. The selections are followed by multiple-choice type questions. Books and grade levels are as follows: Book A—grade two-four; Book B—grade three-five; Book C—grade four-six; Book D—grade five-seven; and Book E—grade seven-twelve.

- *McCall-Harby Test Lessons in Primary Reading,* Teachers College Press.

    These thirty exercises for first and second graders are accompanied by "yes or no" questions that measure reading ability and comprehension.

- *Modern Reading Skilltext Series,* Charles E. Merrill Company.

    These three books, for junior or senior high use, focus on understanding of words, extending ideas, organizing ideas, studying word structure, and knowing the facts. The exercises contain materials dealing with: recognizing the sounds of words; using context clues; using illustration clues; developing dictionary skills; developing map-reading skills; exploring books; reading advertisements; reading at different speeds; locating information; reading graphs; reading the newspaper; reading directions; reading tables and schedules; reading a highway map; and translating formulas. Two diagnostic tests are furnished in each book. Eighteen skill-tapes accompany each of the books.

- *New Goals in Reading*, Steck Company.

    This remedial worktext is designed especially for slow and retarded readers in the middle grades. While reading interesting stories, the pupil learns to obtain the facts, to see how words are formed, to unlock sounds in words, to use the dictionary, and to deal with phonics and structural analysis.

- *New Horizons through Reading and Literature*, Laidlaw Brothers.

    These three books, for grades seven through nine, cover reading, main ideas, vocabulary, details, outlining, and drawing conclusions.

- *New Practice Readers*, Webster Publishing Company.

    These readers for grades two through eight are designed to improve general comprehension skills. They teach the pupil to notice details, to detect opinion, to identify antecedents of words, to select true statements, and to identify words that are similar in meaning.

- *New Reading Skilltext Series*, Charles E. Merrill Company.

    This developmental reading skills program develops skill in getting information, understanding ideas, organizing ideas, making judgments, and studying words. Titles offered are: *Bibs* (grade one), *Nicky* (grade two), *Uncle Funny Bunny* (grade three), *Uncle Ben* (grade four), *Tom Trott* (grade five), and *Pat, the Pilot* (grade six).

- *Progress in Reading*, Steck Company.

    This book for grade seven develops interpretation, critical reading, use of reference tools, reading poetry, skimming, and speed.

- *Read-Aloud Books,* Follett Publishing Company.

  These forty-one books, for use in project Head Start on levels kindergarten through grade three, include such titles as: *Michael Angelo Mouse, A Cow in the House, Martin's Mice, Leander the Gander, Chee Chee and Keeko, The Adventures of Mr. Gilfump, Nail Soup,* etc.

- *Reading Aids Through the Grades,* Bureau of Publications.

  The book offers three hundred activities for grades one through eight useful in remedial programs.

- *Reading Attainment System,* Grolier Educational Corporation.

  This remedial program on third-fourth grade level includes 120 Reading selections, skill cards, answer keys, and student record books.

- *Reading Caravan Series,* D. C. Heath and Company.

  These texts, usable remedially on junior high level and entitled *Peacock Lane, Silver Web,* and *Treasure Gold,* develop comprehension, interpretation and critical thinking, study skills, appreciation, vocabulary, listening skills, oral interpretation, and reading rate.

- *Reader's Digest Reading Skill Builder,* Reader's Digest Services, Inc.

  These readers are useful for independent reading or for corrective instruction in grades two through eight. They develop comprehension and word power.

- *Reading Essentials Series,* Steck-Vaughn Company.

  This is a cumulative skills-building program for grades one through eight consisting of ten worktexts. The worktexts are: *Come and Play, Fun Time, Play Time, Work Time, New Avenues in Reading, New Journeys in Reading, New Adventures in Reading, Progress in Reading, Mastery in Reading* and *New Goals in Reading.*

- *Reading for Meaning Series,* J. B. Lippincott Co.

  This series of three workbooks for grades four through twelve is designed to improve comprehension and speed. Workbooks four and five concentrate on word meanings, total meaning, central thought, and detailed meanings. Workbooks six through twelve include organization and summarization.

- *Reading Skillbooks,* American Book Company.

    These two workbooks, for junior high use, develop word recognition skills, interpretation skills, speed reading skills, and library skills.

- *Reading-Thinking Skills,* Continental Press, Inc.

    These materials, pre-primer level through grade six, develop critical thinking skills. They cover word meaning, relationships, evaluation, inference, generalization, selection, and organization. All materials are available in individual pupil books as well as in carbon masters for liquid duplicating.

- *Reading Workbooks: We Go to School; We Like to Read Books I, II, III,* Harlow Publishing Corporation.

    These four workbooks for grades one through three emphasize vocabulary development, word meanings, proper reading habits, and the teaching of following directions, identification of main ideas, and content comprehension.

- Schmitt, Hall and McCreary Materials.

    The following materials are offered:
    1. *The New A B C Book:* This silent reader and workbook is designed for first graders. It provides an automatic test of the pupil's comprehension.
    2. *First Steps in Reading:* This is a pre-primer workbook that develops word and sentence mastery.
    3. *The New Read and Do:* This book develops understanding and thought reading by requiring the pupil to read and then to do what the words say.
    4. *Something New to Do:* This is a silent reader and workbook with practical comprehension tests for use in advanced first grade or second grade.

- *Sonic Readers,* Educational Projects.

    The *Sonic Reader* is actually an illustrated book with a recorded narration of the story in one compact self-contained unit. Titles available are: *The Night Before Christmas, Mother Goose Favorites, Tommy and His Drum, What Time Is It, Bozo and His ABC Zoo, Bozo's Five Happy Rules, Santa's Missing Reindeer, Little Red Riding Hood, Sylvester: The Little Duck Who Lost His Quack,* etc.

- *Turner-Livingstone Reading Series,* Follett Publishing Company.

  These workbooks for secondary use contain such titles as *The Person You Are, The Money You Spend, The Family You Belong To, The Jobs You Get,* and *The Friends You Make.* These materials develop comprehension and vocabulary skills. They are especially useful with the culturally deprived adolescent, slow learners, and remedial classes.

- *Webster's New Practice Readers,* Webster Publishing Company.

  These high-interest readers are designed for grades two through eight.

Word Attack Materials

Numerous materials also are available for the teaching of word attack skills. The materials listed here offer complete programs in phonetic and structural analysis, including pronunciation, accent, and syllabication. They offer exercises in visual-motor coordination, the use of thinking and context in the identification of words and in word, phrase, and sentence building. They emphasize perceptual skills, visual discrimination, and the development of left-to-right movement in reading.

- *Accelerated Progressive Choice Program,* Institute of Educational Research, Inc., Washington, D.C.

  This program proceeds from phonetically consistent letters to phonetically consistent compounds or letter groups to varying sounds for the same letter and varying letters for the same sound.

- *Alphy's Show and Tell Kits,* Education Services Press.

  The first book teaches the names of the letters of the alphabet, their shapes, the alphabetical sequence, left-to-right projection, writing of the letters, and initial sounds.

- *American Phonetic Reader,* Expression Company.

  This first reader, in which the lessons are graded, introduces phonetic symbols gradually.

- *A to Z Phonics Charts,* Educational Publishing Corporation.

  This is a set of twelve charts teaching the basic elements of phonics. A manual, *A Guide to Teaching Phonics,* is provided to accompany the use of the charts.

- *Audio-Visual Charts*, O'Connor Reading Clinic Publishing Company.

    Designed for primary and upper elementary grades, these charts teach homophonous and homogeneous words. Cards emphasize such aspects as the *f* sound of *ph*, three sounds for *d*, the sound of *gh*, and the *z* sound of *s*.

- *Basic Reading*, J. B. Lippincott Company.

    This is a program for grades one through eight, emphasizing a highly phonetic approach, and is accompanied by workbook and filmstrip materials.

- *Building Pre-Reading Skills: Kit A and Kit B*, Ginn and Company.

    Kit A contains sixteen large illustrations, sixty smaller illustrations, and one hundred and twelve still smaller illustrations. It is designed to help children develop the language, thinking, and perception skills necessary to success in learning to read.

    Kit B includes picture cards, word cards, letter cards, and a teacher's manual. The major purposes of Kit B are:
    1. To develop awareness of likenesses and differences in the initial sounds of spoken words.
    2. To develop auditory perception of the sounds represented by fifteen consonants in the beginning position (*b, c, d, f, g, h, j, l, m, n, p, r, s, t, w*).
    3. To teach association of the fifteen consonant sounds with the names and forms of the letters which represent them (phoneme-grapheme relationship).
    4. To teach use of context plus initial sounds to determine an oral response.
    5. To teach the lower-case and capital-letter forms of fifteen consonants.

- *Beckley-Cardy Aids for Teaching Phonics*, Beckley-Cardy Company.

    1. *Phonics for Reading* (for slow readers)
    2. *Phonetic Word Wheel* (grades two and three)
    3. *Learn to Read Workbooks*

        These two workbooks, the first of which is for grades one, two, and three and the second of which is for grades four and above, provide a program in phonics.

    4. *Phonics Fun* (two workbooks for grades one and two)
    5. *Building Words* (phonics workbook for first grade)

6. *Phonics Skilltexts* (phonics workbooks for grades one through five)

- *Building Reading Skills,* McCormick-Mathers Publishing Company, Inc.

    This phonic series contains workbooks with phonics exercises for grades one through six. Included is a box of Teacher's Phonics Skill Builders—eighty-seven cards and a guidebook.

- *Conquests in Reading,* Webster Division, McGraw-Hill Book Company.

    This workbook, for grades four through six, is designed to review structural and phonetic skills by dealing with the basic relationships between consonant sounds and symbols, short vowel sounds, sound blending, Dolch's 220 Basic Sight Words, silent letters, compound words, syllabication, prefixes and suffixes.

- *Continental Basic Reading Series,* Continental Press, Inc.

    This series, for grades one and two, includes the following materials:

    a. Reading Readiness Materials for Kindergarten and Grade One
      Rhyming, I and *II*
      Visual Motor Skills, I and *II*
      Beginning Sounds, I and *II*
      Independent Activities, I and *II*
      Thinking Skills, I and *II*
    b. *We Get Ready to Read*—————————pre-primer
    c. *We Get Ready to Read*—————————primer
    d. *We Learn to Read* —————————grade one
    e. *We Learn to Read*—————————grade one
    f. *ABC Book*—————————————grades one and two
    g. *Reading-Thinking Skills*—————————grade two

- *Cordts Phonetic Books,* Benefic Press.

    Three books, *I Can Read, Hear Me Read,* and *Reading's Easy,* make up this set for levels one, two and three.

- *Early to Read Series,* Initial Teaching Alphabet Publications.

    This series by Mazurkiewicz and Tanyzer develops a phonetic alphabet of forty-four lower-case characters which represent the phonemes of the language. All the books and workbooks are designed for grade one. The book titles are: *Rides, Dinosaur Ben, Houses, A Game of Ball, The Yo-Yo Contest, Find a Way, The*

Tricks, The Bear That Moped, and *Mr. Pickle's Surprise.* Available also are an alphabet book, a number book, sound symbol cards, vocabulary cards, and a word building kit.

• *Eye and Ear Fun,* Webster Publishing Company.

This is a phonics program for grades one through six. A separate book is provided for each of the first three grades; a fourth covers grades four through six.

• *A First Course in Phonic Reading,* Educators Publishing Service.

This first course is written for children in second and third grade. *A Second Course in Phonic Reading I and II* (grades four and five) is also available. These books are primarily intended for remedial reading.

• *First Phonics,* Educators Publishing Service.

This program of two manuals, with *Stories for First Phonics* and Drill Cards, is intended for first-grade children. It teaches phonics through the use of pictures.

• *A First Course in Remedial Reading,* Educators Publishing Service.

This book for second and third-graders emphasizes phonic and kinesthetic approaches. In preparation are *A Second Course in Remedial Reading* (fourth and fifth grades) and *A Third Course in Remedial Reading* (junior high school).

• *Flight Through Wordland,* Continental Press, Inc.

These thirty lessons for grade four deal with consonant digraphs and blends, long and short vowels, dictionary work, diacritical markings, syllables, prefixes, and suffixes. The lessons are available for duplication.

• *Happy Times with Sounds Series,* Allyn and Bacon, Inc.

This series consists of four books that give a complete course in phonics.

• *Hayes Mastery Phonics Workbooks,* Beckley-Cardy Company.

This series consists of six books that give a complete coverage of the phonic skills.

• *I Learn to Read,* Kenworthy Educational Service.

These two workbooks for grades one through four give a simplified course in phonics.

- *Improving Word Skills,* Educators Publishing Service.

  This is a pupil workbook and an accompanying teacher's manual. It is designed for the intermediate grades and covers phonics, syllabication, and word parts.

- *Instructor Basic Phonics Series,* F. A. Owen Publishing Company.

  This series contains five sets of materials: (1) Initial consonant sounds for grade one; (2) Vowel sounds for grades one and two; (3) Advanced consonants (blends) and prepositions for grades two and three; (4) Compounds, suffixes, prefixes, and syllables for two and three; and (5) Contractions and advanced phonic forms for grades three through five.

- *It's Time for Phonics,* Webster Publishing Company.

  These four workbooks for grades kindergarten through three teach phonics in listening, speaking, reading, and writing.

- *Landon Phonics Program,* Chandler Publishing Company.

  This phonics program for kindergarten through second grade is designed to supplement basic reading series. The program consists of nineteen records (or tapes) and seventy-six worksheets.

- *Learning the Letters,* Educators Publishing Service.

  This series of six booklets teaches the letters of the alphabet, their sounds and common blends. It is intended primarily for remedial use.

- *Lift-Off to Reading,* Science Research Associates.

  This program for grades one through six is designed to provide a basal program to pupils who have poor motor, visual, verbal, or perceptual skills or who are mentally retarded or emotionally disturbed. It teaches reading for meaning and controls the sequence of letter presentations and letter sound-letter shape relations.

- *Magic "e,"* Leona Lennon, Spartanburg, South Carolina.

  This simple cardboard device is designed for teaching vowel sounds and the magic e principle. The adjoining wheels offer initial and final consonants and blends, while a slide between them varies the median vowel. A third wheel, superimposed on the second, adds a final e to show its effect upon the vowel sound.

- *My Word Study Book,* Educational Service, Inc.

  This series of six books, one for each grade, emphasizes

phonetic sounds, syllabication, likenesses and differences, prefixes, and suffixes.

- *New Phonics Skilltexts,* Charles E. Merrill Books, Inc.

   These texts develop phonic skills, structural-analysis skills, comprehension skills, and listening skills. The books range from grades one through six. Book D, for grades four through six, introduces speech sounds, presents sounds in context, develops the association between the sound and the letter, and illustrates the phonic principle.

- *Phonetic Keys to Reading,* Economy Company.

   This is a basal series for grades one through three emphasizing phonics from the beginning. The series consists of *Tag,* the pre-primer; *Dot and Jim,* the primer; *All Around,* the first reader; *Through Happy Hours, As Days Go By,* and *Happy Hours,* the second-grade readers; and *Down Right Roads* and *Tales to Enjoy,* the fourth-grade readers. The series is accompanied by teacher manuals, phonetic cards and charts, and picture cards. The intermediate program is termed *Keys to Independence in Reading.*

- *A Phonetic Reader Series,* Educators Publishing Service.

   These six books use phonetic methods. Although designed for the elementary grades, these readers could be valuable in a remedial junior high situation. Titles included are: *Puss in Boots; Jack, the Giant Giller; Jack and the Beanstalk; Alladin and the Wonderful Lamp; Ali Baba and the Forty Thieves;* and *Robinson Crusoe.*

- *Phonics Is Fun,* Modern Curriculum Press.

   These six books for grades one through three are accompanied by three Phonics Workbooks.

- *Phonics We Use,* Lyons and Carnahan.

   This is a phonics program for grades one through eight.

- *Phonics Slide Rule,* Phonics, 30690 Providence Road, Cleveland.

   This slide rule is useful in teaching initial consonants, long and short vowels, and initial consonant blends and digraphs.

- *Phonics Workbooks,* Modern Curriculum Press.

   This set of three workbooks for grades one through three accompanies Phonics Is Fun books for each grade level. The *Phonics Is Fun* program consists of six books for grades one through three.

- *Phonovisual Skill Builders,* Phonovisual Products Inc.

    Accompanying the Consonant Chart and Method Book are the Readiness Book, the Transition Book, the Game Book, the Consonant Workbook, the Vowel Workbook, the Record of Sounds, the Consonant Flipstrips, the Vowel Flipstrips, the Magnetic Boards, Phonic Rummy Games, Consonant Picture Pack, and the Vowel Picture Pack.

- *A Practice Workbook on Phonetic Instruction,* Hough Community Project, Cleveland, Ohio.

    This workbook is designed for junior high school use.

- *Readiness for Learning Workbook,* J. B. Lippincott.

    The *Readiness for Learning Workbook* provides a carefully structured sequence of perceptual-motor training for kindergarteners or children beginning first grade. It is divided into three levels of training. The first level deals with large-muscle, bilateral activities, aimed at developing coordination, control, comprehension of simple instructions, and conscious awareness of kinesthetic stimuli.

    The second level is concerned with the development of unilateral controls for the establishment of eye-, hand-, and foot-dominance. The top level introduces some of the more specific skills needed in reading, such as knowledge of letter formations, perception of letter-groupings, and the association of printed symbols with the spoken sounds and words they represent.

- *Reading A,* Systems for Education, Inc.

    Reading A, by Doman and Delacato, emphasizes the development of the child's perceptual ability. It consists of 330 Giant Word Cards, one Giant Teaching Book, a color picture book entitled *My Magic Words,* Make It Books, a Teacher's Manual, and thirty-two-frame, four-color slide film of *My Magic Words,* with sound recording pronouncing the words.

- *Reading with Me Series,* Teachers College, Columbia University.

    This series by Allen and Allen is a linguistic approach for teaching reading to pre-school and primary grade children. The child learns the shape of the letters, common spellings for sounds, and learns to read whole sentences. Included are: Story Booklet, Rhyming Words and Simple Sentences Booklet, Alphabet Cards and Anagram Cards.

- *Reading in High Gear,* Science Research Associates.

  This series of workbooks takes the culturally disadvantaged child and nonreader through a basic reading program. It is designed for grades seven through twelve and adult level.

- *Reading Preparation Books,* Beckley-Cardy Company.

  These two books develop left-to-right eye movements and motor coordination.

- *Reading Seatwork Series,* Webster Publishing Company.

  This series of workbooks for preprimer, primer, first grade, and second grade is designed to develop word-recognition skills.

- *Reading Skills,* Holt, Rinehart and Winston, Inc.

  This text, with accompanying text booklet and shutter cards, is directed toward poorer readers at the junior high level. The text includes training the eye to move correctly along the line, correcting lip movement, and subvocal meaning.

- *Remedial Training for Children with Specific Disability in Reading, Spelling, and Penmanship,* Educators Publishing Service.

  This manual comes with phonetic drill cards, phonetic word cards, *Syllable Concept, Little Stories, Introduction of Diphthongs,* and *Dictionary Technique.*

- *Rolling Phonics,* Scott, Foresman and Company.

  This is a set of blocks to be used in teaching phonics, both consonants and vowels. Teacher guides are available. The set is a part of the *Linguistic Block Series,* which includes *First Rolling Reader, Second Rolling Reader,* and *Third Rolling Reader.*

- *Seatwork Books,* Benton Review Publishing Company.

  This series of five books is designed to develop a basic vocabulary. The books are entitled: *Let's Get Started, Fun with Words and Pictures, Fun with Words—Grade I, Fun with Words—Grade II,* and *More Fun with Words—Grade III.*

- *The Sound Way Series,* Benton Review Publishing Company.

  These two books develop the pupil's phonic skills.

- *Sounds We Use,* Wilcox and Follett.

  These three books are useful in grades one through three.

- *Speech-to-Print Phonics,* Harcourt, Brace and World.

This kit is a reading-readiness program. It contains flash cards, phonic lessons, and alphabet and consonant blend pads. Each lesson outlines an inductive introduction to each sound, words in which the sound is used, oral exercises with key words, and practice with flash cards and pupil pads.

- *Steps to Mastery of Words,* Educational Services, Inc.

These workbooks are designed for grades one through six and are accompanied by eight records.

- *Structural Reading Series,* F. W. Singer and Company.

This series begins with the spoken word as the basis of sound analysis. A readiness book, two first-grade readers, two second-grade readers, and phrase cards are available.

- *Syllabascope Materials,* Wordcrafters Guild.

This set of materials consists of: *Teacher and Student Syllabascopes. Christie Word Set:* This contains sixty words of highest frequency in six intermediate readers series; *220 Basic Sight Words; Student Word Set; Guideword Dictionary, and Syllabication Principles.*

The materials are useful in teaching vocabulary, spelling, principles of word analysis, and syllabication. Using sliding panels, the pupil isolates in turn blends, affixes, and syllables from the total word so that he can study them individually and thus arrive at the total word.

- *Syllable Concept,* Anna Gillingham.

These materials consist of sixty-four cards designed for grades three and up and develop the syllabication skill.

- *Through Space to Wordland,* Continental Press, Inc.

These thirty lessons on fifth-grade level, available for duplication, deal with the dictionary, word recognition, and word analysis.

- *Time for Phonics,* Webster Division, McGraw-Hill Book Company.

This is a phonics program for kindergarten through grade three.

Book R is on the readiness level; Book A helps the pupil to

recognize consonant sounds, the five short vowel sounds, and the six consonant digraphs; Book B introduces the consonant blends, the long vowels, the vowel digraphs, phonic families, *y* as a vowel, long and short *oo*, and the diphthongs *ow-ou*, and *oy-oi*. Book C completes the phonics program.

- *Ways to Read Words, More Ways to Read Words,* and *Learning About Words,* Bureau of Publications.

These three books develop fundamental phonic skills usually taught in grades two through four.

- *Webster Word Wheels,* Revised, Webster Publishing Company.

These sixty-three wheels help teach consonant blends, prefixes, suffixes, and word blending. There are seventeen beginning blend wheels, twenty prefix wheels, eighteen suffix wheels, and eight two-letter consonant wheels.

- *Word Analysis Charts,* Webster Publishing Company.

These five charts are entitled: Sounds the Letters Make, One-Syllable Words, Letters That Work Together, Prefixes Help Unlock Big Words, and Reading Big Words. They deal with consonant sounds, vowels, speech blends, vowel digraphs, prefixes, and syllabication.

- *Word Attack: A Way to Better Reading,* Harcourt, Brace and World.

This textbook is intended for remedial reading in high school. It uses contextual, auditory, structural, visual, and kinesthetic approaches. The exercises give training in the association of the printed symbol with the sound, utilization of word clues, analysis of prefixes, suffixes, and word roots, and development of dictionary skills.

- *Word Attack Manual,* Educators Publishing Service.

This manual is designed to strengthen word recognition and word meaning skill. It is to be used with junior high school youngsters. It covers: closed and open syllables, long and short vowels, silent *e*; rules of syllable division; consonant letters and blends; digraphs; diphthongs; vowel *r* combinations; compound words, prefixes, and suffixes; accent; using the dictionary; *sh* sound of *ci, si,* and *ti*; the *y* sound of *i,* and the long *e* sound of *i.*

- *Word Attack Series*, Teachers College Press.

    This series of workbooks for grades two through four offers children a wide variety of approaches to reading new words.

- *Word Clues*, Educational Developmental Laboratories.

    This series, for grades seven through thirteen, teaches word knowledge by requiring the learner to divide the word into syllables, to pronounce it, to read it in a sentence, and to write a definition. It is accompanied by tests, flash-x sets with filmstrips and discs, and tach-x sets with filmstrips.

- *Wordland Series*, Continental Press.

    This is a complete phonics program for grade one through five, with the following titles: *Fun in Wordland*, grade one; *A Trip Through Wordland*, grade two; *Adventures in Wordland*, grade three; *A Flight Through Wordland*, grade four; and *Through Space to Wordland*, grade five.

- *Words in Color*, Learning Materials, Inc.

    This program, described in Chapter 5, contains: *Words in Color: Background and Principles*, twenty-one colored charts, Phonic Code (eight charts in color), Word Cards, Books 1, 2, 3, *Word Building Book, Book of Stories*, and Worksheets.

- *Writing Road to Reading*, Whiteside, Inc.

    This book explains the Unified Phonics Method, using seventy phonogram cards. Cards may be reproduced or bought separately.

Audio-visual materials

Audio-visual materials are used in reading to prepare the pupil for reading, to get his attention, to develop background, to introduce and illustrate new words, and to extend interest and skills.

Among the materials listed in this section are recordings, films, correlated records, textfilms, and audio-books. They cover such areas as readiness, word recognition, comprehension, and critical reading. There are materials directed toward improvement in aural imagery, rhyming, listening, phonics, enunciation, and articulation. Some materials emphasize such study-type reading skills as outlining and note-making. And some materials emphasize choral speaking, appreciation for literature, dictionary skills, library skills, and rate of reading.

- *Basic Primary Phonics Filmstrips Series,* Society for Visual Education.

  This series for grades one through three includes:
  1. Initial Consonant Sounds—b, d, p (19 frames)
  2. Initial Consonant Sounds—h, l, f, k (23 frames)
  3. Initial Consonant Sounds—m, n, t, j (24 frames)
  4. Initial Consonant Sounds—r, s, v, w (25 frames)
  5. Initial Consonant Sounds—c, g, y, q (30 frames)
  6. L and W Blends—bl, cl, fl, gl, pl, sl, sw, tw (30 frames)
  7. R Blends—br, cr, dr, fr, gr, pr, tr (25 frames)
  8. S Blends—sc, sk, sm, sn, sp, st (25 frames)
  9. Two-letter Sounds—ch, sh, wh, ph, th (25 frames)
  10. Two- and three-letter combinations—kn, gn, wr, nd, ng, ck, nk, nt, gh, sch, squ, spl, spr, scr str, thr (29 frames)
  11. Rhyming Words and Final Consonant Sounds (31 frames)
  12. Short Vowel Sounds (24 frames)
  13. Long Vowel Sounds (25 frames)
  14. Y Vowel Sounds (26 frames)
  15. Two-Letter Vowels (25 frames)
  16. Two-Letter Combinations (oo, ow, ou, oi, oy, aw, au—29 frames)
  17. Vowels controlled by R (28 frames)

- *Basic Reading Series,* Society for Visual Education, Inc.

  This basic reading series, in textfilm form to accompany the Lippincott Reading Series, consists of fifty-one filmstrips.

- *Coronet Films,* Coronet Films, Inc.

  1. "Fun with Speech Sounds"—covers the vowels and consonants *p, m, l, r, th,* and *ch* and is designed for the primary level.
  2. "Reading for Beginners: Word Sounds."
  3. "Do Words Ever Fool You?"—deals with listening development (intermediate level).
  4. "Listen Well, Learn Well"—deals with the problems of critical reading (intermediate level).
  5. "Making Sense with Outlines"—teaches outlining (intermediate level).
  6. "We Discover the Dictionary"—intermediate level.
  7. "Who Makes Words?"—word origins—intermediate level.

8. "Maps Are Fun"—how to make and read maps—intermediate level.
9. "How to Read a Book"—junior high.
10. "How to Remember"—junior high.
11. "How to Study"—junior high.
12. "Importance of Making Notes"—junior high.
13. "Improve Your Study Habits"—junior high.
14. "Building an Outline."
15. "Reading Improvement: Comprehension Skills."
16. "Reading Improvement: Effective Speeds."
17. "Reading Improvement: Word Recognition Skills."

• *Dandy Dog's Early Learning Program*, American Book Company.

This is a program for nursery schools, kindergartens, head-start programs, early first grades, programs for slow learners, and non-English speaking children. The program consists of ten "See and Say" story picture books, five "See and Say" story records, two "Do and Learn" records, fourteen "Learning Activities," fourteen "Learning Charts," twenty-eight "Learning Chart Pads," forty-six "Animated Slides" and the teacher's planbook and handbook.

• *EDL Filmstrips*, Educational Developmental Laboratories.

Filmstrips are available from readiness to adult levels. Readiness films are designed to develop concentration, observation, retention, discrimination, and logical reasoning while teaching sixty words. In the first grade the pupil reads stories and adds 218 new words.

• *Filmstrips for Practice in Phonetic Skills*, Scott, Foresman & Co.

There are four filmstrips for the first grade.

• *The Forty Sounds of English*, Initial Teaching Alphabet Publications, Inc.

This film teaches the use of the initial teaching alphabet approach to reading instruction.

• *Fundamentals of Reading*, Eye Gate House.

These nine filmstrips are suitable for remedial junior high use and provide drill in mechanics of reading, phonetics, and reading comprehension.

• *Imperial Instructional Tapes*, Imperial Productions, Inc., Kankakee, Illinois.

The Imperial primary reading program for grades one through

three is a self-teaching program emphasizing readiness, study skills, comprehension skills, and word-attack skills. The program consists of forty tapes. Available from the same company is "The Easy Way to Difficult Sounds" program. This is a remedial phonic program on tape and chart. Available also is "The Magic Road to Sounds" program, on chart and tape, and "Learning the Alphabet and Its Sounds with Amos and his Friends."

- *Language Master,* Hoover Brothers, Kansas City.

   For use with the language master machine are programs usable on all grade-levels: The Vocabulary Builder Program, the Word-Picture Program, the Language-Stimulation Program, the Sounds of English Program, and the Phonics Program.

- *Listen and Do,* Houghton Mifflin Company.

   Sixteen records, duplication masters for pupil worksheets, and a teacher's guide comprise the kit. It teaches the use of the context and initial sound in recognizing new words.

- *Listen and Learn with Phonics,* Americana Interstate Corporation.

   This is a home course in phonics based on records and booklets, plus word and letterstrips. The beginner's set is used with children up to and including second grade and consists of four illustrated booklets and three unbreakable records. An advanced set, the remedial set, is similar to the first, but contains only two records. Accompanying the sets are Funagrams, a domino-like game that uses cardboard strips with phonograms on one end and consonants and consonant blends on the other, and the L & L Educational Game Set, an educational word-building game.

- *Listen and Learn with Phonics Records,* Beckley-Cardy Company.

   Four phonics books, three 78 rpm. records, Turn-a-Word Wheel, and Word Chart are the materials in this program. The set is usable in conjunction with any primers and readers.

- *Listen and Read Program,* Educational Developmental Laboratories.

   This series of thirty tapes and workbook helps the pupil to listen better, to understand words, sentences, and paragraphs, and introduces him to intensive, study-type reading, to critical reading, and to listening. The materials are on a junior high–high school level.

- *New Auditory Visual Response Phonics,* Polyphone Company.

   This phonics program is a series of six teaching tapes, textbook, and worksheets to accompany the tapes and, if desired, the Poly-phone, a ten- or fifteen-outlet listening center. Letter sounds, blends, and various combinations are presented by tape and responded to on the worksheets with the aid of related pictures.

- *Play 'n Talk Phonics Course on Records,* P.O. Box 18804, Oklahoma City.

   There are two series, containing five records and two books. Also available in a *Play 'n Talk Game.*

- *Read Along with Me,* Programmed Records Inc., 154 Nassau Street, New York 38, New York.

   This twelve-inch LP record and accompanying booklet are de-signed for the home instruction of beginning readers. The child follows the booklet as the words are spoken on the record.

- *Readiness for Learning: A Program for Visual and Auditory Per-ceptual-Motor Training,* J. B. Lippincott Company.

   This program provides visual and auditory perceptual-motor training for kindergarten–first grade. It involves bilateral and uni-lateral training and letter and word knowledge.

- *The Reading Series,* Pacific Productions.

   This series of forty-one color filmstrips covers such areas as: learning the use of the dictionary, phonetic analysis—vowels, struc-tural analysis, reading for understanding, and using books efficiently.

- *Sounds for Young Readers,* Educational Record Sales.

   This series from kindergarten to grade five (six records in all) is designed to help children with specific phonetic and auditory dis-criminatory difficulties.

- *Sound Skills for Upper Grades,* Educational Record Sales.

   These six records, for grades five through nine, provide help in consonant and vowel recognition and in word analysis.

- *Sounds We Use,* Ginn and Company.

   These are twelve filmstrips, eight on consonants and four on vowels.

- *The Sound Way to Easy Reading,* Brenner-Davis Phonics, Inc.

   This consists of four records and fifteen wall charts.

- *Tachist-o-Films,* Learning Through Seeing, Inc.

   These filmstrips on four levels, primary (grades one through

three), elementary (grades four through six), junior high (grades
seven through nine), and senior high (grades ten through twelve)
develop attention and concentration, build vocabulary, develop
phrase reading and unitary seeing, and improve retention, comprehension, and reading rate. Special filmstrips cover phonics, prefix
and suffix mastery, and word and phrase mastery. A Tachist-o-Viewer
is available.

- *Telezonia,* Bell Telephone Company.

  Designed for grades four through nine this unit includes tele-
  phones and fifty-one filmstrips. It teaches such reading skills as
  following directions and skimming.

- *Visual-Linguistic Basic Reading Series,* Education Press; Visual
  Products Division, 3M Company, Box 3344, St. Paul, Minnesota.

  This program combines the visual, linguistic, listening, contextual, and programmed approaches. It consists of *Alphy's Show
  and Tell,* which is an alphabet unit; the pre-primers, *Alphy's Cat*
  and *Alphy's Word Kit,* two primers (*Canny Cat* and *Baby Big Ear*),
  one reader (*Bob's Wish Cap*), four programmed texts, and printed
  originals for making transparencies.

- *Visual Perception Skills,* Educational Record Sales.

  These seven color filmstrips deal with visual memory, visual
  motor coordination, visual constancy, visual discrimination, visuali-
  zation, figure–ground perception, and visual matching.

- *Wheel Transparencies,* Cambosco Scientific Co., Inc.

  These fifty-nine wheel transparencies for use with the overhead
  projector teach beginning consonant sounds, beginning consonant
  blends, long and short vowel sounds, and vowel clues.

Mechanical devices

We have grouped mechanical devices into tachistoscopes,
accelerating devices, and other reading-related machines.

TACHISTOSCOPES

Tachistoscopes expose numbers, letters, words, or other images for short periods of time, usually ranging from 1/100th second to 1½ seconds. The tachistoscope, whether individual or
group, primarily develops the person's perceptual intake skills.

By forcing the pupil to cope with intake speeds of ⅒ of a second or less, the tachistoscope requires the pupil to see more rapidly, more accurately, and more orderly; to pay better attention to what was seen; and to organize what he has seen. He also has to develop better directional attack.

Tachistoscopic training has greatest value in the elementary years when the pupil is learning to "see." Since much of the material is designed to develop accuracy of seeing and the retention of the particular placement of certain elements (for example, the pupil needs to see and remember 24571 in a definite order), it may have value in a word attack program.

Here are some tachistoscopes available today:

- *AVR Eye-Span Trainer* (AVR E-S-T 10), Audio-Visual Research.

    This plastic mechanism offers a simple hand-operated shutter device for training in rapid recognition of numbers, words, money amounts, phrases, etc. Slides are available for elementary, junior high, senior high, college, and adult level.

- *AVR Flash-Tachment,* Audio-Visual Research.

    This is a simple attachment that converts any filmstrip projector into a tachistoscope. Speeds range from 1/25 to 1/100 of a second.

- *EDL Flash-X,* Educational Developmental Laboratories.

    In this device the pupil flicks the tab opening the shutter device for 1/25 of a second. The pupil records what he saw and then checks his answer. Discs are provided covering such areas as readiness, primary recognition, numbers, sight vocabulary, arithmetic, and spelling.

- *EDL Tach-X Tachistoscope,* Educational Developmental Laboratories.

    Images (numbers, pictures, letters or words) can be projected on a screen for as long as 1½ seconds or as briefly as 1/100 of a second. The Tach-X is designed to develop visual discrimination and memory. Filmstrips range from the readiness to adult level. Exercises such as the following are very effective. "Watch the screen. Ready?" The Tach-X flashes y j j j j. "Which letter was different?" The letters are shown again so the pupil can check for accuracy. Constant illumination is maintained and the words flash in and out of focus.

- *Electro-Tach*, Lafayette Instrument Company.

   This is a near-point tachistoscopic training instrument for use at all age levels. The exposures are electronically controlled and range from 1/100 to 1 second, Training cards available cover digits, jumbled letters, words, phrases, sentences, and familiar objects.

- *Flashmaster*, Keystone View Company.

   This device used with overhead projector forms a tachistoscope. The flashmeter is multibladed and has the following times: 1/2, 1/5, 1/10, 1/25, 1/50, 1/100 second.

- *Phrase Flasher*, Reading Laboratory, Inc.

   This tachistoscope device is accompanied by a 940-card set of simple digits, words, and paragraphs.

- *Rapid Reading Kit*, Better Reading Program, Inc.

   This is a self-help program designed to develop speed in comprehension. It includes: The Visualizer, practice slides, *Reading Skill Book*, *Progress Records*, *Improvement Guide*, and two *Reading Raters*. Phrases are up to five words long and exposure is up to 1/100 second.

- *Speed-I-O-Scope*, Society for Visual Education.

   This flash mechanism with shutter-like device mounts on a standard still projector. Speeds range from 1/100 second to 1 second.

- *Tachistoscope*, Lafayette Instrument Company.

   This all-purpose group tachistoscope permits exposures of 1, 1/2, 1/10, 1/25, 1/50, and 1/100 seconds. It is usable with any make of projector. The tachistoscopic attachment is adaptable to all makes of projectors.

- *Tachisto-Flasher*, Science Research Associates.

   This shutter mechanism, when set in front of the lens of a filmstrip projector, converts it into a tachistoscope.

- *Tachisto-Viewer*, Learning Through Seeing, Inc.

   This tachistoscope filmstrip viewer has speeds of 1/5 to 1/40 second. Filmstrips are provided to develop word-recognition skills, spelling skills, and speed of visual perception.

ACCELERATING DEVICES

The accelerating devices provide rate training for the competent readers. Such devices lead to a reduction in fixations and regressions, better attention and concentration, more rapid thinking, and improved organization of what is read. Accelerating devices are most useful in the upper elementary years and in junior high school.

Here is a list of some accelerators on the market today:

- *AVR Reading Rateometer*, Audio-Visual Research.

  Three models of this machine are available. The standard model (model A) has a range of from 70 to 2,500 words per minute. Model B offers a range from 20 to 500 words per minute. Model C offers a range of 140 to 5,000 words per minute. Each model is equipped with a pacing T-bar that moves down the page at a constant rate.

- *Cenco Pacer*, Cenco Center, 2600 South Kostner Avenue, Chicago, Illinois.

  A reading pacer with fourteen sequential lesson rolls and a student workbook form the materials for this program usable with the slow learner.

- *Controlled Reader*, Educational Developmental Laboratories.

  A moving slot (picture) travels from left to right across the screen, or a full line may be uncovered at a time. It permits speeds of from 60 to 1,000 words per minute. Filmstrips are available from the kindergarten to the adult level, and question books and story books accompany each level.

- *Craig Reader*, Craig Research, Inc.

  The Craig Reader adjusts to permit reading speeds of 100 to 2,000 words per minute. The machine uses slide units rather than film. The slides contain twelve film frames in each slide. Twelve programs from elementary to university level are available.

- *EDL Controlled Reader Jr.*

  This machine is similar to the Controlled Reader but is more economical for individual use.

- *Keystone Reading Pacer*, Keystone View Company.

  This device has a pointer which moves at speeds from 50 to 1,000 words per minute. The pacer shuts itself off when the bottom of the page is reached and begins as it is moved to the top of the next page.

- *NRI Speed-Reading Machine,* National Reading Institute.

    The automated speed reading program includes this machine, equipped with a self-timing device that enables an automatic increase in speed. This machine comes with programmed reading rolls that are fed through it.

- *PDL Perceptoscope,* Perceptual Development Laboratories, St. Louis 5, Missouri.

    This projector serves as accelerator, projector, tachistoscope, or timer. Speeds may be varied on ten films from 120 to 4,320 words per minute.

- *Readamatic Pacer,* Americana Interstate Corporation, Mundelein, Illinois.

    This pacer, similar in design to the Reading Rateometer, can vary speeds from 100 to 1,000 words per minute.

- *Shadowscope Reading Pacer,* Psychotechnics, Inc.

    The Shadowscope is designed for junior high level and up. The reading speeds may be varied from 125 to 2,000 words per minute.

- *SRA Reading Accelerator,* Science Research Associates.

    Model III offers rate adjustments of from less than 30 to more than 3,000 words per minute. Model IV is a plastic portable.

- *Tachomatic,* Psychotechnics, Inc.

    The Tachomatic film projector is designed for reading training at all levels, including that of adults. It utilizes a special film and high-speed mechanism to project series of words in a narrow band across a screen. The rate may be varied from very slow to motion-picture speeds and the fixations may be one, two, or three per line.

READING-RELATED MACHINES

- *Aud-X,* Educational Developmental Laboratories.

    As students listen to interesting stories, they watch the screen to learn new words. Each time the narrator pronounces one of the several words being taught in a lesson, it appears on the screen in exact synchronization with its pronunciation. In follow-up word-study lessons, students discover the graphic and sound qualities of words through the unique sight-sound synchronization afforded by the Aud-X. Though the students may be part of a small group during Aud-X sessions, each one listens, looks, and responds in an individual manner. Through its auto-instructional capability, the Aud-X makes an important contribution to truly individualized learning.

- *Delacato Stereo-Reading Service,* Keystone View Company.

    This service with stereo reader is designed for remedial use with pupils who suffer from laterality confusions. It develops binocular reading. The Zweig-Bruno Stereo-Tracing Exercises, to be used with the Stereo-Reader, are effective in the correction of letter reversals, letter substitutions, in-word reversals, and poor hand-eye coordination.

- *The EDL Skimmer*

    The only machine available today that is designed to develop the skimming skill is the *EDL Skimmer.* This machine is equipped with a bead of light that travels down the center fold of the book at the rate of one-half minute per page or about 800 to 1,000 words per minute. This informs the reader how rapidly he should proceed and keeps him perceptually alert. The device is useful also in developing scanning skills.

- *Language Master Machine,* Hoover Brothers, Kansas City.

    This machine comes with cards designed to teach vocabulary, sounds of English, phonics, etc.

- *Leavell Language Development Service,* Keystone View Company.

    This service with instrument develops eye control and hand-eye coordination. It is useful with mirror writers and children who reverse.

Professional books

The teacher of reading also needs to become familiar with the professional literature. Of the hundreds of books on the market, the following are especially significant.

- Allen, Roach Van and Lee, Doris May. *Learning to Read Through Experience.* Appleton-Century-Crofts, New York, 1963.
- Anderson, Irving H. and Dearborn, Walter F. *The Psychology of Teaching Reading.* The Ronald Press, New York, 1952.
- Austin, Mary C.; Bush, Clifford L.; and Huebner, Mildred H. *Read-*

ing Education: Appraisal Techniques for School and Classroom. The Ronald Press, New York, 1961.

- Austin, Mary C and others. *The Torch Lighters: Tomorrow's Teachers of Reading.* Harvard University Press, Cambridge, 1961.

- Austin, Mary C. and Morrison, Coleman. *The First R: Harvard Report on Reading in Elementary Schools.* The Macmillan Company, New York, 1963.

- Bagford, Jack. *Phonics: Its Role in Teaching Reading.* Sernoll, Inc., Iowa City, Iowa, 1967.

- Bamman, Henry A.; Hogan, Ursula; and Greene, Charles E. *Reading Instruction in the Secondary Schools.* David McKay Company, New York, 1961.

- Barbe, Walter B. *Educator's Guide to Personalized Reading Instruction.* Prentice-Hall, Englewood Cliffs, New Jersey, 1961.

- Barbe, Walter B. *Teaching Reading: Selected Materials.* Oxford University Press, New York, 1965.

- Betts, Emmett A. *Foundations of Reading Instruction.* American Book Company, New York, 1957.

- Blair, Glenn M. *Diagnostic and Remedial Teaching in Secondary Schools.* The Macmillan Company, New York, 1956.

- Blair, Glenn M. *Diagnostic and Remedial Teaching.* The Macmillan Company, New York, 1956.

- Bloomfield, Leonard and Barnhart, Clarence L. *Let's Read: A Linguistic Approach.* Wayne State University Press, Detroit, 1961.

- Bond, Guy L. and Tinker, Miles. *Reading Difficulties: Their Diagnosis and Correction.* Appleton-Century-Crofts, New York, 1967.

- Bond, Guy L. and Bond, Eva. *Developmental Reading in the High School.* The Macmillan Company, New York, 1941.

- Bond, Guy L. and Wagner, Eva B. *Teaching the Child to Read,* 4th ed. The Macmillan Company, New York, 1966.

- Botel, Morton. *How to Teach Reading.* Follett Publishing Company, New York, 1962.

- Brogan, Peggy and Fox, Lorene K. *Helping Children Read.* Holt, Rinehart and Winston, New York, 1961.

- Bullock, Harrison. *Helping the Non-Reading Pupil in the Secondary Schools.* Bureau of Publications, Teachers College, Columbia University, New York, 1956.

- Carter, Homer and McGinnis, Dorothy J. *Teaching Individuals to Read.* D. C. Heath and Company, Boston, 1962.

- Childs, Sally B. and Childs, Ralph. *Sound Phonics.* Educators Publishing Service, Cambridge, 1962.
- Conroy, Sophie C. *Specifics for You: A Corrective Reading Handbook.* Faculty Press, Brooklyn, 1961.
- Cordts, Anna D. *Phonics for the Reading Teacher.* Holt, Rinehart and Winston, New York, 1965.
- Critchley, Macdonald. *Developmental Dyslexia.* Charles C. Thomas, Springfield, 1964.
- Cutts, Warren G. *Modern Reading Instruction.* Center for Applied Research in Education, Washington, 1964.
- Cutts, Warren G. (ed.). *Teaching Young Children to Read.* (Bulletin No. 19) Office of Education, Washington, 1963.
- Cutts, Warren G. (ed.). *Research in Reading for the Middle Grades.* (Bulletin No. 31) Office of Education, Washington, 1963.
- Darrow, Helen F. and Howes, Virgil M. *Approaches to Individualized Reading.* Appleton-Century-Crofts, New York, 1960.
- Dawson, Mildred A. and Bamman, Henry A. *Fundamentals of Reading Instruction.* David McKay Company, New York, 1963.
- DeBoer, John H. and Dallmann, Martha. *The Teaching of Reading.* Holt, Rinehart and Winston, New York, 1960.
- Dechant, Emerald V. *Improving the Teaching of Reaaing.* Prentice-Hall, Englewood Cliffs, New Jersey, 1963.
- Deighton, Lee C. *Vocabulary Development in the Classroom.* Bureau of Publications, Teachers College, Columbia University, New York, 1959.
- Delacato, C. H. *The Treatment and Prevention of Reading Problems.* Charles C. Thomas, Springfield, 1959.
- Delacato, Carl. *The Diagnosis and Treatment of Speech and Reading Problems.* Charles C. Thomas, Springfield, 1963.
- Delacato, Carl H. *Neurological Organization and Reading.* Charles C. Thomas, Springfield, 1966.
- Diack, H. *Reading and the Psychology of Perception.* Philosophical Library, New York, 1960.
- Dolch, Edward W. *A Manual for Remedial Reading.* Garrard Press, Champaign, 1945.
- Dolch, Edward W. *Teaching Primary Reading.* Garrard Press, Champaign, 1960.
- Dolch, Edward W. *Problems in Reading.* Garrard Press, Champaign, 1948.

- Doman, G. *How to Teach Your Baby to Read*. Random House, New York, 1964.

- Durkin, Dolores. *Phonics and the Teaching of Reading*. Bureau of Publications, Teachers College, Columbia University, New York, 1962.

- Durkin, Dolores. *Children Who Read Early*. Teachers College Press, New York, 1966.

- Durrell, Donald D. *Improving Reading Instruction*. Harcourt, Brace and World, New York, 1956.

- Durrow, Helen and Howes, Virgil M. *Approaches to Individualized Reading*. Appleton-Century-Crofts, New York, 1960.

- Dust, Laurel M. *Teaching the Fundamentals of Reading and Spelling Phonetically*. Vantage, New York, 1962.

- Early, Margaret J. (ed.). *Perspectives in Reading II. Reading in the Secondary School*. International Reading Association, Newark, 1964.

- Ephron, Beulah K. *Difficulties in Reading*. Julian Press, New York, 1953.

- Fay, Leo C. *What Research Says to the Teacher: Reading in the High School*. Department of Classroom Teachers and American Educational Research Association of The NEA, Washington, D.C., 1956.

- Featherstone, W. B. *Teaching the Slow Learner*. Teachers College, Columbia University, 1951.

- Fernald, Grace M. *Remedial Techniques in Basic School Subjects*. McGraw-Hill Book Company, New York, 1966.

- Frank, Josette. *Your Child's Reading Today*. Doubleday and Company, Inc., Garden City, 1960.

- Fries, Charles C. *Linguistics and Reading*. Holt, Rinehart and Winston, Inc., New York, 1963.

- Gans, Roma. *Common Sense in Teaching Reading*. Bobbs-Merrill, Indianapolis, 1963.

- Gans, Roma. *Fact and Fiction About Phonics*. Bobbs-Merrill Company, Inc., 1964.

- Gates, Arthur I. *The Improvement of Reading*. The Macmillan Company, New York, 1947.

- Gattegno, C. *Words in Color*. Encyclopaedia Britannica, Chicago, 1962.

- Gilliland, Hap. *Materials for Remedial Reading and Their Use*. Eastern Montana College, Billings, 1965.

- Gillingham, Anna and Stillman, Bessie E. *Remedial Training for*

Children With Specific Disability in Reading, Spelling, and Penmanship. Educators Publishing Service, Cambridge, 1960.

- Goldstein, Herbert and Levett, Edith. *A Reading Readiness Program for the Mentally Retarded, Primary Level.* R. W. Parkinson, Urbana, 1963.

- Gray, Lillian. *Teaching Children to Read.* Ronald Press, New York, 1963.

- Gray, William S. (ed.). *Basic Instruction in Reading in Elementary and High Schools.* University of Chicago Press, Chicago, 1948.

- Gray, William S. *On Their Own in Reading.* Scott, Foresman, Chicago, 1960.

- Hafner, Lawrence E. *Improving Reading in Secondary Schools: Selected Readings.* The Macmillan Company, New York, 1967.

- Harris, Albert J. *How to Increase Reading Ability.* David McKay Company, New York, 1961.

- Harris, Albert J. *Effective Teaching of Reading.* David McKay Company, New York, 1962.

- Harris, Albert J. *Readings on Reading Instruction.* David McKay Company, New York, 1963.

- Harrison, Lucille and McKee, Paul. *Listen and Do.* Houghton-Mifflin, Boston, 1963.

- Haugh, Oscar M. (ed). *Teaching Reading in the High School.* Kansas Studies in Education, Vol. 10, No. 1. University of Kansas Press, Lawrence, Kansas, February, 1960.

- Hegge, T. G.; Kirk, S. A.; and Kirk, W. D. *Remedial Reading Drills.* Wahr Publishing Company, Ann Arbor, 1945.

- Heilman, Arthur W. *Phonics in Proper Perspective.* Bobbs-Merrill, Indianapolis, 1964.

- Heilman, Arthur W. *Principles and Practices of Teaching Reading.* Bobbs-Merrill, Indianapolis, 1961.

- Hellmuth, Jerome (ed.). *Learning Disorders.* Bernie Straub and Jerome Hellmuth Publishers, Seattle, 1965.

- Herber, Harold L. (ed.). *Perspectives in Reading IV, Study Skills in the Secondary School.* International Reading Association, Newark, 1965.

- Hermann, Knud. *Reading Disability.* Charles C. Thomas, Springfield, 1959.

- Herr, Selma E. *General Patterns of Effective Reading Programs.* C. Brown Company, Dubuque, 1963.

- Herr, Selma E. *Learning Activities for Reading*. Educational Research Associates, Los Angeles, 1961.
- Herr, Selma E. *Phonics Handbook for Teachers*. Educational Research Associates, Los Angeles, 1961.
- Herr, Selma E. *Diagnostic and Corrective Procedures in the Teaching of Reading*. Educational Research Associates, Los Angeles, 1961.
- Hester, Kathleen B. *Teaching Every Child to Read*. Harper and Row, New York, 1964.
- Hildreth, Gertrude H. *Teaching Reading: A Guide to Basic Principles and Modern Practices*. Holt, Rinehart and Winston, New York, 1958.
- Hirsch, Katrina de; Jansky, J. J.; and Langsford, J. *Predicting Reading Failure*. Harper and Row, 1966.
- Hunnicutt, C. W. and Iverson, W. J. (eds.). *Research in the Three R's*. Harper and Row, New York, 1958.
- Ilg, Frances L. and Ames, Louise Bates. *School Readiness*. Harper and Row, New York, 1965.
- International Reading Association. *Individualized Reading*, ed. Harry Sartain. The Association, Newark, 1964.
- International Reading Association. *Providing Clinical Services in Reading*, ed. Roy A. Kress and Marjorie S. Johnson. The Association, Newark, 1964.
- International Reading Association. *Reading Instruction in Secondary School*. "Perspective in Reading," No. 2. The Association, Newark, 1964.
- International Reading Association. *Sources of Good Books for Poor Readers*, ed. George D. Spache. The Association, Newark, 1964.
- Jacobs, L. B.; Vite, Irene; Spencer, Robert; Veatch, Jeannette; McCune, Mary A.; Noel, A. R.; and Miel, Alice. *Individualizing Reading Practices*. Bureau of Publications, Teachers College, Columbia University, 1958.
- Jennings, Frank G. *This Is Reading*. Bureau of Publications, Teachers College, Columbia University, New York, 1965.
- Jewett, Arno (ed.). *Improving Reading in the Junior High School*. Office of Education, Bulletin No. 10, Government Printing Office, Washington, 1957.
- Karlin, Robert. *Teaching Reading in High School*. The Bobbs-Merrill Company, Indianapolis, 1964.

- Kephart, Newell. *The Slow Learner in the Classroom.* The Bobbs-Merrill Company, Indianapolis, 1960.
- Kirk, S. *Teaching Reading to Slow-Learning Children.* Houghton Mifflin, Boston, 1940.
- Kolson, Clifford J. and Kaluger, George. *Clinical Aspects of Remedial Reading.* Charles C. Thomas, Springfield, 1963.
- Kottmeyer, William. *Handbook for Remedial Reading.* Webster Publishing Company, St. Louis, 1947.
- Kottmeyer, William. *Teacher's Guide for Remedial Reading.* Webster Publishing Company, St. Louis, 1959.
- Lazar, May (ed.). *A Practical Guide to Individualized Reading.* Bureau of Education Research, Publication No. 40, Board of Education, City of New York, 1960.
- Lazar, May. *The Retarded Reader in the Junior High School.* Board of Education, City of New York, 1952.
- *Learning to Read: A Report of a Conference of Reading Experts.* Educational Testing Service, Princeton, 1962.
- Lefevre, Carl. *Linguistics and the Teaching of Reading.* McGraw-Hill Book Company, New York, 1964.
- Loretan, Joseph O. and Umans, Shelley. *Teaching the Disadvantaged.* Teachers College Press, New York, 1966.
- MacKinnon, A. R. *How Do Children Learn to Read?* Copp, Clark, Toronto, 1959.
- Malmquist, E. *Factors Related to Reading Disabilities in the First Grade of the Elementary School.* Almquist and Wiksell, Stockholm, 1958.
- Massey, Will J. and Moore, Virginia D. *Helping High School Students to Read Better.* Holt, Rinehart and Winston, New York, 1965.
- Mazurkiewicz, A. A. *New Perceptives in Reading Instruction: A Book of Readings.* Pitman Publishing Corporation, New York, 1964.
- McCallister, James M. *Remedial and Corrective Instruction in Reading.* Appleton-Century-Crofts, New York, 1936.
- McCullough, C. M.; Strang, Ruth; and Traxler, Arthur E. *Problems in Improvement of Reading.* McGraw-Hill Book Company, Inc., New York, 1946.
- McKee, Paul. *The Teaching of Reading in the Elementary School.* Houghton Mifflin, Boston, 1948.
- McKee, Paul and Durr, William K. *Reading: A Program of Instruction for the Elementary School.* Houghton Mifflin, Boston, 1966.

- McKim, Margaret G. and Caskey, Helen. *Guiding Growth in Reading.* The Macmillan Company, New York, 1963.
- Meeker, Alice M. *Teaching Beginners to Read.* Holt, Rinehart, and Winston, New York, 1958.
- Money, John. *Reading Disability Progress and Research Needs in Dyslexia.* Johns Hopkins, Baltimore, 1962.
- Money, John (ed.). *The Disabled Reader.* Johns Hopkins Press, Baltimore, 1966.
- Monroe, M. *Children Who Cannot Read.* University of Chicago Press, Chicago, 1932.
- Monroe, M. and Backus, B. *Remedial Reading.* Houghton Mifflin, Boston, 1937.
- Monroe, Marion and Rogers, Bernice. *Foundations for Reading.* Scott, Foresman, Chicago, 1964.
- Montessori, Maria. *The Montessori Method;* also *Spontaneous Activity in Education;* also *The Montessori Elementary Material.* Robert Bentley, Inc., Cambridge.
- Morris, Ronald. *Success and Failure in Learning to Read.* Oldbourne Book Company, London, 1963.
- Newton, Roy. *Reading in Your School.* McGraw-Hill, New York, 1960.
- Orton, S. T. *Reading, Writing, and Speech Problems in Children.* Norton, New York, 1937.
- Orton, June Lyday. *A Guide to Teaching Phonics.* Educators Publishing Service, Cambridge, 1964.
- Otto, Wayne and McMenemy, Richard A. *Corrective and Remedial Teaching.* Houghton Mifflin, Boston, 1966.
- Pappas, George. *Reading in the Primary School.* The Macmillan Company, New York, 1962.
- Pollack, Myron F. W. and Pierkarz, Josephine. *Reading Problems and Problem Readers.* David McKay Company, New York, 1963.
- Rawson, Margaret B. *A Selected Bibliography of the Nature, Recognition, and Treatment of Language Disabilities.* Educators Publishing Service, Cambridge, 1966.
- Reeves, Ruth. *The Teaching of Reading in Our Schools.* The Macmillan Company, New York, 1966.
- Roach, Eugene G. and Kephart, Newell C. *The Purdue-Perceptual-Motor Survey.* Charles E. Merrill Books, 1966.
- Robinson, H. Alan and Rauch, Sidney J. *Guiding the Reading Pro-*

gram: A Reading Consultant's Handbook. Science Research Associates, Chicago, 1965.

- Robinson, H. Alan and Rauch, Sidney J. *Corrective Reading in the High School Classroom.* International Reading Association, Newark, 1966.
- Robinson, Helen M. (ed.). *Clinical Studies in Reading II.* (Supplementary Educational Monographs No. 68) University of Chicago Press, Chicago, 1953.
- Robinson, Helen M. *Corrective Reading in Classroom and Clinic.* University of Chicago Press, Chicago, 1958.
- Robinson, Helen M. *Why Pupils Fail in Reading.* University of Chicago Press, Chicago, 1946.
- Rogers, John R.; Capps, Edward; and Martin, John E. *Linguistics in Reading Instruction.* The Reading Clinic, University of Mississippi, 1965.
- Roswell, Florence and Natchez, Gladys. *Reading Disability, Diagnosis and Treatment.* Basic Books, New York, 1964.
- Russell, David H. *Children Learn to Read.* Ginn and Company, Boston, 1961.
- Schonell, Fred J. *The Psychology of Teaching Reading.* Oliver and Boyd, London, 1961.
- Simmons, John S. and Rosenblum, Helen O'Hara. *The Reading Improvement Handbook.* Reading Improvement, Pullman, 1965.
- Smith, Donald E. P. and Carrigan, M. *The Nature of Reading Disability.* Harcourt, Brace and World, New York, 1959.
- Smith, Henry P. and Dechant, Emerald V. *Psychology in Teaching Reading.* Prentice-Hall, Englewood Cliffs, New Jersey, 1961.
- Smith, Nila B. *American Reading Instruction.* International Reading Association, Newark, 1965.
- Smith, Nila B. *Reading Instruction for Today's Children.* Prentice-Hall, Englewood Cliffs, New Jersey, 1963.
- Spache, George D. *The Art of Efficient Reading.* The Macmillan Company, New York, 1965.
- Spache, George D. *Good Reading for Poor Readers.* Garrard Press, Champaign, 1966.
- Spache, George D. *Toward Better Reading.* Garrard Press, Champaign, 1963.
- Spalding, Romalda Bishop and Spalding, Walter T. *The Writing Road to Reading.* Whiteside, Inc., and William Morrow and Company, New York, 1962.

- Stahl, Stanley S., Jr. *Teaching of Reading in the Intermediate Grades.* Wm. C. Brown Company, Dubuque, 1965.
- Staiger, Ralph and John, David A. *New Directions in Reading.* Bantam Books Inc., New York, 1967.
- Steere, A.; Peck, C. Z.; and Kahn, L. *Solving Language Difficulties.* Educators Publishing Service, Cambridge, 1966.
- Stern, Catherine and Gould, Toni. *Children Discover Reading.* Random House, New York, 1965.
- Strang, Ruth. *Diagnostic Teaching of Reading.* McGraw-Hill, New York, 1964.
- Strang, Ruth (ed.). *Understanding and Helping the Retarded Reader.* University of Arizona Press, Tucson, 1965.
- Strang, Ruth and Bracken, Dorothy Kenkall. *Making Better Readers.* D. C. Heath and Company, Boston, 1957.
- Strang, Ruth and Lindquist, Donald M. *The Administrator and the Improvement of Reading.* Appleton-Century-Crofts, New York, 1960.
- Strang, Ruth; McCullough, Constance M.; and Traxler, Arthur. *The Improvement of Reading.* McGraw-Hill, New York, 1967.
- Tinker, Miles A. *Bases for Effective Reading.* University of Minnesota Press, Minneapolis, 1965.
- Tinker, Miles A. and McCullough, Constance M. *Teaching Elementary Reading.* Appleton-Century-Crofts, New York, 1962.
- Umans, Shelley. *New Trends in Teaching Reading.* Bureau of Publications, Teachers College, Columbia University, New York, 1964.
- Umans, Shelley. *Designs for Readings Programs.* Bureau of Publications, Teachers College, Columbia University, New York, 1964.
- Veatch, Jeanette. *Individualizing Your Reading Program.* Putnam, New York, 1959.
- Veatch, Jeanette and Acinapuro, Philip J. *Reading in the Elementary School.* Ronald Press Company, New York, 1966.
- Vernon, Magdalen D. *Backwardness in Reading.* Cambridge University Press, Cambridge, 1958.
- Vogts, Caroline F. *Successful Reading in the Elementary School.* Practical Press, Englewood Cliffs, 1961.
- Weiss, M. Jerome. *Reading in the Secondary School.* Odyssey Press, New York, 1961.
- Whipple, Gertrude and Black, Millard H. *Reading for Children Without—Our Disadvantaged Youth.* International Reading Association, Newark.

- Wilson, Robert M. *Diagnostic and Remedial Reading.* Charles E. Merrill, Inc., Columbus, 1967.
- Witty, Paul A.; Freeland, A. M.; and Grotberg, Edith H. *The Teaching of Reading: A Developmental Process.* D. C. Heath Company, Boston, 1966.
- Woolf, Maurice D. and Woolf, Jeanne A. *Remedial Reading: Teaching and Treatment.* McGraw-Hill, New York, 1957.
- Zintz, Miles V. *Corrective Reading.* Wm. C. Brown Company Publishers, Dubuque, 1966.

Conclusion

This book has looked at various aspects of the diagnostic-remedial process. It has outlined the steps of diagnosis as involving over-all screening, diagnostic testing, an investigation of the causal factors, and actual remediation. In addition, the book devoted separate chapters to reading methods, to reading materials, and to the problems of teaching such different learners as the retarded reader, the reluctant reader, the emotionally disturbed reader, and the experientially deprived reader.

Not all children progress at the same rate. Even among pupils of adequate ability, some meet problems that delay or block learning. The effective developmental reading program is thus built on a foundation of early diagnosis of inadequacies, careful evaluation of needs and abilities, and the utilization of professionally designed methods and materials.

A basic thesis in the book has been that diagnostic procedure ought to be aimed at prevention as well as remediation; that prevention is best accomplished by an early identification of the symptoms of incipient reading disability; and that when it is not possible to prevent, when in fact the pupil has already become a reading disability case, that every effort be made to identify the causes and to provide the proper remediation.

Remedial reading instruction is not going to remove all reading disabilities from the educational scene. This would be expecting too much, but remedial instruction has amply proved its effectiveness. Its greatest benefit may be that it focuses the teacher's attention on the pupil's difficulties. Remedial instruction is not magic. Often it is simply a matter of teaching the skills that the pupil does not have.

In summary, diagnosis and remediation are essential elements of a sound developmental program. They are no longer the special privileges of the slow or retarded learner. They must be extended to every child in the classroom.

---

[1] Gilliland, Hap. *Materials for Remedial Reading.* Eastern Montana College Reading Clinic, Eastern Montana College, Billings, 1965, p. 13.

[2] a. Gans, Roma. "Misspent Funds and the Consequences." *The Reading Teacher,* 20 (April, 1967), pp. 595-599.
   b. Johnson, Eleanor M. "Guidelines for Evaluating New Instructional Programs." *The Reading Teacher,* 20 (April, 1967), pp. 600-604.
   c. Durkin, Dolores. "Phonics Materials: A Big Seller." *The Reading Teacher,* 20 (April, 1967), pp. 610-614.

Appendices

Appendix I

Intelligence Tests

The user of tests needs a philosophy of interpretation. In the following principles we have sought to identify at least some aspects of such a philosophy. It is hoped that when tests are utilized to diagnose pupil difficulties and to plan special help to meet the needs indicated by the tests, the following points might be kept in mind:

1. Tests are designed basically for the purpose of understanding children better. Schools at one time got along without tests, but physicians also got along without X-rays. The good teacher can understand children better by using tests. Education without testing may be target practice in the dark.

2. Teachers cannot simply believe or not believe in tests. Tests are not articles of faith. Tests should provide an objective situation for studying a sample of the child's behavior. And, they are useful only if they are interpreted correctly. Testing without the ability to interpret the results is rather useless. And a test score neatly recorded in a folder and never interpreted is a waste of time.

3. Tests do not measure something fixed and immutable that characterizes the pupil for all time. They measure rather how well the pupil performs certain tasks at a given point in time. No test score can determine with complete accuracy what the pupil can or cannot learn in the future. Any one score may be misleading. Tests don't really predict. It is more accurate to say that they estimate. They attempt to forecast a person's chances and express this chance mathematically.

4. The pupil needs to develop the attitude that tests merely offer samples on which he is to try his skill. The tests should be looked

upon as a challenge rather than as an instrument that stigmatizes him.

5. The user of tests should ask four questions about any test that he uses:

a. *Is the test valid?* Does it measure or predict whatever it is supposed to measure or predict? No test is infallible. It is therefore highly important that the teacher utilize the results of more than one test and that he obtain the best test possible.

b. *Is the test reliable?* Does it measure consistently whatever it is measuring? Is the score stable and trustworthy? Does the person taking the test generally maintain about the same ranking in a group of persons upon retaking the test? There is no such thing as reliable performance on an unreliable instrument. A student suffering a severe headache may not do as well as he normally does even on a well-built test. If, on the other hand, the items are ambiguous or the directions are unclear, he may not be able to perform well regardless of how alert he may be when tested.

c. *Is the test usable and objective?* Is it practical? Is it economical? Is the test too long? Is it too expensive? Is it easy to score?

d. What is the norm group? Is the group on which the instrument was standardized representative of the group on which the instrument is to be used? In short, is the student being compared with the correct group? A boy with an IQ of 145 would be classified with the below-average group if the average IQ of the group were 150. In another group, his IQ might be the highest score.

6. It is wrong to assume that a given grade norm for a test is an acceptable standard for a given pupil in a grade. If the average score for a given grade is 65, this does not mean that for a given pupil a score of 65 could be considered acceptable.

7. When achievement scores do not measure up to ability or aptitude scores, it is not always correct to assume that the pupil is lazy or uninterested.

8. Tests do not give answers to problems. They do not tell us what to do. They are designed to give additional information on the basis of which the teacher or pupil can come to wiser decisions. Tests are aids to judgment, not judgment itself. Test results should not be the sole determinant of the course of action which the reading specialist should follow. The remedial program should be based on other data and should be modified as the teacher works

with the pupil, watches his responses, and observes his progress as a result of some activities and his failure as a result of others.

9. Test scores frequently have a direct bearing on the self-concept of the pupil. If the test results, for example, place him in an inferior position with other members of his family or close friends, he may feel threatened by the result. If the intellectual recognition of his limitations is not accompanied by emotional acceptance, the pupil may become hostile, reject the results, and seek compensation in another area. The teacher must understand how the child evaluates himself as a reader and what reading success means to him.

10. Test interpretations to the pupil should not be accompanied by expressions of pleasure or displeasure over the test score. The pupil will infer that the teacher likes him if the score is high and does not like him if the score is low. The teacher is on safer grounds with statements such as the following: "Does this test score fit in with what you think of yourself?" or "Is this about what you expected?"

11. Tests should be given at the beginning of the semester rather than at the end of the school year. The test then is more likely to be interpreted as revealing something about the child rather than about the school or the teacher. To judge a school or teacher on the basis of test data only is invalid and dangerous.

12. The individual child's performance must be interpreted in terms of the curriculum to which he has been exposed. It is reasonable to expect less evidence of ability in reading than in some other areas if the pupil has had substantially less acquaintance with this area.

13. Accurate test results are possible only if the tests are carefully administered, scored accurately, and interpreted in terms of appropriate norms. Numerous errors may and often do creep into testing. Even though the test has been standardized, we need to keep in mind the fact that the persons who administer the tests and who interpret the test data are not standardized.

Let us now list some useful tests of intelligence.

29 *	Arthur	Age 5	This test affords a means of
38	Point	to	measuring the abilities of deaf
42	Scale	15 years	children, those suffering from
	of		reading disabilities, those with
	Performance		delayed or defective speech,

* These numbers refer to the test publishers listed in Appendix VII.

and the non-English speaking population. The test is composed of five non-language subtests which consist of the following: Knox Cube Test, Seguin Form Board, Arthur Stencil Design Test I, Healy Picture Completion Test II, and Porteus Maze Test (Arthur Modification).

7	California Test of Mental Maturity	Grades K–adult	48 min. to 1 hr. 21 min.	Memory, Spatial Relationships, Logical Reasoning, Numerical Reasoning, and Verbal Concepts are measured to determine IQ.
16 29	Chicago Nonverbal Examination	Age 6– adult	25 min.	This test is designed for students handicapped in the use of the English language such as the deaf, those with reading difficulty, and those with a foreign language background. The test has been standardized for both verbal and pantomime directions.
16 19 29	Columbia Mental Maturity Scale	Age 3–12	15–20 min.	This test has 100 items, each printed on a card 6 x 19 and each containing from three to five drawings. This is an individual scale suitable for cerebral palsy patients and others physically handicapped. No verbal response is required. The specific task in each item is to select from a series of drawings the one which does not belong.
30	Full-Range Picture Vocabulary Test	Age 2–16 and adult	5–10 min.	This is an intelligence test based on verbal comprehension using cartoon-like cards. No reading or writing is required of the testee and thus the test can be given to anyone able to signal "yes" or "no" in any interpretable way. The examinee must be able to hear or read words.
29	Gesell Development Schedules	Pre-School Age		These provide measures of mental growth through quantitative measurements of language, motor development, adaptive behavior, and social behavior.
3 11	I. P. A. T. Culture	Age 8–	15–30 min.	This test gives a measure of general intelligence. The IQ

16 21 31 42	Fair Intelligence Tests	Adult		scores are relatively free of educational and cultural influences. It is nonverbal and nonpictorial and uses a perceptual approach. Scale I, ages four–eight or adult defectives, requires 30 minutes. There are two other scales.
30	Kahn Intelligence Tests: Experimental Form	Infant– adult		This test is almost independent of differential educational and cultural learning forces. It requires no reading, writing, or verbal knowledge and includes a scale for assessment of the intelligence of blind persons plus special scales to measure ability in concept formation, recall, and motor coordination.
3 5 27 29 36	Kuhlmann- Anderson IQ Test	Grades K–12	40–50 min.	There are tests at each grade level measuring general learning ability.
2 4 5	Kuhlmann- Finch IQ Test	Grades 1–12	30 min.	This test measures general mental development and provides an IQ score. The predecessor of this test was the Kuhlmann-Anderson. Nonverbal tests only are used through grade 3.
5 16 20 27	Lorge- Thorndike Intelligence Tests	Grades K–12	30–60 min.	A verbal series of these tests is available for grades 4–12. These tests measure scholastic aptitude through subtests of verbal reasoning ability, vocabulary, verbal classification, sentence completion, arithmetic reasoning, and verbal analogy. The nonverbal series is available for grades K–12. These tests measure one aspect of intelligence, namely, abstract reasoning ability, through subtests involving pictorial classification, pictorial analogy, and numerical relationships.
4 5 16 42	Otis-Lennon Mental Ability Test	Grades K–13	25–50 min.	The first two levels (K–3) of these tests contain both pictorial and geometric items sampling the mental processes of classification, following directions, quantitative, verbal conceptualization and reasoning by

analogy. No reading is required at either level.

The upper levels contain both verbal and nonverbal items sampling fourteen different mental processes.

2 4	Peabody Picture Vocabulary Test	Age 2 years 6 mo.– 18 years	15 min.	This is an individual wide-range picture vocabulary test utilizing a graduated series of 150 plates, each containing four pictures.
20	Pictorial Test of Intelligence	Age 3–8	Approx. 45 min.	This is an individual test of general ability designed for administration by a trained examiner to one child at a time. It may be used with normal or handicapped individuals. The child responds to verbal instructions of the examiner by selecting one of four drawings.
5 16 19	Pinter General Ability Tests (Verbal Series)	Grades K–12	25–45 min.	This is a four-battery series measuring a variety of aspects of general mental ability.
4 5	Pinter- Cunningham Primary Test	Grades K–12		A group test for measurement of mental ability, it contains all pictures and no reading.
3	Pressey Classification and Verifying Tests	Grades 1–adult	16 min.	This test provides a quick measure of general intelligence. The primary test (grades 1–2) is composed completely of pictures. The intermediate (grades 3–6) and senior (grades 7 to adult) tests consist of tests of similarities and opposites, information, and practical arithmetic.
30	Quick Test (QT)	Age 2 yrs.– superior adult level	3–10 min.	This is a standardized individual intelligence test in three forms. It requires no reading, writing, or speaking by the testee. Anyone who can see the drawings, hear or read the word items, and signal "yes" or "no" can be tested.
35	Slosson Intelligence Test for Children and Adults.		20 min.	This short individual test takes about twenty minutes to administer and score. It is an abbreviated form of the Stanford-Binet.
34	S. R. A. Primary	Grades K–12	55–60 min.	This test indicates grade placement for ability grouping. The

	Mental Abilities Test			areas tested include verbal meaning, perceptual speed, spatial ability, reasoning, and number sense. The primary battery requires no reading.
4 16 20 29 38 42	Stanford-Binet Intelligence Scales: 1960 Revision	Age 2–adult	1 to 2 hrs.	This latest revision has combined l and m forms of the 1937 revision into one single form. Examiner must have special training.
5 29	Wechsler Intelligence Scale for Children (WISC)	Ages 5–15	1 to 2 hours	Five verbal and five performance-type tests of a spiral omnibus nature are contained in this individual test. IQ can be derived from either the verbal or the performance scale. Special training is required for its administration.

Appendix II

Reading Readiness Tests

3	American School Reading Readiness Test	For first grade entrants	30 min.	This group test provides measures of vocabulary, discrimination of letter forms and letter combinations, discrimination of words by selection and matching, recognition of geometric forms, following directions, and memory of geometric forms.
1	Binion-Beck Reading Readiness Test	Grades K–1	30–45 min.	This readiness test requires the pupil to observe and note details. It consists of four subtests containing a large variety of picture recognition items, likenesses and differences items, motor control items, picture interpretation items, coordination items, visual discrimination items, sustained attention items, etc.
9	Diagnostic Reading Tests: Reading Readiness Booklet	Grades K–1	30–45 min.	This group test measures the child's ability to grasp relationships; his skill in eye-hand and motor coordination; visual and auditory discrimination; and vocabulary.
4 5 6 16 29	Gates Reading Readiness Test	Grades K–1	No time limit	A group and/or individual test, it provides measures of picture directions, word matching, word-card matching, rhyming, and reading and naming letters and numbers. The picture directions test measures the child's ability to listen for directions, to make interpretations of pictures, and carry out verbal directions. The word-card matching test requires the

child to select from four words the one that is like the word shown on a flash card. This test will be replaced in 1968 by the Gates-MacGinitie *Readiness Skills Test.*

20 5	Harrison- Stroud Readiness Profiles	Grades K–1	79 min.	This revision of the Harrison-Stroud Readiness Tests measures using symbols, making visual discriminations, using the context, making auditory discriminations, using context and auditory clues, and how well the pupil knows names of capital and lower-case letters.
7	Lee-Clark Reading Readiness Tests	Grades K–1	20 · min.	This group test measures the ability to note similarities and differences in letter forms; it measures the child's vocabulary and concepts; and it tests the ability to match letters with letters and words with words.
22	Lippincott Reading Readiness Test	Grades K–1		This test measures the pupil's knowledge of printed, spoken, and written letter forms by requiring the pupil to match printed capitals, to identify upper- and lower-case letters, and to write letters from dictation. A Readiness Checklist forms the second part of the test.
2	Maturity Level for School Entrance and Reading Readiness	Grades K–1	60 min.	This test helps to identify children mature enough to enter first grade, having readiness in reading regardless of high or low chronological age. It is a revision of the School Readiness Inventory. It yields a maturity level score and a reading readiness score.
4 5 16 19 29	Metropolitan Readiness Test	Grades K–1	60 min.	This group test contains measures of (1) word meaning (the child selects from four pictures the one that is a picture of the word used by the examiner); (2) sentence meaning (the child must comprehend a sentence); (3) information (child picks the picture that depicts what the tester is describing); (4) matching (child must select from four pictures one that matches a sample picture); (5)

numbers (various knowledge about numbers is tested); and (6) copying (this measures visual perception, motor control, and the tendency toward spatial reversal). A supplementary test requires the child to draw a man. It measures perceptual maturity and motor control.

5 16 20	Monroe Reading Aptitude Test	Grades K–1	30–40 min.	This test, part group and part individual, yields five scores: visual discrimination, auditory discrimination, motor control, oral speed and articulation, and language.
5 19	Murphy-Durrell Diagnostic Reading Readiness Analysis	Grades K–1	60 min.	This instrument tests for identifying separate sounds in spoken words, identifying capital and lower-case letters named by the examiner, and recognizing sight words one hour after they have been taught. It thus measures auditory and visual discrimination and learning rate.
43	Perceptual Forms Test	Ages 6–8½		This test measures visual development either in groups or individually.
37	Reading Readiness Test (Steck-Vaughn)	Grades K–1	80 min.	The test has ten parts: differentiation of letters; differentiation of pairs of letters; differentiation of words; differentiation of phrases; differentiation of pictures and designs; recognition of words; recognition of patterns; familiarity with names of objects; functions of objects; and interpretation of spoken sentences.
33	Scholastic Reading Readiness Test	Grades K–1	30–45 min.	This test measures knowledge and understanding of facts, visual discrimination, and sound-symbol association.
33	Steinbach Test of Reading Readiness	Grades K–1		This test measures letter identification, word identification, ability to follow directions, and ability to relate words and pictures.
33	STS Reading Readiness	Grades K–1		This test measures knowledge and understanding of facts, events, and objects; visual discrimination; and ability to associate sounds and symbols.

Appendix III

Reading Survey Tests

3	American School Achievement Reading Tests	Grades 1–9	65–137 min.	This is a battery of tests for various grade levels which provides information material on ability, skill, progress, and reading difficulties. The reading test measures sentence and word meaning and paragraph meaning.
14	Botel Reading Inventory	Grades 1–12		This test measures word recognition, listening comprehension, and phonics. It is used to determine whether a pupil is reading at an instructional, frustrational, or free-reading level.
7	California Reading Test	Grades 1–14	23–68 min.	This is a battery divided into two major areas: reading vocabulary and comprehension.
12	Cooperative English Tests: Reading Comprehension	Grades 8–13		This test measures reading vocabulary, general comprehension and speed of comprehension, and accuracy.
16 29	Davis Reading Test	Grades 8–13	40 min.	This test is used to assess the reading comprehension and skills of individuals and groups. It provides scores of level of comprehension and speed of comprehension.
5 19	Detroit Reading Test	Grades 2–9	26 min.	This test consists of four reading tests of twenty-five items each and twelve paragraphs. It is useful for preliminary classification of pupils with ability.
22	Developmental Reading Test	Grades 1–3	40 min.	These tests are designed to provide a measure of basic vocabulary, general comprehension, and specific comprehension.

251

5	Durrell-Sullivan Reading Capacity and Achievement Test	Grades 2–6	30–55 min.	The purpose of this test is to determine whether or not a pupil is reading up to his capacity. It is designed for grades 2–6; the primary level for grades 2–5 to 4–5; the intermediate for grades 3–6. It has two sections: a reading capacity section and a reading achievement section. The reading capacity section, composed entirely of pictures, has subtests on word-meaning and on paragraph meaning. It is a hearing comprehension test. The reading achievement section contains a word meaning test, a spelling test, and written recall test. The reading capacity section requires no reading. The comprehension test (word meaning and paragraph meaning) of the reading achievement test is read by the pupil without help from the examiner.
6	Gates-MacGinitie Reading Tests	Grades K–12	40–45 min.	This test is available on different levels. Primary A, Grade 1, and Primary B, Grade 2, and Primary C, Grade 3, measure vocabulary and comprehension. Primary CS, Grades 2 and 3, measures speed and accuracy. It is only seven minutes long. Survey D, for grades 4, 5, and 6, measures speed and accuracy, vocabulary, and comprehension. Survey E does the same for grades 7, 8, and 9.
5	Haggarty Reading Examinations	Grades 1–3 and 6–12	40 min.	This examination is a survey test covering vocabulary, sentence reading, and paragraph reading.
1	High School Reading Test: National Achievement Tests	Grades 7–12	Approx. 40 min.	This test measures reading vocabulary, sentence meaning, specific comprehension, and paragraph meaning.
4 5 16 19 20 29	Iowa Silent Reading Test	Grades 4–13	45–50 min.	This test is designed on two levels: grades 4–8 and grades 9–13. The elementary test measures rate and comprehension, directed reading to locate answers to factual questions, word meaning, paragraph compre-

hension, sentence meaning and location of information (alphabetizing, using guide words, and use of index). On the advanced level there are measures of rate of comprehension of connected prose, directed reading to locate answers to factual questions, poetry comprehension, word meaning in content areas, sentence meaning, paragraph comprehension, and location of information.

5 16 19 29	Kelley-Greene Reading Comprehension Test	Grades 9–13	75 min.	This is an overall measure of retention, comprehension, and ability to find answers to questions.
7	Lee-Clark Reading Tests (1963 Revision)	Grades K–2	K–20 min. 1–15 min. 2–25 min.	These tests measure readiness, reading achievement and silent reading skills. The four subtests are auditory stimuli, visual stimuli, following directions, and completion.
19	Metropolitan Reading Test	Grades 2–9	40–50–60 min.	This test is designed for five levels: primary I (last half of grade 1), primary II (grade 2), elementary (grades 3–4), intermediate (grades 5–6), and advanced (grades 7–9). The primary tests measure word knowledge and word discrimination; the elementary test adds reading comprehension, and the intermediate and advanced tests measure word knowledge and reading comprehension.
3	Monroe Revised Silent Reading Tests	Grades 3–12	4 min.	The tests, consisting of exercises in which the student is asked to read seventeen short paragraphs and answer a question on each, measure both reading comprehension and reading rate.
1	National Achievement Test	Grades 4–9		This test measures sentence meaning, paragraph meaning, and speed.
5 16 20	Nelson-Denny Reading Test, 1960 Revision	Grades 9–16	30 min.	This test has three purposes: (1) to predict a student's probable success in college; (2) to assist in classifying incoming college or high school classes; (3) to aid in the diagnosis of

students' reading difficulties. Subtest scores in vocabulary, comprehension, and reading rate are provided.

2	Nelson-Lohmann Reading Test	Grades 4–8	Untimed, approx. 50 min.	This test measures comprehension with a graduated sequence of difficulty.
20	Nelson Silent Reading Test	Grades 3–9	30 min.	This test measures the ability to comprehend words, to comprehend the general significance of a paragraph, to note details, and to predict outcomes.
16 20	Nelson Reading Test (1962 Edition)	Grades 3–9	30 min.	This test is designed to measure reading ability in terms of vocabulary and comprehension. This test replaces the Nelson Silent Reading Test.
3	Pressey Diagnostic Reading Tests	Grades 3–9		This test measures speed, vocabulary, and paragraph meaning.
1	Primary Reading Test: Acorn Achievement Tests	Grades 2–3		This test measures word recognition, sentence meaning, and paragraph meaning.
33	Pupil Progress Series: Reading	Grades 1–8	40 min.	This is a reading achievement test, measuring total comprehension, rate, vocabulary, and knowledge and use of sources.
12	Sequential Tests of Educational Progress: Reading	Grades 4–14	70 min.	This test measures five major categories of comprehension skills, abilities, and attitudes: ability to recall ideas, to translate ideas and make inferences, to analyze motivation (of the author), to analyze presentation, and ability to criticize (constructively).
34	SRA Reading Record	Grades 6–12	45 min.	This test by Guy T. Buswell measures ten basic reading skills: rate of reading, reading comprehension, paragraph meaning, directory reading, map-table-graph reading, advertisement reading, index reading, sentence meaning, and technical and general vocabulary.
34	SRA Achievement Series: Reading	Grades 1–9	65–120 min.	This test measures comprehension, vocabulary verbal-pictorial association, and language perception.

19	Stanford Achievement Test	Grades 1–5 to intermediate		These test batteries each measure word meaning, paragraph meaning, vocabulary, spelling, and word study skills.
19	Stanford Reading Tests	Grades 3–9	35–40 min.	This series consists of three tests that measure reading comprehension and vocabulary or word meaning. The range includes grades 3–4, 5–6, and 7–9.
5 20	Stroud-Hieronymus Primary Reading Profiles	Grades 1–2		This test is designed to evaluate pupil progress upon the completion of the usual first-grade reading program. Level 2 helps the teacher to determine the relative strengths and weaknesses in the pupil's ability to read by the time he has reached the end of the second year of the instruction. Each level consists of a battery of five tests to be administered to the class as a group: Aptitude for Reading, Auditory Association, Word Recognition, Word Attack, and Comprehension.
7	Survey of Reading Achievement	Grades 7–12	40 min.	This test measures vocabulary, ability to follow directions, reference skills, and comprehension.
24	Tinker Speed of Reading	Grades 7–10		This test measures rate, story comprehension, word meaning, paragraph meaning and total comprehension.
3 16	Traxler High School Reading Test	Grades 10–12	40 min.	This test measures rate, story comprehension, main ideas, and total comprehension.

Appendix IV

Diagnostic Reading Tests

22	Bond-Clymer-Hoyt Silent Reading Test	Grades 3–8	45 min. in two sessions	This group test is made up of eleven subtests. These are: (1) recognition of words in isolation; (2) recognition of words in context; (3) recognition of reversible words in context; (4) location of parts of words useful in word recognition; (5) syllabication; (6) locating root words; (7) phonetic knowledge—general word elements; (8) recognition of beginning sounds; (9) selecting rhyming words; (10) identification of letter sounds; and (11) ability to blend visually and phonetically.

The test is basically a test of silent reading skills. The chief weakness of the test is that it cannot be used with children who are nonreaders or who have serious reading problems. |
| 38 | Diagnostic Reading Examination for Diagnosis of Special Difficulty in Reading | Grades 1–4 | | This is a combination of assessment procedures consisting of Revised Stanford-Binet Scale, Gray's Standardized Oral Reading Paragraphs, Monroe's Standardized Silent Reading Tests, adaptation of Ayres Spelling Scale, arithmetic computation from Stanford Achievement Test, Iota Word Test, and eight other additional tests of special areas in reading. |
| 7 | Diagnostic Reading Scales (Spache) | Grades 1–8 | No time limit | These scales are individually administered tests designed to identify reading deficiencies that hinder pupils from reading |

256

adequately. The scale is recommended for normal and retarded readers at the elementary, junior high, and senior high levels. The test battery comprises three word-recognition lists, twenty-two reading passages, and six supplementary phonics tests; consonant sounds, vowel sounds, consonant blends, common syllables, blends, and letter sounds. Three reading levels are yielded for each pupil: instructional level in oral reading, independent level in silent reading, and potential level in auditory comprehension.

9	Diagnostic Reading Tests (Committee on Diagnostic Reading Tests, Inc.)	Grades K–16		These tests are composed of three batteries which are: K–4, grades 4–8, and grades 7–16. These tests provide a comprehensive diagnostic testing program covering word recognition, comprehension, vocabulary, story reading, story comprehension, and, at the upper levels, rate of comprehension.
33	Diagnostic Reading Test: Pupil Progress Series	Grades 1.9–2.1, 2.2–3.0, 4–6, 7–8	40–60 min.	This test covers vocabulary, rate of reading, reading for meaning, comprehension, and knowledge and use of sources.
2 16	Doren Diagnostic Reading Test	Grades 1–9	Untimed, 3 hrs. needed	This group test for children in need of remedial instruction tests for beginning sounds, sight words, rhyming, whole word recognition, speech consonants, blending, vowels, ending sounds, discriminate guessing, and letter recognition.
5 16 19 29	Durrell Analysis of Reading Difficulty	Grades 1–6	30–45 min.	This test is designed for grades 1–6 and is made up of the following subtests: (1) the Oral Reading Test; (2) the Silent Reading Test; (3) Listening Comprehension Test; (4) Word Recognition and Word Analysis Test; (5) Naming Letters; (6) Identifying Letter Names; (7) Matching Letters; (8) Writing Letters; (9) Visual Memory of Words; (10) Hearing Sounds in Words; (11) Learning to Hear Sounds in Words; (12) Learning Rate;

(13) Phonic Spelling of Words; (14) Spelling Test; and (15) Handwriting Test.

This test is generally recommended for less severe cases. The profile is not so adequate as it might be in that it makes no provision for recording tests 5 through 13. The checklist of errors that accompanies the test is probably the best of its kind.

6	Gates-McKillop Diagnostic Tests	Grades 1–8	No time limit	This battery is for detailed diagnosis of specific deficiencies in reading performance. It is a revision of the Gates Reading Diagnostic Tests and includes a battery of individually administered tests. It tests oral reading, word perception, phrase perception, blending word parts, giving letter sounds, naming letters, recognizing visual form of sounds, auditory blending, spelling, oral vocabulary, syllabication, and auditory discrimination.
25	Group Diagnostic Reading Aptitude and Achievement Tests	Grades 3–9	60–70 min.	This test provides fifteen scores: paragraph understanding, speed, word discrimination (four subtests), arithmetic, spelling, visual ability (two subtests), auditory ability (two subtests), motor ability (two subtests), and vocabulary.
15	McCullough Word-Analysis Tests, Experimental Edition	Grades 4–6	70 min. in 7 sessions	This test provides ten scores: initial blends and digraphs, phonetic discrimination, matching letters to vowel sounds, sounding whole words, interpreting phonetic symbols, phonetic analysis, dividing words into syllables, root words in affixed forms, structural analysis, and total score.
38	Monroe Diagnostic Reading Test			This test offers a diagnostic profile showing specific reading retardations as well as arithmetic, spelling and mental age.
38	Pupil Progress Diagnostic Reading Tests	Grades 1–8	Approx. 40 min.	This series of tests is offered on four levels: primary level I, primary level II, elementary (grades 4, 5, 6), and advanced (grades 7 and 8). The primary

level I test measures vocabulary, rate, and comprehension and provides diagnostic subscores for word recognition, word to content relation, words in use, recalling information, locating information, and reading for descriptions. The primary level II provides subscores also for reading for meaning and following directions. The elementary and advanced levels measure rate, comprehension, and knowledge and use of sources. They provide additional subscores for functions of common sources, selection of suitable sources for a specific purpose, use of the index, and use of the table of contents.

3 7	Pressey Diagnostic Reading Test	Grades 3–9	50 min.	This instrument consists of three tests covering vocabulary, speed, and paragraph meaning.
6	Reading Diagnostic Record for H. S. and College Students	Grades 8–16	50 min.	This is a comprehensive study of reading ability which facilitates unification, recording, ascertaining of performance level, and aids in the collection of data for reasonable purposes.
13	The Roswell-Chall Diagnostic Reading Test of Word-Analysis Skills	Grades 2–6	5 min.	This is a test of word analysis skills, constructed for teachers and psychologists who need a simple test to supplement information obtained from standardized silent and oral reading tests. The basic skills measured by this test provide the teacher with a qualitative evaluation of the pupil's strengths and weaknesses in word recognition. The five parts deal with single consonants and combinations, short vowel sounds, rule of silent e, vowel combinations, and syllabication.
33	Scholastic Diagnostic Reading Test	Grades 1–3, 4–6, and 7–9		This test is similar to Diagnostic Reading Test, Pupil Progress Series. It consists of twelve scores on vocabulary, rate, and comprehension on the Primary Test; fourteen scores on knowledge and use of sources, rate, comprehension, and total on

the Elementary and the Advanced Test.

| 34 | S. R. A. Diagno.tic Reading Test | Grades 4–13 | 50 min. | This test measures word recognition, comprehension, vocabulary, story reading, story comprehension, and rate of comprehension. |
| 19 | Stanford Diagnostic Reading Test | Grades 2.5–8.5 | 1 hr. 50 min. to 2 hrs. 40 min. in 3 or 4 sittings | This test aids in the identification of specific strengths and weaknesses in reading comprehension, vocabulary, syllabication, comprehension, auditory skills, various aspects of phonetic analysis, and rate of reading. The tests are auditorily loaded. |

Appendix V

Oral Reading Tests

16 19 29	Gilmore Oral Reading Test	Grades 1–8	15–20 min.	This individual test consists of ten paragraphs, measuring comprehension, speed, and accuracy of comprehension. Pupil errors can be recorded: substitutions, mispronunciations, insertions, and omissions.
3	Gray Standardized Oral Reading Check Tests	Grades 1–2, 2–4, 4–6, and 6–8		This test can be used to get measures of progress of pupils in rate and accuracy of oral reading. The information obtained will aid the teacher in determining the specific nature of problems which poor readers have and what can be done to correct difficulties.
3	Gray Standardized Oral Reading Paragraphs Test	Grades 1–8	3–8 min.	This test is designed for grades 1–8 and measures rate and accuracy of oral reading. As the child reads the various passages aloud, all errors and hesitations are recorded: gross mispronunciation, partial mispronunciation, omission, insertion, repetition, substitution and inversion. Other observations include word-by-word reading, poor phrasing, lack of expression, monotonous tone, poor enunciation, overuse of phonics, no method of word attack, head movement, finger pointing, and loss of place. The teacher underlines mispronounced words, encircles omissions, writes in substitutions, and indicates any repetitions with a wavy line. This test emphasizes the *proc-*

ess rather than the end *product* of reading. It represents a record of the errors that can be studied rather than a total score that may mean little or nothing. It is an individual test and consists of twelve paragraphs progressing from simple to more difficult material.

| 2 | Leavell Analytical Oral Reading Test | Grades 1–10 | Approx. 10 min. | This is an oral reading test, administered individually, in which the content is a continuous story. It is made up of paragraphs of increasing difficulty. The first paragraph is adapted to beginning readers and the last presents difficulty to high school students. It provides measures for comprehension, mechanical errors, and rate. |

The following errors are noted: repetition of words, unknown words, oral spelling of words, inserted or miscalled words, omitted words, lines skipped, and lines reread.

| 3 | New Gray Oral Reading | Grades 1–12 | | This test consists of thirteen graded passages in each of four forms. It is designed to measure growth in oral reading, to help in diagnosing reading difficulties, and to provide beginning placement in grade or reading groups. |
| 35 | Slosson Oral Reading Test | Grades 1–12 | 3 min. | This is an individual test and is based on the ability to pronounce words at different levels of difficulty. |

Appendix VI

The Role of the
Reading Specialist

As we begin to specialize in reading teaching, we find a need to differentiate the roles of various people functioning in the process. At the outset, we have the regular classroom teacher who, among a myriad of other duties, is supposed to be well versed in developmental reading teaching. He is the first person who formally introduces the pupil to reading instruction.

Unfortunately, some of the pupils in some classrooms do not learn to read so well as they might. This has created a need for specialists in reading. Today we have corrective teachers, remedial teachers, and reading consultants.

We use the term "special teacher" to identify an individual who is a specialist in reading and who works most directly with those youngsters who have been taken out of the regular classroom for special instruction.

As Robinson and Rauch[1] note, the title of "remedial reading teacher," or "helping teacher," or "special reading teacher" is reserved "for those teachers with special training or for those wholly engaged in teaching reading under the direction of the consultant."

We have used the term "reading consultant" to refer to a person largely freed of classroom teaching so that he may concentrate on helping the staff in the coordination and facilitation of efforts to improve the total reading program.

The special reading teacher

The role of the special reading teacher is that of corrective and remedial teaching. We already have described his role.

The minimum standards for specialists in reading, prepared by the International Reading Associations Committee on Professional Standards, suggest the type of preparation needed and the type of role and responsibilities that the position involves. The standards are the following:

I. A minimum of three years of successful teaching and/or clinical experience.

II. A master's degree or the equivalent of a bachelor's degree plus 30 graduate hours in reading and related areas as indicated in the following:

A. A minimum of twelve hours (semester) in graduate-level reading courses with at least one course in 1 and 2 and in 3 or 4:

1. Foundations or survey of reading.

   The content of this basic course is related exclusively to reading instruction or the psychology of reading. Such a course ordinarily would be the first in a sequence of reading courses.

2. Diagnosis and correction of reading disabilities.

   The content of this course or these courses includes the following: causes of reading disabilities; observation and interview procedures; diagnostic instruments; standard and informal tests; report writing; materials and methods of instruction.

3. Clinical or laboratory practicum in reading.

   A clinical or laboratory experience might be an integral part of a course or courses in the diagnosis and correction of reading disabilities. Students diagnose and treat reading disability cases under supervision.

4. Supervision and curriculum in reading.

   This course involves the study of selected curriculum in reading; an understanding of the functions and duties of the reading supervisor or consultant and the effective ways of implementing them.

B. At least one graduate-level course in each of the following content areas:

1. Measurement and/or evaluation.

This course includes one or more of the following studies: the principles and practices of test construction and the selecting, administering, scoring, and interpreting of group standardized tests; the nature, theory, function, and use of individual intelligence tests; the theory, function, and use of tests of personality.

2. Child and/or adolescent psychology or development.

This course stresses how children and/or adolescents mature and develop with emphasis on school activities and their relation to normal, healthy development.

3. Personality and/or mental hygiene.

This course includes one or more of the following studies: the nature, development, and patterns of personality and the methods of change; personality theories and their contributions to understanding the dynamics of personality; integration of psychological knowledge and principles and their relation to mental health; etiological factors, differential diagnosis, and methods used in the correction of behavior problems.

4. Educational psychology.

This course includes one or both of the following studies: the study of behavior, development, school environment, conditions for learning, and methods of assessment; the theories of learning and their implications for classroom practices.

C. The remaining semester hours in reading and/or related areas—the following courses being recommended:

1. Literature for children and/or adolescents
2. Organization and supervision of reading programs
3. Research and the literature in reading
4. Foundations of education
5. Principles of guidance
6. Nature of language
7. Communications

8. Speech and hearing
9. Exceptional child
10. Any additional courses listed under A and B

From a conference in St. Louis in 1966, there emerged the following identifications of the types of reading specialists and the respective roles of each: [2]

The *Reading Teacher* is one who devotes full time to corrective and remedial teaching at the elementary level or to developmental, corrective, or remedial teaching at the junior or senior high level. We prefer that this person be called the special remedial reading teacher. This special reading teacher should:

1. Be an extraordinarily fine teacher of reading—he should excel in know-how.
2. Possess more than average knowledge of the reading process.
3. Have developed clinical competence in diagnosis and correction.

Some specific duties are:

1. Plans with the classroom teacher methods and materials for use with small groups experiencing specific reading problems.
2. Diagnoses reading difficulties so pupils may be appropriately grouped or referred for special help.
3. Works with seriously retarded readers either individually or in small groups.

The *Reading Consultant* is a person who works directly with teachers and administrators to develop and implement the total reading program.

The *Reading Coordinator* provides leadership in all phases of the system-wide reading program and interprets the program to the administration. He works with the consultant, the special reading teachers, and the classroom teachers.

The *Reading Clinician* diagnoses and aids teachers in diagnosing remedial cases and in planning and carrying out remedial work for persistently difficult reading disability cases.

The *College Instructor* teaches reading courses concerned

with reading methodology on both undergraduate and graduate level and advises, directs, and carries out research.

Let us look at the role of the reading consultant in more detail.

The reading consultant [3]

The reading consultant is a resource person, an adviser to administrators and teachers, an in-service leader, a researcher, a diagnostician, an evaluator, and even an instructor. His role is to perfect "the teaching of reading within a school or school system," [4] perhaps a county or a state.

His position grew out of the fact that remedial teachers were simply not able to cope with all the reading disability cases. His role is that of assisting classroom teachers and remedial teachers to provide more effective reading programs. He works with the staff to develop, implement, coordinate, and evaluate the reading program. In some schools, especially the small schools, the special teacher assumes a consultant role.

The reading consultant is directly responsible to the reading coordinators or director or perhaps to the superintendent working as a member of the superintendent's staff on instruction. He may at times perform any of the duties outlined for the special teacher, but will be concerned primarily with assisting teachers. He will, as Robinson points out, have the following duties:

1. In-Service Education
2. Methods, Materials, and Procedures
3. Curriculum Development
4. Administration
5. Research
6. Evaluation
7. Public Relations

IN-SERVICE EDUCATION

1. Interprets the reading program to teachers, especially by orienting new teachers to the reading program.
2. Keeps the staff up to date on new developments in reading, new research, and possibilities for experimentation.
3. Conducts demonstration lessons in the classrooms of individual teachers or before groups of teachers.

4. Conducts short-term workshops for teachers.
5. Prepares brief bulletins of a practical nature for teachers.
6. Conducts large-group in-service programs through workshops for teachers of all levels, administrators, and particularly the new teachers and demonstrates new programs or specific teaching techniques.

METHODS, MATERIALS, AND PROCEDURES

1. Helps to select appropriate materials and tests.
2. Advises on the prevention of disabilities.
3. Assists with class organization for corrective and remedial instruction.
4. Directs the development of reading programs for gifted children and rapid learners in reading.
5. At times works with a few severely retarded readers, but his function is not to teach pupils. Superintendents often conceive the role of the reading consultant to be primarily in the area of corrective reading, expecting him to spend his time working with nonreaders or underachieving readers.
6. Directs diagnoses of pupils who are severly retarded, helps teachers to diagnose and interpret the results of diagnoses.
7. Helps teachers to carry out remedial procedures.
8. Helps teachers to identify children's preferred modalities of learning.

CURRICULUM DEVELOPMENT

1. Works with the curriculum committee in developing, revising, or evaluating the curriculum guide in reading and in the other language arts.
2. Tries to integrate the reading skills into the curricula of the content areas.
3. Helps subject-matter teachers to develop more effective ways of teaching reading.
4. Meets with elementary and secondary teachers to discuss with them the reading skills pupils need at the respective levels.

ADMINISTRATION

1. Assists in the development of proposals for reading projects that might be financed by state, federal, or private agencies.
2. Directs projects.
3. Is a direct counselor to the administration as to how the educa-

tional dollar should be spent in the reading area by submitting a well-thought-out budget.

4. Plans facilities for the reading program.
5. Writes detailed reports of reading projects and research.
6. Assists in the program for first-grade admission.
7. Is directly responsible for the conduct of the remedial program by supervising other special teachers of reading.
8. Provides leadership by directing the reading committee.
9. Helps to select, develop, and evaluate the physical and material side of the program: the supply of reading materials—basal, cobasal, and supplementary; the availability of classroom libraries; the use of workbooks and teachers' manuals, etc.
10. Helps to improve the quality of instruction through supervision, demonstration, visitation, selection of reading materials, and the organization of instruction.
11. Interprets the reading program to the administration. Central administrative officers frequently are unaware of the strengths and weaknesses of their own programs.
12. Develops with the administration clear guidelines as to who should assume major responsibility for the success of the reading program. Too often elementary supervisors are hindered by their more generalized duties and interests and assistant superintendents have too little experience in teaching in the elementary school or too little understanding of the reading program.
13. Assists in the articulation between the elementary and secondary programs.

RESEARCH

1. Keeps the staff informed of the implications of specific research studies in reading.
2. Interprets research to the staff.
3. Promotes and helps teachers to design research plans for a given teacher or the total school. Encourages teachers to try out new programs.
4. Helps teachers to prepare materials for publication.

EVALUATION

1. Supervises or directs the school-wide testing of reading achievement.
2. Helps teachers to select the proper tests and to make the proper use of tests.
3. Helps teachers to develop competency in diagnosing pupil strengths

and weaknesses in reading and to combine diagnosis with instruction—to teach reading diagnostically.

4. Conducts periodic evaluations of the reading program. *The First R: The Harvard Report on Reading in the Elementary School,* suggests that the reading consultant often has less to say about the appraisal of the reading program than three or four other administrative officers and that he may have even less authority in the selection of materials.

PUBLIC RELATIONS

1. Interprets, describes, and explains the reading program to the administration, staff, and community.
2. Works with content-area teachers as a member of the team. Team teaching activities should take a good deal of the reading consultant's time and are good public relations for the reading program.
3. Presents demonstrations, question-and-answer programs, and exhibits of materials at PTA meetings.

---

[1] Robinson, H. Alan, and Rauch, Sidney J. *Guiding the Reading Program: A Reading Consultant's Handbook.* Science Research Associates, Chicago, 1965, p. 1.

[2] Dietrich, Dorothy M. "Standards and Qualifications for Reading Specialists." *The Reading Teacher,* 20 (March, 1967) 483-486.

[3] Volume 20 of *The Reading Teacher,* March, 1967, is devoted entirely to the role of the reading specialist and the reading consultant. For a discussion of the discrepancy between what ought to be the role of the reading consultant and what it actually is, see: Lerner, Janet W. "A New Focus in Reading Research: The Decision-Making Process." *Elementary English,* 44 (March, 1967) 236-242, 251.

[4] Robinson, H. Allen. "The Reading Consultant of the Past, Present, and Possible Future." *The Reading Teacher,* 20 (March, 1967) 475-482.

Appendix VII

Test Publishers

1. Acorn Publishing Company, Rockville Centre, New York.
2. American Guidance Service, Inc., 720 Washington Avenue, S.E., Minneapolis 14, Minnesota 55414.
3. The Bobbs-Merrill Co. Inc., or the Public School Publishing Co., or the C. A. Gregory Co., 4300 West 62nd Street, Indianapolis 6, Indiana.
4. Bureau of Educational Measurements, Kansas State Teachers College, Emporia, Kansas.
5. The Bureau of Educational Research and Service, Extension Division, State University of Iowa, Iowa City, Iowa.
6. The Bureau of Publications, Teachers College, Columbia University, New York 27, New York.
7. California Test Bureau, Del Monte Research Park, Monterey, California.
8. The Center for Psychological Service, Suite 419, Columbia Medical Building, 1835 Eye Street, N.W., Washington 6, D.C.
9. Committee on Diagnostic Reading Tests, Mountain Home, North Carolina.
10. Educational Developmental Laboratories, 75 Prospect, Huntington, New York.
11. Educational and Industrial Testing Service, P.O. Box 7234, San Diego 7, California.
12. Educational Testing Service, Cooperative Test Bureau, 20 Nassau Street, Princeton, New Jersey.
13. Essay Press, Box 5, Planetarium Station, New York 24, New York.
14. Follett Publishing Company, 1010 West Washington Boulevard, Chicago 7, Illinois.

15. Ginn and Company, 205 West Wacker Drive, Chicago 6, Illinois.

16. Guidance Centre, Ontario College of Education, University of Toronto, Toronto 5, Ontario, Canada.

17. Guidance Testing Associates, 6516 Shirley Avenue, Austin, Texas 78752.

18. C. S. Hammond & Co., Maplewood, New Jersey.

19. Harcourt, Brace and World, 7555 Caldwell Avenue, Chicago 48, Illinois.

20. Houghton Mifflin Co., 2 Park Street, Boston 7, Massachusetts.

21. Institute for Personality & Ability Testing, 16024 Coronado Drive, Champaign, Illinois.

22. Lyons & Carnahan Co., 407 East 25th Street, Chicago 16, Illinois.

23. The Mills Center, 1512 East Broward Boulevard, Fort Lauderdale, Florida.

24. University of Minnesota Press, 2037 University Avenue Southeast, Minneapolis 14, Minnesota.

25. C. H. Nevins Printing Co., 311 Bryn Mawr Island, Bayshore Gardens, Bradenton, Florida.

26. O'Connor Reading Clinic Publishing Co., 1040 E. Maple Road, Birmingham, Michigan 48011.

27. Personnel Press, Inc., 20 Nassau Street, Princeton, New Jersey.

28. Phonovisual Products, Inc., P.O. Box 5625, Friendship Station, Washington, D.C. 20016.

29. The Psychological Corporation, 304 East 45th Street, New York 17, New York.

30. Psychological Test Specialists, Box 1441, Missoula, Montana.

31. Psychometric Affiliates, Box 1625, Chicago 90, Illinois.

32. Reading and Study Skills Center, Inc., 15 Washington Place, New York, N.Y.

33. Scholastic Testing Service, Inc., 480 Meyer Road, Bensenville, Illinois.

34. Science Research Associates, Inc., 259 East Erie Street, Chicago 11, Illinois.

35. Slosson Educational Publications, 140 Pine Street, East Aurora, New York 14052.

36. State High School Testing Service for Indiana, Purdue University, Lafayette, Indiana.

37. The Steck Company, Austin, Texas.

38. C. H. Stoelting Company, 424 North Homan Avenue, Chicago 24, Illinois.

39. Charles C. Thomas, 301-327 East Lawrence Avenue, Springfield, Illinois.

40. United States Employment Service, Washington, D.C.

41. Mazie Earle Wagner, 400 Klein Road, Buffalo, New York.

42. Western Psychological Services, 12035 Wilshire Boulevard, Los Angeles 25, California.

43. Winter Haven Lions Research Foundation, Inc., P.O. Box 1045, Winter Haven, Florida.

Appendix VIII

Book Publishers

Abelard-Schuman, Limited, 6 West 57th Street, New York 19, New York.

Abingdon Press, 201 Eighth Avenue, South, Nashville 2, Tennessee.

Allyn and Bacon, Inc., 150 Tremont Street, Boston 11, Massachusetts.

Affiliated Publishers, Inc., Division of Simon & Schuster, Inc., 630 Fifth Avenue, New York, New York.

Americana Interstate Corporation, Mundelein, Illinois.

American Book Company, 300 Pike Street, Cincinnati, Ohio.

American Education Publications, 1250 Fairwood Avenue, Columbus 16, Ohio.

American Guidance Service, Inc., Publishers Building, Circle Pines, Minnesota.

American Library Association, 50 E. Huron Street, Chicago 11, Illinois.

Amidon, Paul S. and Associates, Inc., 1035 Plymouth Building, Minneapolis, Minnesota.

Apollo Editions, 425 Park Avenue South, New York 16, New York.

Appleton-Century-Crofts, Inc., 440 Park Avenue South, New York 1, New York.

Association Films Inc., 347 Madison Avenue, New York 17, New York.

Association for Childhood Education International, 3615 Wisconsin Avenue, N.W., Washington 16, D.C.

Audio Education, Inc., c/o American Book Company.

Audio-Visual Center, Kent State University, Kent, Ohio.

Audio-Visual Research, 1509 Eighth Street, S.E., Waseco, Minnesota.

Bailey Films Inc., 6509 De Longpre Avenue, Hollywood 28, California.

Barnell Loft, Ltd., 111 South Center Avenue, Rockville Centre, New York.

Barnes & Noble, Inc., 105 Fifth Avenue, New York 3, New York.

Barrons Educational Series, Inc., 343 Great Neck Road, Great Neck, New York.

Bausch and Lomb, Inc., Rochester 2, New York.

Beckley-Cardy Company, 1900 N. Narragansett, Chicago 39, Illinois.

Behavioral Research Laboratories, Ladera Professional Center, Box 577, Palo Alto, California.

Benefic Press Publications, 10300 West Roosevelt Road, Westchester, Illinois.

Robert Bentley, Inc., 872 Massachusetts Avenue, Cambridge, Massachusetts.

Benton Review Publishing Co., Inc., Fowler, Indiana.

Better Reading Program, Inc., 230 East Ohio Street, Chicago 1, Illinois.

Walter J. Black, Inc., Flower Hill, Roslyn, New York.

Bobbs-Merrill Company, Inc., 4300 West 62nd Street, Indianapolis 6, Indiana.

Book of the Month Club, Inc., 345 Hudson Street, New York 14, New York.

R. R. Bowker Company, 1180 Avenue of the Americas, New York 36, New York.

Milton Bradley Company, 74 Park Street, Springfield 2, Massachusetts.

Brenner-Davis Phonics, Inc., 161 Green Bay Road, Wilmette, Illinois.

Silver Burdett Company, 460 South Northwest Highway, Park Ridge, Illinois.

Bureau of Publications, Teachers College, Columbia University, 525 West 120th Street, New York 27, New York.

Burgess Publishing Co., 426 South Sixth Street, Minneapolis 15, Minnesota.

California Test Bureau, Division of McGraw-Hill Book Company, Del Monte Research Park, Monterey, California.

Cambosco Scientific Co., Inc., 342 Western Avenue, Boston, Massachusetts.

Cambridge University Press, American Branch, 32 East 57th Street, New York 22, New York.

Cenco Educational Aids, 2600 South Kostner Avenue, Chicago, Illinois.

Chandler Publishing Company, 124 Spear Street, San Francisco, California.

Chester Electronic Laboratories, Chester, Connecticut.

Childrens Press Inc., Jackson Boulevard and Racine Avenue, Chicago 7, Illinois.

Children's Reading Service, *CRS Audio-Visual Catalog*, Brooklyn, New York.

Chilton Company, 525 Locust Street, Philadelphia 39, Pennsylvania.

Columbia Records, 799 Seventh Avenue, New York 19, New York.

Combined Book Exhibit, Inc., 950 University Avenue, New York 52, New York.

The Continental Press, Inc., Elizabethtown, Pennsylvania.

Coronet Films, 65 East South Water Street, Chicago 1, Illinois.

Coward-McCann, Inc., 200 Madison Avenue, New York 16, New York.

Craig Research, Inc., 3410 South LaCienega Boulevard, Los Angeles 16, California.

Criterion Books, Inc., 6 West 57th Street, New York 19, New York.

Thomas Y. Crowell Company, 201 Park Avenue South, New York 13, New York.

Denoyer-Geppert Company, 5235 Ravenswood Avenue, Chicago 40, Illinois.

Developmental Reading Distributors, 1944 Sheridan, Laramie, Wyoming.

The Dial Press, Inc., 750 Third Avenue, New York 16, New York.

Dodd, Mead & Co., 432 Park Avenue South, New York 16, New York.

Dover Publications, Inc., 180 Varick Street, New York 14, New York.

Doubleday & Company, Inc., Garden City, New York.

Dowlings, Inc., 607-11 West Sheridan Avenue, Oklahoma City 2, Oklahoma.

Duell, Sloan and Pearce, Inc., 60 East 42nd Street, New York 17, New York.

E. P. Dutton & Company, Inc., 300 Park Avenue South, New York 10, New York.

Economy Company, 24 West Park Place, Oklahoma City, Oklahoma.

Educational Developmental Laboratories, 75 Prospect, Huntington, New York.

Educational Film Library Association, Inc., 250 West 57th Street, New York 19, New York.

Educational Projects, Dept. CO-12, 488 Madison Avenue, New York, New York.

Educational Publishing Corporation, Darien, Connecticut.

Educational Record Sales, 153 Chambers Street, New York 7, New York.

Educational Service, Inc., P.O. Box 112, Benton Harbor, Michigan.

Educational Stimuli, 2012 Hammond Avenue, Superior, Wisconsin.

Educational Test Bureau, Educational Publishers, Inc., Minneapolis 14, Minnesota.

Education Services Press, 3M Company, Box 3100, St. Paul, Minnesota.

Educators Progress Service, Randolph, Wisconsin.

Educators Publishing Service, 301 Vassar Street, Cambridge, Massachusetts.

Encyclopaedia Britannica, Educational Department, 425 North Michigan Avenue, Chicago 11, Illinois.

Encyclopaedia Britannica Films, Inc., 1150 Wilmette Avenue, Wilmette, Illinois.

Enrichment Teaching Materials, 246 Fifth Avenue, New York 1, New York.

Essay Press, Box 5, Planetarium Station, New York 24, New York.

Expression Company, P.O. Box 11, Magnolia, Massachusetts.

Eye Gate House, Inc., 146-01 Archer Avenue, Jamaica 35, New York.

Faber and Faber Books, 24 Russell Square, London, W.C. 1.

Fideler Company, 31 Ottawa Avenue, N.W., Grand Rapids, Michigan.

Field Enterprises Educational Corporation, 510 Merchandise Mart Plaza, Chicago, Illinois.

Follett Publishing Company, 1010 West Washington Boulevard, Chicago 6, Illinois.

Folkways Records and Service Corporation, 121 W. 47th Street, New York 36, New York.

Friendship Press, 475 Riverside Drive, New York 26, New York.

Garrard Press, 510 North Hickory Street, Champaign, Illinois.

Ginn and Company, Arlington Heights, Illinois.

Globe Book Company, Inc., 175 Fifth Avenue, New York 10, New York.

Golden Gate Junior Books, San Carlos, California.

Golden Press, Inc., Educational Division, 850 Third Avenue, New York 18, New York.

Graflex, Inc., Dept. AV-111, Rochester 3, New York.

Stephen Greene Press, 120 Main Street, Brattleboro, Vermont.

Grolier Educational Corporation, Dept. RA-7, 845 Third Avenue, New York, New York.

Grosset and Dunlap, Inc., 51 Madison Avenue, New York, New York.

E. M. Hale and Company, 1201 South Hastings Way, Eau Claire, Wisconsin.

C. S. Hammond and Company, 515 Valley Street, Maplewood, New Jersey.

Harcourt, Brace and World, Inc., 7555 Caldwell Avenue, Chicago 48, Illinois.

Harlow Publishing Corporation, 532-536 N.W. Second Street, Oklahoma City 2, Oklahoma.

Harper and Row, Publishers, 49 East 33rd Street, New York 16, New York, and 2500 Crawford Avenue, Evanston, Illinois.

Harvey House, Irvington-on-Hudson, New York.

Hastings House Publishers, Inc., 151 East 50th Street, New York 22, New York.

Hayes School Publishing Company, 321 Pennwood Avenue, Wilkinsburg, Pennsylvania.

D. C. Heath & Company, 1815 Prairie Avenue, Chicago, Illinois.

Heritage Press, c/o Dial Press, Inc., 461 Park Avenue South, New York 16, New York.

Highlights, 2300 W. Fifth Avenue, Columbus 16, Ohio.

Holiday House, 8 West 13th Street, New York 11, New York.

Holt, Rinehart & Winston, Inc., 383 Madison Avenue, New York 17, New York.

Horn Book, Inc., 585 Boylston Street, Boston 16, Massachusetts.

Houghton Mifflin Company, 1900 South Batavia Avenue, Geneva, Illinois.

Hubbard Company, P.O. Drawer 100, Defiance, Ohio.

Ideal School Supply Company, 8316 South Birkhoff Street, Chicago, Illinois.

Initial Teaching Alphabet Productions, Inc., 20 East 46th Street, New York 17, New York.

Instructional Materials Associates, 175 Fifth Avenue, New York, New York.

Instructo Products Company, Philadelphia 31, Pennsylvania.

Instructor Subscription Agency, Instructor Park, Dansville, New York.

International Visual Educational Service, Inc., 300 South Racine Avenue, Chicago 7, Illinois.

Iroquois Publishing Company, Inc., 1300 Alum Creek Drive, Columbus 16, Ohio.

The John Day Company, Inc., 210 Madison Avenue, New York 16, New York.

Judy Company, 310 North Second Street, Minneapolis 1, Minnesota.

Junior Literary Guild Books, Garden City, New York.

Kenworthy Educational Service, Inc., P.O. Box 3031, Buffalo 1, New York.

Keystone View Company, Department RT 93, Meadville, Pennsylvania.

Alfred A. Knopf, Inc., 501 Madison Avenue, New York 22, New York.

Lafayette Instrument Company, North 26 Street and 52 By Pass, P.O. Box 57, Lafayette, Indiana.

Laidlaw Brothers, Thatcher & Madison, River Forest, Illinois.

Learning Materials, Inc., 100 East Ohio Street, Chicago 11, Illinois.

Learning Through Seeing, Inc., P.O. Box 368, Sunland, California.

J. B. Lippincott Co., East Washington Square, Philadelphia 5, Pennsylvania.

Little, Brown and Company, 34 Beacon Street, Boston 6, Massachusetts.

Liveright Publishing Corp., 386 Fourth Avenue, New York 16, New York.

Longmans, Green & Co., Inc. See David McKay Company, Inc.

Lothrop, Lee & Shepard Co., Inc., 419 Fourth Avenue, New York 16, New York.

Lyons and Carnahan, 407 East 25th Street, Chicago 16, Illinois.

The Macmillan Company, 866 Third Avenue, New York 11, New York.

Macrae Smith Co., 225 South 15 Street, Philadelphia 2, Pennsylvania.

Mafex Associates, Inc., Box 519, Johnstown, Pennsylvania.

Marand Publishing Company, Inc., 152 East 23rd Street, New York, New York.

Materials for Learning, Inc., (formerly Children's Reading Service), 1078 St. John's Place, Brooklyn 13, New York.

McCormick-Mathers Publishing Company, Inc., 1440 East English Street, Wichita, Kansas.

McGraw-Hill Book Company, Inc., 330 West 42nd Street, New York 36, New York.

McGraw-Hill Text Films, 327 West 41 Street, New York, New York.

David McKay Company, Inc., 119 West 40th Street, New York 18, New York.

Melmont Publishers, Inc., Jackson Boulevard & Racine Avenue, Chicago 7, Illinois.

Meredith Press, 60 East 42nd Street, New York, New York.

Meredith Publishing Company, 440 Park Avenue South, New York, New York.

Meridian Books, 2231 West 110th Street, Cleveland 2, Ohio.

G. & C. Merriam Company, 47 Federal Street, Springfield, Massachusetts.

Charles E. Merrill Books, Inc., 1300 Alum Creek Drive, Columbus 16, Ohio.

University of Minnesota Press, 2037 University Avenue S.E., Minneapolis 14, Minnesota.

Modern Curriculum Press, P.O. Box 9, Berea, Ohio.

William Morrow & Co., Inc., 425 Park Avenue South, New York 16, New York: distributor for William Sloan Associates, M. Barrows and Company, Inc., M. S. Mill Company, Inc., Whiteside Inc., Jefferson House, Inc., Reynal & Company, Inc., and Apollo Editions.

National Council of Teachers of English, 508 South Sixth Street, Champaign, Illinois.

National Education Association, 1201 Sixteenth Street, N.W., Washington 6, D.C., Department of Audio-Visual Instruction.

National Reading Institute, 24 Rope Ferry Road, Waterford, Connecticut.

Thomas Nelson and Sons, Copewood and Davis Streets, Camden, New Jersey.

C. H. Nevins Printing Company, 311 Bryn Mawr Drive, Bayshore Gardens, Bradenton, Florida.

New American Library of World Literature, Inc., 501 Madison Avenue, New York 22, New York.

New York Public Library, Fifth Avenue and 42nd Street, New York 18, New York.

Noble & Noble, Publishers, Inc., 750 Third Avenue, New York, New York.

Ivan Obolensky, Inc., 219 East 61st Street, New York 21, New York.

Ohio State University, 1945 North High Street, Columbus, Ohio; Center for School Experimentation, College of Education.

Open Court Publishing Company, Box 399, LaSalle, Illinois.

F. A. Owen Publishing Company, Dansville, New York.

Oxford Book Company, 71 Fifth Avenue, New York, New York.

Oxford University Press, Inc., 200 Madison Avenue, New York, New York.

Pacific Coast Publishers, Campbell Avenue at Scott Drive, Menlo Park, California.

Pacific Productions, 2614 Etna Street, Berkeley, California.

Pantheon Books, Inc., 333 Sixth Avenue, New York 14, New York.

Parents' Magazines' Publications, Inc., 80 New Bridge Road, Bergenfield, New Jersey.

Parker Publishing Company, Inc., West Nyack, N.Y.

Perceptual Developmental Laboratories, 6767 Southwest Avenue, St. Louis 17, Missouri.

Phonovisual Products, Inc., Box 5625, 4708 Wisconsin Avenue, N.W., Washington 16, D.C.

Pitman Publishing Corporation, 20 East 46th Street, New York, New York.

The Platt & Munk Co., Inc., 200 Fifth Avenue, New York 10, New York.

Plays Inc., 8 Arlington Street, Boston 16, Massachusetts.

Prentice-Hall, Inc., Englewood Cliffs, New Jersey.

Psychotechnics, Inc., 105 West Adams Street, Chicago 3, Illinois.

Purdue University, The Audio-Visual Center, West Lafayette, Indiana.

G. P. Putnam's Sons, 200 Madison Avenue, New York 16, New York.

Rand McNally & Co., P.O. Box 7600, Chicago 80, Illinois.

Random House, 501 Madison Avenue, New York 22, New York.

Reading Circle, Inc., Box 55, North Manchester, Indiana.

Reading Laboratory, Inc., New York 36, New York.

Reading Laboratory, Inc., Developmental Research Institute, Inc., 500 Fifth Avenue, New York, New York.

Reader's Digest Educational Division, Pleasantville, New York.

Record, Book, and Film Sales, Inc., 165 West 46th Street, New York, New York.

Remedial Education Center, 1321 New Hampshire Avenue, Washington 6, D.C.

Row, Peterson and Company, 2500 Crawford Avenue, Evanston, Illinois. (See Harper and Row.)

Saalfield Publishing Company, Akron 1, Ohio.

St. Martin's Press, Inc., 175 Fifth Avenue, New York 10, New York.

Porter Sargent, Publisher, 11 Beacon Street, Boston, Massachusetts.

Schmitt, Hall and McCreary Company, 527 Park Avenue, Minneapolis 15, Minnesota.

Scholastic Book Services, 900 Sylvan Avenue, Englewood Cliffs, New Jersey.

Science Research Associates, Inc., 259 E. Erie Street, Chicago 11, Illinois.

Scott, Foresman & Company, 1900 East Lake Avenue, Glenview, Illinois.

Charles Scribner's Sons, 597 Fifth Avenue, New York 17, New York.

Silver Burdett Company, 460 South Northwest Highway, Park Ridge, Illinois.

Simon & Schuster, Inc., Rockefeller Center, 630 Fifth Avenue, New York, New York.

L. W. Singer Company, Inc., a division of Random House, 249-259 West Erie Boulevard, Syracuse 2, New York.

Turner E. Smith & Company, 680 Forrest Road, N.E., Atlanta 12, Georgia.

Society for Visual Education, Inc., Subsidiary of General Precision Equipment Corporation, Diversey Broadway, Chicago 14, Illinois.

Spencer International Press, Inc., 575 Lexington Avenue, New York, New York.

The Steck-Vaughn Company, P.O. Box 2028, Austin 61, Texas.

Syracuse University Press, Box 87, University Station, Syracuse 10, New York.

Systems for Education, Inc., 612 North Michigan Avenue, Chicago, Illinois.

Taplinger Publishing Company, Inc., 119 West 57th Street, New York 19, New York.

University of Iowa, Bureau of Audio-Visual Instruction, Iowa City, Iowa.

University of Pittsburgh Press, Pittsburgh 13, Pennsylvania.

The Viking Press, Inc., 625 Madison Avenue, New York 22, New York.

Harr Wagner Publishing Company, 609 Mission Street, San Francisco, California.

George Wahr Publishing Company, 316 South State Street, Ann Arbor, Michigan.

Henry Z. Walch, Inc., 101 Fifth Avenue, New York 3, New York.

Frederick Warne and Co., Inc., 101 Fifth Ave., New York, N.Y. 10003.

Ives Washburn, Inc., 119 West 40th Street, New York 18, New York.

Washington Square Press, Inc., Educational Department, 630 Fifth Avenue, New York, New York; a division of Simon & Schuster.

Franklin Watts, Inc., 575 Lexington Avenue, New York 22, New York.

Webster Division, McGraw-Hill Book Company, Manchester Road, Manchester, Missouri.

Wenkart, 4 Shady Hill Square, Cambridge 38, Massachusetts.

Westminster Press, Witherspoon Building, Philadelphia 7, Pennsylvania.

Weston Woods Studios, Weston, Connecticut.

Wheeler Publishing Company. (This is now a subsidiary of Harper and Row.)

Whiteside, Inc., 325 Fourth Avenue, New York 16, New York.

Albert Whitman and Company, 560 West Lake Street, Chicago 6, Illinois.

Wilcox and Follett, 1000 West Washington Boulevard, Chicago 7, Illinois.

H. W. Wilson Co., 950 University Avenue, Bronx, New York.

Wisconsin State Reading Circle Board, State Department of Public Instruction, Madison, Wisconsin.

Wordcrafters Guild, St. Albans School, Washington 16, D.C.

World Book Company, see Harcourt, Brace & World, Inc.

World Publishing Company, 2231 West 110 Street, Cleveland 2, Ohio.

World Trade Academy Press, Inc., 50 East 42nd Street, New York 17, New York.

Index

A

A Comparative Study of the Reading Achievement of German and American Children, 108n

A Comprehensive Linguistic Approach to Reading, 160n, 161n

A Description of the Gillingham Method, 107n

A Diacritical Marking System to Aid Beginning Reading Instruction, 159n

A First Course in Phonic Reading and A Second Course in Phonic Reading, 129

A Guide for Establishing a Corrective Reading Program, 134, 139n

A Guide to the Teaching of Reading, 170

A New Focus in Reading Research: The Decision-Making Process, 270n

A Phonetic Reader Series, 129

A Reading List for Disadvantaged Youth, 170

A Title I Short Course for Reading Teachers, 192n

Accelerating devices for teaching reading, 224-226

Achievement in reading, tests to determine, 18-24

Acuity of vision, 79

Adams, Ruth, 174

Allen, Claryce, 150, 160n

Allen, R. V., 150, 160n

Alphabet systems, 141-144
  diacritical marking system, 143
  Initial Teaching Alphabet, 141-142
  ten-vowel modification model, 142-143
  Unifon system, 143
  words in color, 143-144

American Journal of Orthopsychiatry, 193n

American Optical Company, 82, 84

Analysis of causal factors of reading disability, 54-108
  (see also "Causes of reading disability")

Analytic phonics, 145

And Now—The Package Deal, 192n

Aniseikonia, 81

Ansara, Alice, 170

A O Sight Screener, 82-83

Aptitude tests, values and limitations of, 10

ARA, 141

Artley, A. Sterl, 61-62, 107n

Assessing reading potential, 10-18

Association areas of brain, 92-94

Astigmatism, 79

Atlantic City Eye Test, 83

Audiometer, use of in hearing tests, 91

Audio-visual materials, 217-222

Auditory deficiencies, types of, 89-90

Auditory Discrimination Test, 42, 98

Augmented Roman Alphabet, 141

B

Backus, 166

Baldwin, Maurine, 138n

Baller, Warren, R., 64, 107n

Bamman, Henry A., 128

Bank Street College, 171

Bannatyne, Alex D., 184-188, 193n

Barbe, Walter B., 160n

Barnhart, C. L., 145, 160n

Bartkowiak, Deanna, 160n

Basal reading series, lists of, 195-1o7

Basic Reading Series, 129